FALLEN
HEROES

FALLEN HEROES

Sports Stories of Madness, Resilience, and Inspiration

Jeffrey A. Kottler, Ph.D.

Baylor College of Medicine

Bassim Hamadeh, CEO and Publisher
Amy Smith, Project Editor
Sean Adams, Production Editor
Emely Villavicencio, Senior Graphic Designer
Sara Schennum, Licensing Associate
Natalie Piccotti, Senior Marketing Manager
Kassie Graves, Vice President of Editorial
Jamie Giganti, Director of Academic Publishing

Cover image copyright © 2016 iStockphoto LP/Savushkin; © 2015 iStockphoto LP/ViewApart; ©
2017 iStockphoto LP/Serikbaib.

Printed in the United States of America.

ISBN: 978-1-5165-3874-4 (pbk) / 978-1-5165-3875-1 (br)

Cognella Books by Jeffrey Kottler

Kottler, J. A., & Safari, S. (2019). *Making a difference: A journey of adventure, disaster, and redemption inspired by the plight of at-risk girls*. Cognella.

Kottler, J. A., Banu, S., & Jani, S. (Eds.). (2019). *Handbook of refugee experience: Trauma, resilience, and recovery*. Cognella.

Kottler, J. A., & Englar-Carlson, M. (2019). *Learning group leadership: An experiential approach* (4th ed.). Cognella.

Kottler, J. A., & Montgomery, M. (2019). *Theories in counseling and therapy: Experiential and practical approaches*. Cognella.

Safari, S., & Kottler, J. (2018). *Above the mountain's shadow: A journey of hope and adventure inspired by the forgotten*. Cognella.

Kottler, J. A., & Sharp, L. (2018). *Understanding research: Being a competent and critical consumer*. Cognella.

Kottler, J. A. (2018). *Living and being a therapist: A collection of readings*. Cognella.

Brief Contents

Detailed Contents

Preface

This book has been percolating within me for over a decade since I completed *Divine Madness*, a volume that presented psychobiographies of 10 creative geniuses who all struggled with extreme forms of mental illness. Those profiled in that project represented a variety of disciplines, including art (Mark Rothko), music (Judy Garland), poetry (Sylvia Plath), fiction (Ernest Hemingway), dance (Vaslav Nijinsky), acting (Marilyn Monroe), and comedy (Lenny Bruce). I was fascinated by the intersection between extraordinary innovators of their crafts and the emotional demons that, ultimately, destroyed their lives. In most cases, their stories ended in tragedy. Yet, interestingly, it was precisely their suffering and rather unique outlooks that allowed them to achieve such eminence in their creative endeavors. In some ways, their emotional struggles ended up informing and shaping their life's work.

Once that project was completed, I started thinking about a sequel that might be far more uplifting. I wanted to dig more deeply into the realm of emotional disorders but with a greater emphasis on the human capability for resilience and recovery in overcoming such life challenges. I was drawn to sports figures—in many cases among the best in the world—because of their extraordinary levels of self-discipline and achievement. I wondered what we might learn from their struggles, even of those whose lives ended tragically.

I'd gotten sidetracked during the ensuing years with so many other interests and projects to complete, but this one was always simmering on the back burner. After having written so many books about psychotherapy and the treatment of psychological disorders, I welcomed the opportunity to return to a more intensive study of how extraordinary individuals are both handicapped and empowered by their sometimes tortured inner lives. I have also always admired people who can do things that I could never dream of doing.

I am hardly an elite athlete. I jumped into sport, literally, with both feet as a way to manage my anxiety during a time of extraordinary stress and grief. I was a young man in my mid-20s. At the time, my mother had just died of cancer, and my father was in another hospital undergoing quadruple bypass heart surgery; soon afterward, he had a debilitating stroke that left him wheelchair bound and brain damaged.

I stood in the hallway outside my mother's room, sobbing uncontrollably. I had driven for 16 straight hours to say goodbye to her, but I had arrived too late. My life was in turmoil, and I'd never felt so alone. To add to my misery, the attending physician approached me tentatively and casually remarked that with my genes, I'd be lucky to live to 40. As he walked away, he added over his shoulder, "You better take care of yourself."

I wanted to punch the insensitive bastard. I couldn't believe he could be so rude, especially at a time when I felt so vulnerable and lost. But his words have haunted me ever since—and I started running the next day.

I have never been particularly athletic. I played right field and batted last in Little League. Team sports never appealed to me, either because I didn't have the skills or I felt too shy to join in the easy camaraderie. But I always had a talent in one area that allowed me to excel: I have a first-rate tolerance for pain. This is what allowed me to wallow in my emotional suffering during my early years and to do so without the need to medicate myself in the usual ways of my generation—with alcohol or hallucinogenic drugs. When I was a kid, I used sheer will to set the record at summer camp for doing sit-ups; it was no big deal, since it was only pain.

When I began running the morning after my mother's death, I could only make it about a quarter mile before I ran out of breath. The next day I made it a hundred meters further, adding to the distance incrementally until I could run a mile. For the next 20 years or so, I didn't skip a single day of exercise—not a single one. That means that during blizzards, bouts of the flu, torrential rain storms, ice-slickened streets, and sprained ankles, I still managed to hit the road, training for races or marathons. The truth is that I didn't have a choice: Running became my lifeline to manage stress, to help me sleep at night, and to save my life.

Even though I train psychotherapists and write books about the profession for a living, I've been a lousy patient during the times I've sought help for my own problems. I think and overanalyze too much. I play games to avoid stuff I'd rather not talk about. I can't stop myself from critiquing the interventions rather than actually responding to them. But once I went out on the road, everything that bothered me seemed to disappear. I felt grounded and relaxed even when I could barely catch my breath and my muscles were aching.

I have since become a mountaineer and competitive cyclist for much the same reason I continued running (but to preserve my knees). Like most recreational athletes, I enjoy sport for reasons other than glory, financial riches, or professional ambition; it is just something I do to keep myself together. But it gives me the barest glimpse into what a world-class athlete must do in order to attain the status of being the best. I can only imagine the sacrifices, single-minded dedication, and compulsive work it must take to realize those physical gifts.

Professional athletes live with unimaginable pressure. They prepare and train their whole lives in order to perform in front of millions of people. Their livelihood, not to mention their whole self-worth, is based solely on their latest achievements. They put their mental and physical health at risk, living with chronic stress that floods their endocrine and nervous systems with cortisol and other biochemical reactions that break down their immune systems. They risk injuries that can cripple or incapacitate them for life. They live with constant pain and disabilities. They are at greater risk for emotional problems as a function of their background—many have escaped poverty, dysfunctional families, and early trauma.

The lifestyle of sports figures is hardly conducive to emotional stability. They are constantly traveling, living in hotels, and relocating their residences—they're always on the move. Their primary relationships are often unstable and ever changing; trust issues are a major concern when they are so often targets of exploitation. Then there is the hero worship they "suffer," creating a burden as well as a sense of entitlement that leads them to make impulsive decisions and consider themselves exempt from the limitations the rest of the population faces. They are told over and over how special they are—and they come to believe it.

Athletes carry the burden of impossible expectations. No matter how good they are—no matter how much they prepare and train—occasional failures are inevitable. And the consequences of going through a bad streak are catastrophic, since they might very well be cut from the team or lose their ability to work. Add to that the number of people in their entourages who have a vested interest in their continued success: teammates, coaches, managers, agents, accountants, handlers, trainers, consultants, fans, groupies, and a world-wide audience as well as extended family members and friends who enjoy the fruits of their labor. In addition, no matter how well they do, most athletes feel like they never really live up to their own ambitions. In spite of the adulation and attention they receive (along with the generous financial benefits), deep down inside, many elite athletes are barely keeping feelings of failure at bay. On some level, they feel like frauds who can't possibly meet their own expectations, much less those of others.

Despite these challenges, both physical and emotional, most athletes are pretty well adjusted. The same drive, determination, and self-discipline that allow them to excel in sports provide them with parallel skills that help them function well in a competitive world. Yet single-minded devotion to one pursuit also leaves them vulnerable, especially those who are pushed beyond what they can handle. The emphasis on performance without excuses is so prevalent that it is no wonder that athletes resort to desperate coping strategies in order to remain at the top of their games. They take performance-enhancing substances to gain an edge, especially when they feel their physical gifts are waning. They medicate their stress and depression with drugs and alcohol in order to manage their anxiety and depression. They act out in all kinds of ways to let off steam and express their frustration, or they even sabotage themselves as a means of escape from a kind of indentured servitude (however well compensated). They are also not permitted to show any kind of weakness or admit any doubts or vulnerability. Emotional problems, in particular, must remain closely guarded secrets, or their careers will end abruptly.

We have long had a fascination with fallen heroes. Whether profiling movie stars, celebrities, or sports figures who self-destruct, the public remains riveted by such stories that dominate the media. It is like watching a car wreck: It is both horrifying and difficult to avert your gaze. We admire prominent sports figures, fantasizing that they are idealized versions of ourselves, yet we resent their special status, arrogance, and self-indulgence. On some level, we are both saddened and delighted by their fall from grace, especially when it results from their own self-indulgent or inexplicable behavior.

This book explores the tragedy of mental illness, particularly the incredible (and often silent) suffering of those who have attained special status in our culture as gladiators and champions. There are indeed some awfully sad stories of notable figures who self-destructed and died of their mental afflictions in poverty and disgrace. Yet more often than not, elite athletes have been able to demonstrate a degree of determination and courage that allowed them to manage, if not overcome, their personal struggles. It is their stories that inspire the rest of us to look at our own problems and challenges with renewed commitment to follow in their extraordinary footsteps.

1

The Sport of Madness

There are many tragic, poignant, even amusing examples of athletes losing control, if not their minds. Some slipped permanently into madness, while others found that they had the ability to not only recover from their affliction but to inspire others through their commitment to promoting mental health issues.

The public is generally tolerant of, and sometimes even entertained by, dramatic emotional meltdowns. Whenever an athlete throws a temper tantrum, behaves impulsively, or is caught doing something extravagant or ridiculous, the story hits the news cycle for days afterwards. But underneath the seemingly imprudent actions are often deeper, darker problems that signify much more than merely temporarily losing one's composure. Some famous incidents of athletes losing control become indelible in fans' memories. Boxer Mike Tyson once chomped on Evander Holyfield's ear during a fight. Tennis great John McEnroe routinely threw tantrums when a call didn't go his way, often stopping the game in a fit of rage. Basketball player Dennis Rodman, somewhat notorious for bizarre behavior, once tripped over a photographer during a game and then kicked him in the groin in frustration. Heck, O. J. Simpson believed his status as an athlete and celebrity was so special he could murder people in a jealous rage and get away with it.

Emotional difficulties can manifest themselves as situational and contextual, triggered by particular stressors or circumstances as well as by life crises. They can also represent entrenched personality features or deeper mental illness. Whereas in this volume we explore more than a dozen cases that cover much of the landscape, there is a long and checkered history of athletes falling apart while the world was watching. Unlike the rest of us who may lose our tempers, act inappropriately, behave impulsively, or spin out of control in far more private circumstances, cameras record almost every facet of these athletes live, whether during performances or when they think nobody is looking.

It is more than a little ironic that if an athlete is physically injured on the field, a phalanx of trainers, assistants, team doctors, and even the coach race onto the field in seconds to lend assistance. Everything comes to a standstill. There is a hush over the crowd. The athlete is immediately taken by golf cart, ambulance, or helicopter to the nearest medical facility to receive treatment, all while the spectators rise to their feet in applause for the fallen hero. If injured, he or she will be given the best care available in the world, followed by rehabilitation and physical therapy. But if that same person is crippled by a mental illness, it is a whole different story altogether. Treatment is not only withheld completely, but the athlete's whole career can go down the drain just by admitting there's a problem.

A Brief Survey of the Landscape

Before we get into several stories in depth, it is interesting to review the sheer number of prominent athletes in a variety of sports who struggled mightily as much with the demons inside them as with their adversaries in the stadium or arena. Many of these figures are household names from popular sports, while others operated in relative obscurity. All of them had secrets they tried to cover up because of shame and fear of being stigmatized, if not marginalized.

Here is just a brief sampling of athletes who dealt with significant forms of emotional disorders and mental illness. Some of them recovered, finding resilience and strength in their struggles, while others were destroyed by the toxic conditions as well as the shame, humiliation, and stigma they encountered. It's not that any of them experienced problems that are not faced daily by a significant percentage of the general population; it's that they were held to a higher standard and afforded little privacy because of their status as notable sports figures. They had nowhere to hide.

Let's begin with professional hockey, the most viciously uncontrolled sport, the one where teams have designated "enforcers" whose main job is to start fights while the referees stand around and watch and the crowds go wild. Those players whose principal purpose is to act as intimidators and instruments of retribution seem to be disproportionately at risk for mental disorders. Perhaps this is not all that surprising, considering what they do for a living.

Is it the repeated concussions from being pummeled like boxers that does serious brain damage and leads to chronic depression? Is it the frustration from being relegated to a subservient role on the team? Is it a particular kind of personality that leads one to seek such responsibility? In any case, there have been a number of suicides among hockey players in general, and among enforcers in particular. Three of them committed suicide in the same year!

It may have been not only the pressures within the sport that led to such self-destructive despair but also the adjustment to life after their careers ended. Wade Belak, Rick Rypien, and Tom Cavanagh all took their own lives. Rypien was just 27 years old and had struggled with depression for some time, having taken several leaves of absences from the team in order to deal with his problems. In each case he'd return, but the recovery didn't last because of a lack of support and effective treatment for his condition.

Along with hockey, football is one of the more physically violent sports that has produced a number of brain injuries and other devastating consequences. While we will look at hockey player Theo Fleury in one chapter and Lionel Aldridge, defensive back for the Green Bay Packers, in another chapter, several other players are worth mentioning. Kenny McKinley, a wide receiver for the Denver Broncos, blew his brains out at the age of 23 because of despondency over a season-ending injury. Barret Robbins, a center for the Oakland Raiders, disappeared the day before the Super Bowl because of a manic episode sparked by bipolar disorder. Dimitrius Underwood, a defensive end, repeatedly tried to kill himself, once by slashing his neck with a knife and another time by running in front of a car. Perhaps most notorious of all was star running back Ricky Williams (University of Texas and New Orleans Saints), who had so much social anxiety he would conduct media interviews with his helmet on and remained isolated in his home or room as much as possible. And then there is Terry Bradshaw, Hall of Fame quarterback and sports commentator, who suffered so much anxiety and depression he could barely function off the field. "Shoot, the football was the easy part," he said. "I could concentrate for 3 hours, and the games were an escape. It was the rest of my life that was going to hell in a handbasket."

Once again, it probably isn't that sports like hockey and football lead to emotional problems—at least not any more than other stressful jobs like air traffic controller, police officer, special forces operator, or neurosurgeon—but athletes function so much in the public eye that their problems are magnified. In addition, many such athletes come from backgrounds that leave them completely unprepared for the pressures they face. Eighty-six percent of all college athletes live below the poverty line, and half of all NFL players grew up in areas where poverty was the norm. With their compromised education (not having to perform well academically because of their exceptional athletic talent) as well as limited mentoring and role models, it is no wonder that some would struggle mightily when shoved into the limelight, especially when showered with unimaginable riches and told their talent and fame made them exempt from the rules mortal beings had to follow.

Here is a sampling of athletes from different sports, each of whom struggled with a serious debilitating emotional disorder or mental illness. Many recovered and led relatively functional, productive lives, while others remained incapacitated and took their own lives out of despair.

Athlete	Sport	Emotional Disorder or Mental Illness
Julie Krone	Hall of Fame jockey	Depression, posttraumatic stress disorder, migraines, insomnia, eating disorder
Chuck Knoblauch	Yankee Golden Glove second baseman	Paralyzing anxiety that left him suddenly unable to make the throw to first base without the ball careening into the stands
Pål Arne Fagernes	Norwegian Olympic javelin thrower	Emotional outbursts, violent episodes, substance abuse; died in car wreck
Wendy Williams	Champion diver and Olympic medalist	Suffered depression and suicidal ideation for 15 years to the point where she gave up driving because of fears of harming herself or others
Joe Louis	World heavyweight champion boxer for 12 years	Financial problems; physical deterioration led to increased depression, paranoia, drug abuse, and psychiatric hospitalizations
Dorothy Hamill	Olympic gold medalist in figure skating	Bipolar disorder, anxiety, and lifelong depression that were eventually treated with medication and therapy
Kamara James	Olympic fencer (epée)	Schizophrenia that led to homelessness and suicide
Aaron Lennon	English soccer player at wing in World Cup	Chronic stress, depression, and suicidal ideation requiring hospitalization
Jennifer Capriati	Tennis Olympic gold medal winner and Grand Slam champion	Depression, suicidal ideation, self-destructive behavior including arrests for shoplifting and drug possession
Shayne Corson	NHL hockey player for 17 years	Panic attacks and social phobia so severe he was forced to retire and seek treatment
Jim Shea	Gold medal winner in skeleton racing	Depression; appetite and sleep disruptions eventually diagnosed as anhedonia, an absence of joy
Amanda Beard	Winner of four Olympic medals from ages 14–18	Depression, obsessive-compulsive disorder, self-mutilation

Athlete	Sport	Emotional Disorder or Mental Illness
Bert Yancey	Golfer for 15 years on PGA tour	Bipolar disorder treated with lithium, but side effects created hand tremors that forced retirement
Chamique Holdsclaw	Leading scorer in the Women's NBA	Depression forced her to disappear in middle of season, resign from Olympic team, and miss All-Star game
Picabo Street	Alpine skier and Olympic gold medalist	Chronic depression exacerbated by devastating injuries that kept him isolated and literally living in the dark
Greg Louganis	Olympic gold medalist in diving	Sexual abuse, sexual identity issues led to depression; afraid he would die of AIDS but is actually very much alive
Bruce (aka Caitlyn) Jenner	Olympic gold medal decathlete	Anxiety and depression related to sexual identity and gender dysphoria issues; came out as transgender with sexual reassignment surgery
Rob Krar	Ultramarathon runner	Depression
Ronda Rousey	Ultimate fighter	Depression
Duncan Bell	Rugby	Depression

An Identity of Perfection

The incredible levels of stress in performance-oriented sports would logically lead to emotional consequences no matter how well trained and prepared athletes might be. Any athlete's value is always in flux, depending on their latest performance. Any injury can end their careers, often with no other viable option available after forced retirement. They are has-beens or what-might-have-beens. From their preschool years, they were likely tracked into rigid schedules and given singular identities as athletes, sacrificing many other aspects of healthy functioning along the way. They were coached, trained, mentored, and carefully supervised, surrendering much of their personal autonomy. They consistently received messages that their value and status were directly related to their athletic ability. Yet they were always in competition with others trying to knock them off their pedestal. Mark Fidrych, a quirky All-Star baseball pitcher from the 1970s, once said, "When you're a winner, you'll always be happy, but if you're happy as a loser, you'll always be a loser." Imagine living with that view of life—you can only be happy if you are a winner. In Fidrych's case, his mercurial and temporary success as a winner was unfortunately cut short by a career-ending rotator cuff injury. He later died of an unfortunate accident working on his farm.

The pressure from sport also leads to dramatic meltdowns that are situational rather than characterological, so to speak. In other words, specific dramatic emotional outbursts don't necessarily imply some underlying mental disorder as much as expressions of frustration or anger. On the other hand, there have been several infamous examples of coaches or players with "explosive personalities." These are individuals with hair triggers who may be repeatedly abusive toward others. The Detroit Pistons' Ron Artest (aka Metta World Peace) famously started a riot after going into the stands to brawl with fans who'd offended him. Other athletes like tennis players John McEnroe and Ilie Nastase, basketball player Dennis Rodman, baseball manager Lou Piniella, and basketball coach Bobby Knight were also known for their explosive tempers, but they were tolerated, if not enabled, because of their special status in our culture, which allows, if not encourages, such behavior.

Fig. 1-1. Although swimmer Amanda Beard was a media sensation (having appeared in her first Olympics at the age of 14 and winning seven medals in three different Olympics), she kept a dark secret related to her chronic depression, obsessive-compulsive disorder, perfectionism, and self-mutilation. Many girls who participate in competitive gymnastics, swimming, and figure skating admit to problems with eating disorders and body image.

For many years, it was assumed that elite athletes were largely exempt from the emotional difficulties and personal problems that bother the rest of us. With their fame, wealth, adulation, and prestige—not to mention their exceptional physical health and extraordinary fitness—it was assumed that they were better equipped to handle life's stressors. After all, they were (and still are) perceived as superhuman, with abilities and attributes that make them literally one in a million.

Although the research investigating the mental health and emotional problems of elite amateur and professional athletes is spotty and incomplete, it is increasingly clear that they are certainly no more well-adjusted than the normal population—perhaps somewhat less so because of their additional stressors. Consider that they are expected to be role models in *every* aspect of daily life. They are, by definition, perfectionists who hold standards for themselves by which every lapse, mistake, or failure has the potential to sully their reputations, invalidate their contracts, or even end their careers. Throughout their lives, they have been told they are special, privileged, and exceptional because of their unique ability to do one thing better than others. Yet there will come a time when all that ends, when they have to adjust to life without the opportunity to continue doing the one thing—perhaps the only thing—they can do well.

If your identity is defined primarily through sport, such a self-narrative is difficult to change. When mental illness compromises the continued viability of that personal story, the prevailing theme changes from one of empowerment to deficit, helplessness, and dysfunction. Depression and anxiety are not only possible but almost inevitable, making recovery that much more difficult for those who are forced to deny and disown their problems.

Stories With Different Endings

During those rare times when an athlete does recognize that his or her life is out of control and actually asks for help, the response from team staff, media, or the public often reinforces the notion that it's just best to keep your mouth shut and endure the suffering. You will find this theme prevalent in the stories that follow—once athletes admit to some emotional problem, they are considered damaged goods. They lose market value. Their coaches and teammates lose confidence in their abilities. The media and fans jump all over their cases. They suffer a subsequent loss of faith in their own capacity to operate at their previous high levels. Performance drops off and becomes a self-fulfilling prophecy. Careers come to crashing conclusions.

Pete Harnisch had been a dominating pitcher at the college level, with 21 wins, only three losses, and an earned run avrage of 2.29. He was drafted in the first round and ended up playing for the New York Mets in one of the most challenging markets—there's an incredible amount of media scrutiny in New York. When Harnisch confided to his manager that he hadn't slept in five days and was having trouble holding things together, he was simply ignored and told to stop complaining. When things continued to get worse, he approached other staff on the team and received the same response. Finally, the trainer just offered him a package of over-the-counter allergy medication and walked away. When things still didn't improve, the team insisted that his problem must be due to Lyme disease, then tobacco withdrawal—anything except what was really going on with him, which was severe depression. Rather than offering sympathy and support, the manager humiliated him in front of the team, calling him gutless. This often happens when an athlete asks, even begs, for help, and that helps to explain why the incidence of mental illness among athletes is vastly underreported. Their whole image and value is based on an illusion of perfection.

Another example from baseball demonstrates the sort of perfectionistic standards that can lead to debilitating emotional disorders. Rick Ankiel, a pitcher for the St. Louis Cardinals, had always been a prodigy. He was drafted out of high school and awarded one of the highest signing bonuses ever for an amateur player. In his first years in the minor leagues, he was selected as an All-Star. With a commanding 97-mile-per-hour fastball, a wicked curveball, and a mean sinker, he had all the tools he would ever need to succeed as a starting pitcher in the major leagues. He was even compared to the great Sandy Koufax.

His team won their division championship in 2000, and Ankiel was called on to pitch the first game of the playoffs against future Hall of Famer Greg Maddux of the Atlanta Braves. During the first two innings, he didn't allow a run, but in the third inning, something inexplicable occurred. He ended up facing eight different batters, all of whom either walked or got hits, but that isn't what was most strange: He threw five wild pitches that sailed over the batters' heads, setting a record for the most erratic performance in history, a record that has never been duplicated. For some reason, he could no longer throw the ball over the plate, no matter how hard he tried. "For anyone who hasn't had it happen to them," he explained, "they don't understand how deep and how dark it is. It consumes you." He was talking not just about baseball but all facets of his life. He described the feeling as "an ongoing battle with your own brain"—a brain that will no longer obey instructions or at least hold the power to make your body respond.

Fig. 1-2. Rick Ankiel struggled with anxiety and depressive disorders to the point where he could no longer work as a pitcher. Incredibly, he is one of the few players in history to make the transition to outfielder, a position he played for the St. Louis Cardinals (see photo above), having been a starting pitcher and hit a home run in the postseason.

Rick Ankiel had been ridiculed for his strange anxiety and obsessive disorder. They said he lacked mental toughness. He was "weak" and "fragile." His teammates who had physical injuries were coddled and given time and rehabilitative treatment, but he was shamed and called a malingerer.

Ankiel tried medicating his jitters with marijuana and alcohol, but they didn't put a dent in his level of anxiety. He was terrified of going back on the mound again and feeling the helplessness that came with not being able to throw a ball over the plate—something he'd been doing better than anyone else since he was a child. The magic was gone. Forever. And he had no possible way to understand or explain what had happened.

But that's not the end of the story. Instead of giving up, Ankiel decided to become an outfielder. He switched positions, something that until that time only Babe Ruth had done successfully at the highest level.

It was a sports psychologist who came to Ankiel's rescue, helping him counter the anxiety and subsequent depression with alternative ways of thinking about his situation. It was an opportunity, not a failure. Such an attitude adjustment allowed him to make the switch to a completely new role in his sport, and he rose once again to the highest level. Besides Babe Ruth, he is the only starting pitcher in history to hit a home run in the postseason. And his story is still not over, as he is currently considering renewing his career as a pitcher.

These cases have been referred to as the "perfectionistic paradox": Athletes develop extremely high standards for themselves, internalizing the expectations of their parents and coaches over the years. They flat out work harder than others around them and find it difficult to tolerate lapses or mistakes. This actually serves them well with respect to maintaining high standards of performance in their competitive sports, but it also leads to obsessive-compulsive tendencies. If these habits are left unchallenged, full-blown anxiety disorders can, and do, result.

The stories in this book feature two basic narratives and themes that are highlighted in the introductory stories and the two chapters that follow. Whereas the first chapter describes the journey of an All-Star baseball pitcher who sank into the depths of depression, drug abuse, and disgrace and eventually recovered, reclaimed his life, and helped others with such problems, the second story is about one of the world's greatest surfing champions, who struggled with a psychotic disorder that eventually destroyed him in the end. There are object lessons in both examples and many of the others that follow, featuring incredible resilience as well as despair. If there is a single message that flows through all of the stories, it is that we can hope to address emotional problems and mental illness only by talking more openly about them. If elite athletes are supposed to be role models during their performances onstage, then it is time for us to allow them to lead us through their courage and commitment to their own mental health.

Sources

Bar, K. J., & Markser, V. Z. (2013). Sport specificity of mental disorders: The issue of sport psychiatry. *European Archives of Psychiatry and Clinical Neuroscience, 263*, 205–210.

Biggin, I. J. R., Burns, J. H., & Uphill, M. (2017). An investigation of athletes' and coaches' perceptions of mental ill-health in elite athletes. *Journal of Clinical Sport Psychology, 11*, 126–147.

Chen, S., Magner, M., Leadingham, M., & Ahmadi, S. (2017). Mental illness and sport. *KAHPERD Journal, 54*(1), 25–34.

Gleeson, S., & Brady, E. (2017, August 30). When athletes share their battles with mental illness. *USA Today.* https://www.usatoday.com/story/sports/2017/08/30/michael-phelps-brandon-marshall-mental-health-battles-royce-white-jerry-west/596857001/

Gucciardi, D. F., Hanton, S., & Fleming, S. (2017). Are mental toughness and mental health contradictory concepts in elite sport? A narrative review of theory and evidence. *Journal of Science and Medicine in Sport, 20*, 307–311.

Hughes, L., & Leavey, G. (2012). Setting the bar: Athletes and vulnerability to mental illness. *British Journal of Psychiatry, 200*(2), 95–96.

McLean, B. (2014). Stigma of mental health in sports remains an opponent. *National Alliance on Mental Health.* https://www.nami.org/About-NAMI/NAMI-News/2014/Stigma-of-Mental-Health-in-Sports-Remains-an-Oppon

Rhoden, W. C. (2012, October 29). With no one looking, a hurt stays hidden. *New York Times.* https://www.nytimes.com/2012/10/30/sports/with-no-one-looking-mental-illness-in-athletes-can-stay-hidden.html

Rice, S. M., Purcell, R., De Silva, S., Mawren, D., McGorry, P. D., & Parker, A. G. (2016). The mental health of elite athletes: A narrative systematic review. *Sports Medicine, 46*(9), 1333–1353.

2

Dock Ellis

Controlled Crazy

It was the bottom of the sixth inning. The Pittsburgh Pirates were up one to nothing after a solo home run by Willie Stargell in the second inning. Dock Ellis, the volatile starting pitcher, was struggling on the mound, in more ways than one. Not only had he lost his pitching control, but he also seemed to be having trouble picking up the ball sitting on the mound.

The pitcher looked up, momentarily startled, as if a few minutes earlier he had been lying in bed drunk and tripping out of his mind and then all of a sudden found himself dropped into the middle of a major league baseball game. That wasn't far from the truth.

Ellis visibly shook his head and took a deep breath, then another. It didn't seem to help. With the ball now firmly trapped in his glove, he looked at the catcher for the sign, but that seemed hopeless. In truth, he couldn't even *see* the catcher, much less the batter or umpire. He just felt—no, *sensed*—that the batter must be standing there waiting for the pitch, although at that point he couldn't even tell if he was batting right- or left-handed. Maybe it would be better to kind of aim down the middle and hope for the best.

In spite of his resolve, the pitches were sinking into the dirt or flying high out of control; sometimes he couldn't even tell where the throws were going. He could hear people yelling, all excited about something, but he couldn't quite figure out what was so damn important that it was worth screaming about.

Shit, he must have walked the first batter, because now he could see him on first base, although he couldn't remember exactly how he got there. "Gotta concentrate. Gotta *focus*," he said to himself. But it was so damn hard when the ball kept changing size and shape. Sometimes it was so big he could barely lift it in his arm or even hold it in his oversized hand, then suddenly, it was reduced to the size of a grape, so he could barely see the damn thing, much less grab it with two delicate fingers.

What was he thinking? Oh yeah, new batter. Time to start over.

Ellis looked over his shoulder and noticed that Nate Colbert, the guy who had been on first, wasn't there anymore! He looked around, confused, and saw the smug son of a bitch standing on second. Shit, the guy stole the base when he wasn't looking!

Ellis regained his composure, at least enough to sort of remember what was going on. He was "high as a Georgia pine," as he would later describe his internal state after ingesting LSD hours before the game and then taking a handful of amphetamines to help him stabilize enough to walk out to the mound.

He looked up at the scoreboard and noticed that not much had changed in the seconds (minutes? hours?) he had been standing there. Then he turned and saw Jimi Hendrix standing at the plate, ready to take a swing with his Stratocaster guitar. Ellis just started to giggle into his glove, pretty sure this part wasn't real. A few innings earlier, he'd thought he'd seen Richard Nixon behind the plate calling balls and strikes.

He shook his head, closed his eyes for a moment, and tried to keep his focus. It was hard, so hard, because he couldn't keep track of the count, much less the score. "I'm throwing a crazy game," he recalled thinking. "I'm hitting people, walking people, throwing balls in the dirt, they're going everywhere." Yet in a very strange way, Ellis found it easier to pitch when he was high. Or at least he'd gotten so used it that it had become normal for him.

Miraculously, the next two batters flied out, and the sparse crowd of less than 10,000 people seemed to get all excited about something again. They were making noise, but it seemed very far away. *Everything* seemed very far away—especially home plate.

Rather than feeling better as things progressed, Ellis felt himself drifting away and losing his focus again. It was like there was a war going on inside his head, a battle between the hallucinogenic drug that should be wearing off soon and the speed that was now kicking in with its full power. He was sure that if he could just get out of this inning, he could get back into a groove.

There had been one point earlier in the game when he felt especially proud of himself because he had remembered to cover first base when a hard grounder was hit to an infielder. Somehow he managed to catch the throw and tag the bag, but when he shouted, "Touchdown!" he got a very strange look from the runner. That was the least of his worries, although he could tell that everyone was looking at him like he was doing something crazy. At the time he thought it was because he was so incredibly high, but later he realized it was because he was pitching a no-hitter!

Ellis walked the next batter. Now there were two guys bothering him on the bases, sending him weird telepathic messages. He couldn't figure out how to get rid of them, so he decided he just had to get this next guy, Tommy Dean, out so he could get back to the dugout. At least when he was sitting down he could concentrate on cleaning the cleats on the bottom of his shoes. They kept getting dirty, and he didn't like that. They weighed him down so he could barely move.

The next thing he knew, Ellis was back on the bench, so he must have struck the last guy out. At least now he could get some real work done and get back to his cleats. He appreciated that everyone was staying the hell away from him—everyone except the stupid rookie Dave Cash, who was too dumb to know that you *never* talk to a pitcher during a possible no-hitter.

Somehow—and even Ellis doesn't remember much about exactly how—he completed the "perfect" game, a no-hitter, even though he had ended up walking eight batters and throwing pitches high, low, and everywhere else. He had so much trouble concentrating that he gave up paying attention to any runners who managed to get on base through walks. Three players had stolen bases, but he didn't care as long as they didn't get past second. He even had trouble catching the ball when it was lobbed back to the mound. Eventually, the catcher, Jerry May, had to put white tape on his fingers because Dock claimed he couldn't see the signals. The catcher wasn't sure that helped much.

Willie Stargell ended up hitting a second home run in the seventh inning, which sealed the victory for the team. The Pirates were ecstatic, especially Dock's teammates

Fig. 2-1. In the photo above, we see Dock Ellis pitching for the Pirates. When Dock Ellis was in the groove, he was one of the most dominant players of his era, a master of five different pitches. It is all the more remarkable that he maintained such excellence over so many years, all while he was addicted to alcohol and a staggering assortment of drugs.

who knew him well enough to recognize that the dude had been *way* out of control, far more than usual for him. This was their chance to win a National League championship and eventually a World Series title—and Dock Ellis was critical to their success.

Ellis had made history as the first person to pitch a no-hitter—maybe the first athlete ever to reach the pinnacle of his sport—while tripping on LSD (there is another documented case of the whole offensive line of a football team tripping on LSD and playing flawlessly, but that's another story). It is from such stuff that legends are made. But it is also because of such myths that a man's struggles and suffering are overlooked because it all makes for such an amazing story, one that has found its way into articles or films that celebrate the improbability of the whole crazy episode. But that one afternoon in Dock Ellis's life, and even the 12 years he spent in the major leagues as an eventual Hall of Fame player, were only a small part of his life and his legacy.

Earlier in the Day

Ellis had arrived in Southern California a few days earlier than his scheduled game so he could hang out in Los Angeles with his childhood friend, Rambo, and his girlfriend, Mitzi. This was a frequent refuge for him, a place he felt safe, where nobody could bother him. He had grown up in this part of the city, and it was still the only place he felt he could be himself.

As was their custom, the three of them went on a 24-hour drug-fueled binge, smoking marijuana, drinking vodka, snorting lines of cocaine, and popping amphetamines. Ellis just liked to tune out all the pressures of the world, all the stress of being a starting pitcher in the major leagues. It was just unbelievable what everyone expected from him, what everyone wanted from him. Every few days he'd have to put his whole job on the line. Teammates were depending on him. The manager was always on his ass. The racist media was driving him crazy with their critical comments about his rather eccentric outspoken style. His fucking arm hurt all the time, but he couldn't say anything; he had to just suck it up and get ready for the next start. Fans were always pestering him for autographs and pushing him to say something funny or memorable. He could hardly trust anyone except those in the 'hood, and even they were sometimes suspect. When he was home, when he was high, nobody could get to him. He'd listen to Jimi Hendrix sing "Purple Haze," which had become his anthem. He *lived* in a haze.

Upon arrival back in Los Angeles, Ellis started to relax and unwind. "So I took some LSD at the airport," he said, "cause I knew where it would hit me. I'd be in my own area, and I know where to go. So that's how I got to my friend's house."

They'd been partying for hours when it was time to crash. He felt like he'd just closed his eyes for a moment when Mitzi started shaking him. "What's *wrong* with you? You gotta get up. You gotta pitch today."

"Leave me alone," he moaned. "Hell, what are you talking about? I don't pitch 'til tomorrow." Then he took another hit of LSD to prove his point.

The girl then grabbed the sports section of the paper and shoved it in front of his face. Sure enough, he was scheduled as the starting pitcher in the first game of a doubleheader. The game was due to start in just a few hours, and the acid was really starting to kick in.

"Oh wow!" Ellis giggled. "What happened to yesterday?"

"I don't know," she scolded him, "but you better get to San Diego."

Ellis had exactly four hours to compose himself, get something to eat, drive to the airport, catch the short flight to San Diego, warm up, and get ready to pitch. He was 25 years old, one of the greatest pitchers in baseball, and already a wreck—addicted to all kinds of drugs, impulsive, and totally unpredictable.

Ellis managed to arrive at Jack Murphy Stadium just a few minutes before game time. He settled himself in the dugout and started scanning the crowd for a particular woman who supplied him with amphetamines. "I went out of the dugout and reached up because she was standing there over the rail, and she had a pretty little gold pouch. So I got the bennies [Benzedrine] and went back into the clubhouse to take them." Ellis took a handful of pills and ran outside to get ready.

"Just as the game started," Ellis remembered, "the mist started, a misty rain." Ellis was having trouble seeing clearly. Almost everyone, even the opposing team, could tell he was high, but they didn't know what he was on. "They had no idea what LSD was all about except what they saw on TV with the hippies."

Ellis was just hoping the umpires would cancel the game because of the rain. No such luck. "Damn, looks like I'm going to have to pitch," he muttered to himself.

Much of what happened on that day remained a secret for years until he disclosed to a writer the real reason he had been so erratic that day. There are some who question just how high Ellis was by the time he started pitching. There were witnesses who could testify that he had taken LSD and others who didn't find it the least surprising that he would pop some "bennies" prior to starting the game (this was not uncommon among players at the time), but nobody really knows just how high Ellis really was during that career-defining moment. What *is* clear is that once the story got out, Dock Ellis became a legend who transcended his sport, celebrated by stoners and worshipped by rebels everywhere.

Dock Ellis become famous not just for his extraordinary athletic prowess as one of the most dominant pitchers of his era but also for his eccentricities and erratic behavior. For anyone who knows his story, it is hard to say his name without giggling. Indeed, throughout his lifetime, Ellis loved to kid with people, repeat the legend of his LSD trip on the mound, and talk about his drug-crazed adventures. Songs, poems, and graphic novels have been written, paintings created, and short films produced about perhaps the greatest performance in history made under the influence of hallucinogenic drugs. Comedian Robin Williams put together a whole routine to reenact that event.

Underneath all the comic antics was a deeply wounded man who did the best he could to hold his life together under the harsh glare of public scrutiny. He was perceived by many as a big, angry black man who didn't give a shit about anything. As is the case with many addicts, the drugs he relied on were as much to help him get through the day as to have fun. He *needed* the drugs to function in his job as well as to deal with the pressures of daily life. It wasn't just his insanely difficult job as a starting pitcher that got to him—it was dealing with money, health, relationships, and ghosts from his past.

Ellis has been repeatedly, annoyingly interviewed about that fateful day. When one reporter remarked that it must have been the scariest experience of his life—trying to keep himself together and perform at the highest level when he could barely keep himself grounded—Dock just laughed.

"That's not true," he said. "The scariest time was in 1973, when I tried to pitch completely sober. We were in San Francisco, and when I went to the bullpen to warm up, I couldn't even figure out how to wind up."

On that day, when the catcher, Manny Sanguillén, asked him what the hell was wrong because he looked so out of sorts, Ellis just shrugged. "I don't have my shit."

"Well, you better go get it then."

Ellis nodded. He went back into the clubhouse, located some amphetamines, downed them with strong coffee, and started to feel normal again. "I pitched every game in the major leagues under the influence of drugs," he once confessed. He'd used uppers, downers, alcohol, marijuana, and hallucinogens, often mixed together.

Thinking back on that day in the spring of 1972, Ellis could only shake his head in wonder. "It was [actually] *easier* to pitch with the LSD because I was so used to medicating myself. That's the way I was dealing with the fear of failure. The fear of losing. The fear of winning. It's part of the game, you know. You get to the major leagues and you think, 'I got to stay here. What do I need to do?' I was functioning as a baseball player, but I was addicted to drugs and alcohol."

It got to the point where his tolerance level for Dexamyl was so high that he'd reach into a bowl and throw a handful of the "greenies" on the table and then swallow all those that landed on their sides. Sometimes that could amount to more than a dozen, which is roughly the equivalent of drinking 20 cups of coffee. Needless to say, his energy and concentration level went through the roof.

Instilling Fear

Dock Ellis was an integral and significant part of the Pittsburgh Pirates pitching staff when they won the World Series in 1971, the year after he pitched his no-hitter. He was also part of the Yankees team that won the World Series five years later, when he was voted the "comeback player of the year."

If, as Sandy Koufax once observed, "pitching is the art of instilling fear," then Ellis was a master at this craft. Opposing players were afraid of him. He was once pepper-sprayed by a security guard at a visiting stadium because he appeared menacing. Huge, hulking, 6 feet 4 inches of chaos in action. Even Ellis didn't know what he would do next.

One of Dock's most fearsome weapons was his complete willingness to deliberately hit batters. He would stand on the mound chewing a big wad of gum, glassy-eyed, sometimes brimming with rage fueled by the amphetamines coursing through his system. He once announced to his teammates that he intended to hit every player in the famed Cincinnati Reds' "Big Red Machine" just to teach them a lesson and command respect. He was tired of hearing all this crap about the great Pete Rose, Joe Morgan, and all the rest. His friends laughed at this crazy boast, but Ellis was serious.

Pete Rose was the leadoff batter, and Ellis promptly hit him in the side. He followed this by hitting Joe Morgan in the hip and Dan Driessen in the back, loading the bases. Tony Perez, the cleanup batter, managed to duck out of the way of two pitches aimed at his head and got on base on a walk. After Ellis then tried his best to hit Johnny Bench in the head with the next two pitches, the manager had no choice but to pull him out of the game. But Ellis had made his point to his teammates: Those guys were not to be feared; *he* was the one to be feared.

To prove his point again, after Reggie Jackson hit his famous monstrous home run off the light tower at Tiger Stadium during the 1971 All-Star game when Ellis was pitching, Dock carried a grudge for five long years. When he faced Jackson again, he hit him in the head with a ball in retaliation for the humiliation.

Fans would yell racist taunts at him. "I couldn't stand to hear that shit," Ellis remembered. "I'd go crazy. I was up in the stands swinging a leaded bat. They had to come and get me in a hurry."

Yet at another time, after he heard fans call him a "nigger," he just calmly climbed up into the stands and sat next to them, not saying a word at first. The fans started to freak out, expecting an outburst. "What happened to all the niggers up here?" he simply asked them. "All the niggers calling me a nigger?" Nobody said a word. And a good thing, too, considering Ellis allegedly carried a gun with him.

Fig. 2-2. Dock Ellis was one of the first athletes to take a public stand against racism. He was also rather unorthodox, testing the limits of what he could get away with and challenging the powers of professional baseball. His hairstyles (as seen in the photo above) and protest gestures drove the team owner crazy and led to a series of suspensions. This made him both a hero to many and an object of revulsion for others. No player since Jackie Robinson, who broke the color barrier in the sport, received as much hate mail and as many death threats.

Source: https://bit.ly/2teAhsw

No player, other than Jackie Robinson, ever received more hate mail than Ellis, most of it virulently racist and threatening. "You're just a street nigger that [sic] never become [sic] civilized," one person wrote, demonstrating his own illiteracy. Another angry fan wrote: "I suppose like all the other niggers you wear those carnival type clothes too—big hats, the whole bit ... P.S.: I hope Murtaugh [the manager] runs your black ass out of the league."

Just imagine what that must have felt like, to have some people hate you so much they threaten violence and death. And yet Ellis became so used to this sort of thing he kept a file organized by familiar racist themes.

Even though opposing players, critical sports writers, and some (racist) fans were afraid of Ellis, his friends described him as one of the most entertaining, spontaneous, generous, and kind people they'd ever known. Brad Corbett, the owner of the Texas Rangers, one of the last stops in Dock's career, absolutely adored Ellis and spoke for legions of his admirers: "The biggest misconception about Dock is that he's this untamed, self-destructive wild man. And part of that is true; he was crazy, but in a good way. He was fun. He had a way of keeping people loose. He was a practical joker. He had character." Even when Ellis's career was almost over, his arm gone, Corbett still couldn't trade him or let him go.

Sure, Ellis was wounded, haunted, and at times spectacularly self-destructive, but Dock Ellis was drowning and had no idea where and how to get help. It was only the bennies, pot, acid, booze, and cocaine that seemed to bring relief.

"In spring training," Ellis recalled, "I'd walk all the way out to the backstop of the field and sit out there and drink, get high, and smoke weed, and they wouldn't bother me because they'd say, 'He's here. He's not out on the streets.'" But in a sense, he *was* lost out on the streets—separated from his wife, isolated and homesick on the road, and his drug use escalating to the point where he'd party all night with booze and whatever else he could get his hands on and then need speed in the morning to get out of bed and put himself back together enough to face the day. This cycle continued until he lost his control and mastery on the mound. The Pittsburgh Pirates had enough of his shenanigans, so they traded him away when his career eventually bottomed out.

Early History

Dock Ellis, Jr., so named because his grandfather wanted his father to be a doctor, grew up in a relatively loving, stable home in Los Angeles. His father owned a small business repairing shoes, doing his best to support the family during difficult times in Compton, South Central Los Angeles. Both of Dock's parents did their best to raise their son to do something important with his life.

While a teenager, Ellis first got involved in drugs, and later he started drinking heavily while being passed around the minor leagues in baseball. Yet he held on to a clear dream that he would someday achieve greatness.

It was no picnic for a black minor league player in the '60s. They were segregated into their own hotels, taunted by the Ku Klux Klan, and barely surviving on minimal compensation. Drugs were just part of Ellis's life, a means of self-medication as much as any form of entertainment. By the time he broke into professional baseball at the highest level, he was a major addict. "From there I was off and flying ... because when you get to the big leagues, you start getting big league dope." By that, he meant that he added "juice," liquid amphetamines, to his regular diet, and he loved it. Throughout the 12 years of his major league career, he never pitched without it. "It got to the point where I had to take it just to be on the bench, when I'm not pitching."

Indeed, the life of a starting pitcher in the major leagues is one of the most stressful jobs in existence. Although they only play once or twice per week, perhaps 50 times during the preseason and regular season, they must alternate the intense periods of complete engagement in a game—monitoring their own mechanics, selecting pitches, watching base runners, dealing with three or more hours of constant pressure—with extended periods of inactivity and boredom sitting on the bench. No matter how good they are, no matter how well they take care of business, they are totally dependent on their teammates to score runs and field balls. Uniquely, in baseball—as opposed to any other sport—there is *way* too much time to think between pitches, between innings, and between games. For this reason, Ray Karesky, a sports psychologist who specializes in treating baseball players, observed that God invented baseball in the first place because he wanted to distract men from war and drive them crazy.

If the excessive idle time isn't enough to drive even a professional a little off his rocker, then the continuous solitude will do the job. There is no lonelier job in the world than that of a baseball pitcher, standing alone on the mound, with everyone screaming and everything on the line. Pitchers in particular are separated from the rest of the team, as much competitors with one another as they are with opponents.

Anxiety disorders and depression are not uncommon reactions to such pressure, especially given the stress associated with constant travel, changing teams, unstable relationships, and the temptations that sudden wealth and easy access to drugs can bring. That is one reason that in just the last few years, Major League Baseball, more than any other professional sport, has made it a priority to acknowledge the mental health problems its players face.

For Ellis, drugs and alcohol weren't just a tool with which to deal with the unrelenting stress but also a way to stave off his fear of failure. Yet far more than that, he also struggled with what it meant for him to truly excel: "I was frightened to death of succeeding, and subconsciously, I did a lot of things to tear that down." Indeed, Ellis's career was filled with volatile ups and downs that reflected his own ambivalence about what he'd accomplished—and what he really could have done if he'd set his mind and will to it. Although Ellis earned a spot in the Hall of Fame, he never managed to maintain enough consistency to win 20 games in a season. Ellis believed he could have reached that milestone "if I'd had a chance to consult someone who was an authority on stress management. I felt my drug problem would have been arrested."

"I Was an Angry Black Man"

Dock Ellis described himself as the first "baseball militant," one of the first black men to speak out passionately, and without reserve, against racism and injustices toward minorities, both within sports and society at large. Although that might be an exaggeration, he was certainly one of the vocal advocates during his era, along with his hero Muhammad Ali.

Ellis was provocative, impulsive, and self-described as a loudmouth. He wore flashy clothes and drove an orange Corvette and a yellow Cadillac. His friends and teammates described him as "controlled crazy," able and willing to push himself and others to the brink.

This was a time when players were paid significantly less money than they are today and when they had significantly less power. And yet Ellis and his Pittsburgh teammates inspired a book, *The Team That Changed Baseball*, because 1971 was the first time in history in which every starting player was a minority. This was an era of social change, of revolution and rebellion, and Ellis was a vocal voice within his own professional domain, fearless in advocating for himself and others.

Mention Ellis's name to any baseball aficionado and they are likely to grin, associating him with descriptions as a free spirit, temperamental, brash, outspoken, rebellious, or just plain crazy. He has been profiled as the ultimate "counterculture" athlete of the '70s, saying and doing the most outrageous things not because he wanted the attention but because he didn't take shit from anyone. Many in the media were less enthralled with his behavior, and one sports columnist, Dick Young, said about him: "There is nothing wrong with Dock Ellis's arm. What's wrong is his head. It's not screwed on right. He is, to put it tastefully, a pain in the butt. He is profane, even bigoted, churlish, troublesome, and irreverent." And that was the "tasteful" description! Other even more blunt writers said he inflamed racial issues because he was so outspoken. Another interpretation might lead one to conclude that Ellis was threatening to the establishment because he wouldn't play the game by their rules.

Ellis's tempestuous nature led his Pittsburgh manager to dump him on the Yankees even though he played a significant role in their World Series title. The media expected real fireworks once Ellis started working under Billy Martin, the most intense and unpredictable manager ever to coach the game. Much to everyone's surprise, Ellis actually reached the height of his athletic prowess under Martin's tutelage because he always knew where he stood. Unfortunately, he also had to deal with the most controlling owner in the world, George Steinbrenner, of whom he once remarked during spring training of 1978: "Every time we make trouble, old George flies out here from another part of the country and gets in our way. Maybe we should make a lot of trouble so he'll keep flying out here. Sooner or later, his plane's gonna crash."

Dock wasn't just making trouble for the sake of sticking it in his arrogant boss's eye; he was standing up for his manager, who he felt was being treated disrespectfully by the meddling owner. He wasn't going to allow this rich white guy to push him or his friends around. As is so often the case with individuals who take a strong stand against perceived injustice, Steinbrenner dumped the mercurial pitcher as soon as he could in spite of how important he was to the team. The two of them eventually shared mutual respect, and Steinbrenner hired Ellis many years later to serve as a drug counselor to his team.

From the earliest age, Ellis took stands based on principle (or, as some say, stubbornness). Although he had the size and talent to stand out in almost any sport in high school, he refused to play for his school's baseball team because he believed the coach was a racist.

Without any deliberate intention, Ellis became an outspoken civil rights advocate during his playing days. He had been subjected to racism his whole life and just wasn't going to take it any longer. Yes, he would challenge racist fans in the stands, but he also took the fight to the media. When he was chosen to play for the National League team in the All-Star game, he publicly challenged his manager's assertion that he'd never start a black man in the game. There was a public outcry. The sports writers turned on Ellis. He was called "militant" and "uppity." Pressure mounted, and he *was* assigned as the starting pitcher, a result that the cynical writers said was his agenda all along.

Soon after the incident, Ellis received a letter from none other than Jackie Robinson, the first and foremost African American baseball player. "I wanted you to know how much I appreciate your courage and honesty," Robinson wrote him. Ellis sobbed as he read the letter, a validation that in some ways was more important than pitching in the World Series or starting an All-Star game.

Ellis claimed he didn't care much for the trappings of fame and attention; he just wanted to be left alone. Perhaps that was the case after his baseball career ended, but he certainly conducted himself in a way that made sure he received a disproportionate amount of attention on his team. He was once asked by his manager to fill out the pitching charts, and instead he chose to burn them in the locker room, setting off the sprinklers. He found as many ways as possible to test the limits of what he could get away with. Reflecting the larger culture of the times, he took it upon himself to fight for players' rights to free agency and more fair contracts. He was a thorn in the side of management and the baseball commissioner. He was perhaps the first player to "take a knee," so to speak, in the same manner that NFL football players protested against racism.

Once Ellis started to lose velocity on his fastball and his pitches stopped sinking, the Yankees traded him to the Rangers, then to the Mets, then finally back to the Pirates again, who eventually released him. His depression and volatility deepened, his behavior became more erratic, and his dependence on drugs worsened. "Anything that would get me high, I was doing—cocaine, heroin, mescaline, crank, alcohol. I mean, I had guys that would give me stuff on the street and say, 'Dock, I wonder how high *this* will get you. Check it out.'"

During his career, Ellis earned two World Series rings during the '70s. Eventually, he lost both rings. "I left one in the bathroom of Highway 10 in Arizona and the other on top of a car that my nephew was washing."

Life After the Major Leagues

After his retirement from baseball in 1980, Ellis's first priority was to get himself clean and sober. He told his sister to buy him one last bottle of vodka so he could take his last drink, and then he entered a treatment program to become serious about his recovery. "There was a big old redheaded dude in my face every day, and he had a lot experience with what I was going through." Ellis paused for a moment, remembering that his mentor had killed himself. "Some of us live. Some of us don't make it."

Whereas it usually takes an addict a few tries, with a lot of relapses and failures, to recover from a lifetime of abuse, Dock Ellis seemed to virtually change overnight, or at least after he started a family. "Then my son was born," he explained. "I was wearing a lot of jewelry at the time, and when I'd hold him, I'd grab his arms and whatnot. Then I read these stories about parents who shake their kids and kill them. I asked myself, 'I wonder how hard I'm grabbing him.' Then I realized the truly fucked-up thing: that I had to ask myself at all. That's when I knew something's wrong with me. I went to treatment the next day."

It's not like things were easy for Ellis in his recovery. He struggled and fought with the staff, just as he had opposed anyone else in his life who had tried to control him. He actually tried sniffing ping pong balls to try and get high. When one of the psychiatrists interviewed him during the intake and asked him to list all the drugs he'd taken in his life, the doctor concluded that Ellis had to be suicidal, since anyone ingesting that many substances *had* to be trying to kill himself. "I looked at him," Ellis recounted, "and thought about that. After a minute, I told him nobody will ever have to worry about me getting high ever again."

Dock remained true to his word, remaining clean and sober for the rest of his life. Yet Ellis wanted to do something to redeem himself. He moved to the remote desert town of Victorville, California, a mere rest stop on the way to Las Vegas known for housing a few outlet malls and state prisons. Ellis worked as a drug counselor for the Department of Corrections, living with his fourth wife in a tract neighborhood. He had all but separated himself from his previous life, or perhaps baseball had chosen to abandon him.

Although Dock Ellis gained notoriety through his acid-fueled no-hitter, which transformed him into a cult figure and even the subject of a documentary film, it was also an event about which he carried ongoing shame. "It was pretty painful for him," his fourth and last wife told an ESPN reporter. "I think it was something he kinda, sorta wished would go away." But of course it didn't—so he eventually came to terms with that, realizing that the attention from that fateful day, perhaps far more memorable than anything he'd accomplished during his distinguished baseball career, gave him the leverage he needed to assist others struggling with addictions. During the latter stage of his life after baseball, he finally found his calling as a mentor for other players and kids incarcerated in juvenile detention centers.

"If I had never met Dock, I would probably be dead or doing life in prison," one of his protégés admitted. "That dude changed my life. He changed my world."

Ellis devoted the rest of his life to helping others maintain sobriety and avoid some of the mistakes that had ruled his life. He became a spokesperson for the dangers and seduction of celebrity status among elite athletes. When testifying before Congress, which was investigating the rampant drug use among professional players, he described the vicious cycle and toxic culture of major sports. "The money causes a lot of problems," he explained. "The problems cause a lot of stress. The stress causes a lot of need for medication. And to medicate these problems, a lot of athletes seek drugs and alcohol."

Bottom of the Ninth Inning

Once he was in his 60s, Ellis's body began to betray him—the consequence of so many years of abuse. He began to lose weight at an alarming rate. His 6'4" frame seemed to shrink in size. His liver was damaged from years of alcohol and drug abuse. He had no health insurance, so he depended on the assistance of friends to pay his medical bills.

During his last years, Dock Ellis devoted himself to his family, including his wife, three daughters, and grandchild. Whereas once he had been known for his volatile mood swings and craziness, Dock's priority was to teach others the hard lessons he had learned that destroyed his health. From his own reservoir of suffering, he found the tools to help others who had lost hope.

Ellis is a prime example of the fallen hero—plagued by insecurities, emotional problems, addictions, and impulsive, self-destructive behavior—who managed to recover and rededicate himself to teaching and mentoring others through sharing his own hard life lessons. His resilience and willingness to move forward, even when he was broke and estranged from his family, stands as a monument to persistence and courage. He brought the same determination and strength to his later life that he'd once demonstrated so ably on the pitching mound.

In an interview shortly before his death, Ellis remained unapologetic about his past, even though he had rehabilitated himself over the previous 20 years. It was precisely the experience with his dark side that made him so effective as a counselor for other addicts and incarcerated inmates. One of his previous clients, Dwayne Ballard, observed that it was Dock's own checkered past that gave him credibility with the "losers" who had been abandoned by everyone else.

It was Dock's stories that were so inspirational and transformative for the prisoners, children, and professional athletes he sought to help. He could get their attention by describing what it felt like to strike out Willie Mays, deliberately hit Pete Rose with a pitch, play in the World Series, or pitch a no-hitter. And then he could scare them straight by talking about drinking two bottles of vodka a day, the blackouts and debauchery, and the losses and suffering that resulted. He would often break down in tears in front of an audience, using himself as an example of a fall from grace. But he had also eventually found peace and redemption.

During one of his last public statements before he succumbed to liver failure, he summarized the most important accomplishment of his life—which wasn't pitching a no-hitter, winning the World Series, or being elected to the Hall of Fame. "I try to help people," he said simply with a shrug, "but I can't save them. They have to do that themselves."

Sources

Baseball-Reference.com. (n.d.). Pittsburgh Pirates at San Diego Padres box score, June 12, 1970. http://www.baseball-reference.com/boxes/SDN/SDN197006121.shtml

Crasnick, J. (2008, December 19). Ex-pitcher Ellis dies of liver disease. *ESPN*. http://sports.espn.go.com/mlb/news/story?id=3782859

de la Cretaz, B. (2017, December 19). How Dock Ellis, player who pitched a no-hitter on LSD, is misremembered. *Rolling Stone*.

Elliot, H. (2008, May 13). Ellis is trying to strike back at a tough foe. *Los Angeles Times*.

Former star Dock Ellis says fear of success drove him to use drugs. (1984, April 30). *Jet, 66*(8).

Goldstein, R. (2008, December 21). Dock Ellis, All-Star pitcher who overcame longtime addictions, dies at 63. *New York Times*, p. 43.

Hall, D. (1989). *Dock Ellis in the country of baseball*. Fireside.

Ilel, N., & Alexander, D. (2008, March 29). An LSD no-no. *Weekend America*. American Public Media. http://weekendamerica.publicradio.org/display/web/2008/03/28/pitch/

Illest, Bruce. *June 12, 1970: Dock Ellis took a bunch of LSD and pitched a no-hitter.* YouTube. http://www.youtube.com/watch?v=PgOqHLeKGHo

Madden, B. (2008, December 22). From no-hitter on LSD to hair curlers to feuds, Dock Ellis was free spirit. *New York Daily News*. http://articles.nydailynews.com/2008-12-20/sports/17912792_1_dock-ellis-no-hitter-yankees

Mcalester, K. (2005, June 16). How to throw a no-hitter on acid, and other lessons from the career of baseball legend Dock Ellis. *Dallas Observer*. http://www.dallasobserver.com/content/printVersion/286078/

Mikkelson, B., & Mikkelson, D. P. (2003). Did Dock Ellis pitch a no-hitter on LSD? http://www.snopes.com/sports/baseball/ellis.asp

Nesteroff, K. (2009, September 13). Just what the doctor ordered [blog post]. http://blog.wfmu.org/freeform/2009/09/just-what-the-doc-ordered-lsd-and-the-strangest-moment-in-major-league-history.html

Radice, J. (Director). (2014). *No no: A dockumentary.* The Orchard Studio.

Silver, M. (2007). Dock Ellis. *Sports Illustrated, 107*(1), 126.

Tayler, J. (2017, June 12). Today is the 47th anniversary of Dock Ellis's acid-fueled no-hitter. *Sports Illustrated.*

Torre, P. S. (2010). A light in the darkness. *Sports Illustrated, 112*(26), 72–79.

Walker, R. (2017). The day Pittsburgh Pirates pitcher Dock Ellis threw a no-no while high on LSD. *The Undefeated.* https://theundefeated.com/features/pittsburgh-pirates-pitcher-dock-ellis-threw-a-no-no-while-high-on-lsd/

Witz, B. (2010, September 4). For Ellis, a long, strange trip to a no-hitter. *New York Times.*

3

Michael Peterson

National Icon and Antihero

The year was 1975, and Mick, or MP, as he was known by his mates, was the only Australian surfer in history who'd won a national championship three years in a row. He had already dominated the contests of the previous years and was now in a position to further demonstrate his dominance. Unfortunately, he was being soundly beaten by his main rival, who had won six of the previous rounds and had a commanding lead of more than 1,000 points. It was virtually impossible to overcome such a deficit.

Peterson was on fire that day, paddling like a madman back and forth at a furious pace. It takes an extraordinary amount of energy to just get past the break of the waves, yet he managed to catch more than a dozen consecutive waves. He carved each turn with his characteristic aggression and artistry, which blew the South African opponent out of the water.

Nobody thought this was remotely conceivable, especially considering that Peterson was riding his so-called "secret weapon" with the unwieldy shape. The board was alleged to look more like a weird torture device from the Middle Ages than a functional surfboard. Peterson was a noted board shaper, but this monstrosity seemed to defy the laws of physics with its triple flyer pintail. Nevertheless, Mick was quite attached to it and felt it would bring him good luck. Indeed it did.

In order to claim his trophy and prize money, Peterson was expected to appear at the award ceremony in front of the crowd. It was the usual convention for the winner to take a few bows, offer a short speech, and stick around for media interviews and autographs. This he refused to do. Instead, Peterson was lurking in the bushes, hiding and watching the award event from afar. When a friend found him kneeling there and begged him to come up and accept his trophy, he just shook his head vigorously, whispering to the guy to leave him alone. He couldn't stand to have people stare at him. He didn't understand why he was that way, but he later explained, "It's mainly the way I look. It's the way I act. I try to be like everybody else, but it's hard." He avoided people whenever possible, especially when attention was drawn to him. He felt like he was "condemned to live like a hermit, to live in a dark room, and just survive." Once he emerged from the dark room—or the bushes—it felt like everyone would pick at him relentlessly, and he had no armor, no protection.

He did show up the next day at the reception, where he was required to give a champion speech. He delivered one of the most unusual such talks in history: "I could tell you what my strategy was for winning, but I'm not going to. Thanks very much." Then he walked away and out the door.

To say that Michael Peterson was shy can't possibly do justice to his pathological avoidance of attention in any form. He once claimed that one reason he loved surfing so much was because nobody could see him when he was hiding inside the barrel of a wave. As a shaper and board designer, he had developed a radical template for his "Moon Rocket," a board with three fins and a more centered underside curvature. This allowed him to lean back and slow his speed inside the tube for so long it would sometimes seem as if he had disappeared.

In the Beginning

Michael never knew his father, never even discovered who he was. Nobody knew. And if his mother, Joan, could identify the man, she wasn't saying. There was a rumor that she had once been gang-raped and her son was the result. Joan said she was dragged off the street into a boarding house and raped by three different men, and she was forever uncertain which one could have been the father.

"The greatest surfer of his time drowned long before he ever caught his first wave." So begins Sean Doherty's comprehensive and remarkable account of MP's life. Doherty describes MP's initial experience with water, falling into the river and floating downstream "dead as driftwood. Mouth-to-mouth resuscitation brought him back to life, and he never looked back after this baptism."

His single mother was a strict, controlling disciplinarian, although she did have a succession of temporary husbands living in the house. Not surprisingly, the family struggled financially, living on the edge of poverty for many years. Joan worked hard for a long time in a variety of difficult jobs—peeling shrimp, running a pool hall, working in a laundry, making change in a pinball parlor—doing whatever it took to support her family.

The kids hit the jackpot when the family relocated to a famous surfing community on the Australian east coast. Michael (aka "Mick," aka "MP") joined the lifesaving club when he was just five years old, giving him unlimited access to a locker, a shower, and the beach. He spent so much time in the water he seemed to grow scales. By the time he was 11, he was already winning youth titles. By age 16, he had dropped out of school to devote himself full-time to the water.

Two of his friends and surf mates, Wayne "Rabbit" Bartholomew and Peter Townsend, would frequent the Queensland beaches near their homes. Each of them would one day win the World Surfing Championship, so the competition among them was fierce. Bartholomew would later claim that MP was "flat out the best surfer in the world." Even though they were friends since childhood, Rabbit would often feel intimidated by MP's spooky stare. "He'd chop your head off in the water," he laughed and then remembered how Peterson once shaped a "special" board for him, one he said would guarantee him a victory. But in fact it was specifically designed to sabotage him, and the thing could barely float. Even MP's brother, Tommy, admitted, "He had a nasty competitive edge."

From the earliest age, MP showed signs of emotional instability. He was a compulsive hand washer from the age of two, scrubbing his hands over and over. Although almost totally indifferent to friendships, he was meticulous about his appearance, his clothes orderly and pressed. Mostly all he cared about was surfing.

A Surfer Without a Board

MP could never scrape together enough money to buy a surfboard to pursue his passion in the water. His family had enough trouble just trying to survive and put food on the table. Fortunately, this was during the days before leashes (straps that would tether the trailing ankle to the board), so a lot of broken boards would wash up on remote parts of the beach. He and his brother, Tommy, would go on hunting expeditions trying to find a board that was repairable. MP also got jobs working as a surf lifesaver when he was 15, which gave him continued access to a locker and showers as well as time to work the surf and become intimately familiar with its moods and nuances.

With an entrepreneurial spirit, the two brothers set up a business carrying the huge 12-foot boards of the era that tourists would bring to the beach. Then they set up their own board-shaping business, and they became instrumental in launching the "short

Fig. 3-1. **Above we see Michael (MP) Peterson making one of his signature cutbacks with his unique aggressive style, which featured incredible power and acrobatics that had never been seen before. He seemed to defy the laws of physics with his extraordinary strength and sense of balance. Riding a wave was the only time he felt truly sane and in control of his life.**

board" revolution. They would take the standard-length longboards and cut them down to six feet, making them far more maneuverable and allowing surfers to make radical cutbacks on the waves.

Just as soon as Michael and Tommy would finish shaping an experimental board, they'd immediately run out to the surf before the paint even dried. Of course, Tommy would usually have to wait impatiently on the sand for hours until his brother would relinquish control. They tried all kinds of creative variations regarding where to place the fin or even multiple fins. They'd try relocating the rails in different spots, depending on the surf conditions and the beach. They'd also keep cutting down the size of the boards from the standard eight feet to all kinds of adaptations. And remember, these were just kids who were revolutionizing the sport in their backyard.

MP was already winning contests before he was even 16. During one such tournament on the Gold Coast, there was uncharacteristically huge swell for that area, and a film-maker was shooting footage for his movie *Morning of the Earth*. Peterson was a madman that day, making turns and taking risks that spectators couldn't believe. MP was featured prominently in the film, showcasing his muscular, lean, statuesque body, his long hair flying in the wind, and a ferocious expression on his face. He looked like a surfing god.

MP was expected to attend the premiere of the film, which was being screened in a local hall. His mother went so far as to drive him to the event, but Peterson refused to go inside. He just wasn't comfortable with any attention and was quite apprehensive about his newfound notoriety. In addition to his appearance in the movie, an iconic photo of him taken from the film (and considered an archetypal image of surfing to this day) was displayed on the cover of a popular surfing magazine. The dude was famous.

MP would become highly anxious in almost any social situation. People wanted to talk to him. Girls tried to get his attention. Other surfers wanted to engage him about some of his unique tricks. Only marijuana seemed to calm him down enough to function. And he would smoke a *lot* of it. The drug seemed to slow down the chaos whirling around inside his head and silence the voices that were whispering to him. Whereas most athletes were inclined to use performance-enhancing substances such as amphetamines, steroids, and human growth hormones, MP needed drugs to *decrease* his reaction times and processing. He was likely already showing the early signs of mental illness that typically become symptomatic during adolescence, so he was doing his best to hold himself together. Only the weed and water could keep him calm.

Over time, Peterson's reliance on illicit drugs to maintain some semblance of sanity escalated. Heroin hit the surfing scene big-time during the '70s, and that provided an even more potent option for him to moderate his symptoms. His friends made allowances for his erratic moods, unpredictable behavior, and strange claims about voices inside his head, perhaps attributing them to chronic drug use. By that time, there had been dozens of fatal overdoses from injecting heroin, so MP limited himself solely to snorting the drug for its effects.

After the early years cobbling together boards from leftovers, MP's mother enticed him with the ultimate irresistible challenge: if he could win the upcoming club championship—populated by many older, more experienced surfers—she'd buy him his first brand-new customized board. It hardly needs to be mentioned that he won the contest easily and earned his first tool to eventually become a professional surfer.

A Measure of Success

After dropping out of school to devote more time to surfing, MP tried to support himself as a bricklayer, but, not surprisingly, his heart wasn't in it. Instead he began spending more time shaping boards, a skill that seemed to be in great demand. Shaping is an art form, combining engineering with aesthetics to create a tool that can maximize both speed and maneuverability. Nobody doubted that Peterson was a genius at this craft, but the problem was that he kept designing boards according to his own preferences and specifications. There was status associated with owning such a coveted board—it's just that nobody could control it quite like he could. In one sense, that says it all: MP seemed absolutely incapable of figuring out that his job was actually to satisfy his customers' needs rather than his own.

Michael Peterson's surfboard business was flourishing in spite of his poor business decisions and volatile moods. He never made any significant income from surfing, even during the time when he won every contest he entered. The cash prizes would be blown within a few weeks to pay off debts or purchase drugs.

Yet orders were flooding in for his newly designed products, which revolutionized the maneuvers that could now be expanded on the waves. Unfortunately, many of the orders could not be filled because of a shortage of supplies. Whatever income came in MP would impulsively squander on things he couldn't even remember purchasing. By the time his mother stepped in to stop the financial hemorrhaging, it was far too late, and the business crashed. His sole source of income was now whatever he could win during competitions—a few hundred dollars here and there.

The early years of the '70s were a golden time for Peterson as he earned international recognition for his domination of the sport. His signature style was quite unlike anything that had been seen before. "He demonstrated a full-power style," remembers writer Nick Carroll, "that combined an acute tube sense with fast, deep rail carves." In layman's language, he was ferocious out in the waves. If anyone got too close to his tubes, he'd launch a shrill whistle to intimidate them out of the way.

On land, MP was sometimes a frightening figure, stomping around, brooding, muttering to himself in a leather jacket and aviator sunglasses. Although he was "aloof, awkward, and monosyllabic on land," recalls writer Martin Childs, "he was transformed by the sea. His surfing was frenetic and savage." His legs would fold underneath each other and then straighten out as if propelled by some magic force, twitching into contorted shapes as he guided his board into crazy angles along the face of the waves. He had an uncanny ability to read the ocean, to talk to the water, to know just when a perfect set was on its way to him.

MP was certainly shy and obviously eccentric, but his personal habits would drive others up the wall. He would usually show up at a contest just seconds before he was due for a heat, and then he would fade away immediately afterwards like a wisp of smoke. His violent temper was as legendary as his surfing prowess. He was especially inclined to get into violent brawls with his brother, Tom, often in public or while they were out on the surf. One time while they were out on the water, MP perceived that his brother got in his way, so he ripped the surfboard out of Tom's arms and lobbed it over the shark nets, where the predators were known to hunt for prey. Tom was so furious that, in retaliation, he swam to shore, opened up the hood of his brother's car, detached the battery and distributor, and hurled them into the ocean.

Cult Figure

It wasn't just Peterson's moves on the waves that made him a cult figure; it was also his prowess at shaping boards to his singular purpose. He constantly sanded and resanded the surfaces, jiggled with the fin placements, and tightened the angles, almost like alchemy. Adding to the mystery was the complete paranoia and secrecy he attached to his work, refusing to allow anyone to watch him do his magic.

Michael Peterson was a physical freak in his sport, in the same way that Olympic swimmer Michael Phelps has size-14 flipper feet attached to double-jointed ankles. According to observers, MP's hands (the size of dinner plates) were made for paddling, his arms were elastic, and his shoulders were so tireless that he could paddle for hours without seeming to slow down. If you've ever tried surfing, you know that the toughest part of the sport isn't just managing to catch a wave but also paddling back out past the break against the current, riptides, and crashing surf. And do it again and again. And again.

MP's cult status also permitted him to intimidate other surfers out on the water, sometimes terrifying them if they got in his way. Nobody was ever allowed to drop into a wave in front of him, or he would seek retribution, even sacrificing his board to aim for the offender's head. He *owned* the waves and would tolerate no infringement on his personal territory. His temper and erratic behavior were sometimes so capricious that nobody would even think of challenging his reign.

The cult surrounding Peterson only began to grow as he won more tournaments, and his behavior became more eccentric. He won the Australian National Championship in 1972 and became the country's most notorious surfer. Tourists started to flood into town just to watch him at work. Other surfers would just hang out on the water, waiting and watching his signature moves.

As the surfing culture and its accompanying drug use started to grow on the Queensland coast, the local police became more focused on trying to snag some arrests. In addition to weed, LSD, and magic mushrooms, other more dangerous drugs were now openly commonplace. This put a target squarely on MP's back, since he was viewed as the leader of this pack of unruly potheads. Whatever paranoia was part of his normal psyche was ramped up to much higher levels, especially after he was arrested and threatened with jail. He was also the subject of attempts by the local surf club to disqualify him from some competitions. He was garnering just too much attention, which threatened others, and many waited, even hoped, for his inevitable fall from grace.

The Last Wave

MP flamed out as fast as he rose within the sport. He had plenty of excuses for his collapse, attributing some of his losses to jealous judges, a government conspiracy, or the fact that he just surfed too fast to be rewarded appropriately by the points system. He was supposed to defend his Australian championship in 1975 but arrived in South Australia after the contest had already started. Once again, he offered a lot of excuses: The waves were too small, and there were too many sharks around for him to compete. During one interview, he said he was just sick of winning all the time and wanted to give others a chance.

The truth was that the voices inside his head were now starting to take over. He talked more often about conspiracies and being followed everywhere. He was showing many of the classic signs and symptoms of schizophrenia, even if others attributed his behavior to drug abuse. He was becoming increasingly withdrawn, even for him, barely bothering to respond to others around him. Just as his abilities in the water were waning, he became more convinced than ever of his invincibility and specialness as a surfing god.

After a string of losses when he barely showed up at contests (physically and sometimes literally), he competed in 1977 in the Stubbies Event at Burleigh Heads in front of over 20,000 spectators. This was the birth of pro surfing's world tour and its first official event. It was also the first time that a system was introduced in which two surfers would compete against one another at the same time, a structure that is still currently in use by the World Surf League. It was a close race between MP and his main rivals and childhood friends, Wayne "Rabbit" Bartholomew and Peter Townsend, who would someday each win their own world championships.

MP tried his best to get his head back together for what would become his final hurrah. He changed his diet, abstained from sex, and tried some rather unusual forms of therapy to get the voices out of his head. Whatever heroin, cocaine, and weed couldn't fix he addressed with self-administered acupuncture by sticking needles all over his body.

The waves were perfect that day, head-high and glassy, and this was on his home turf, where he was totally familiar with the break. Rabbit and Townsend wondered if MP would even show up. There'd been a rumor that he might have even overdosed on heroin.

After annihilating the competition in the initial heats, MP's name was called for the final, but he was nowhere to be found; he'd disappeared once again. They finally found him sitting in his car, nodding off in a drug-steeped daze. After he was pulled out of the car and pointed in the direction of the beach, he seemed to come alive. And come alive he did, earning 47 out of a perfect 50 points. It was the closest possible match anyone had ever seen between MP and Mark Richards, who would soon dominate the sport. It turned out to be a split decision among the judges, but MP prevailed, mostly based on one ride during which he slipped inside a tube by a rock pile and everyone wondered if he'd even survive, much less emerge from the wave. Sure enough, he popped out in a crouch.

MP earned $5,000 in prize money that day, an astronomical amount for him at the time. Years later, his friends wondered if his life might have been different if someone else had won and deprived him of that money, which allowed him to go off on a crazed drug binge. That was to be his last major victory before he slipped into obscurity. At the award ceremony afterwards, in front of international media and a crowd, he just stood on stage, frozen and mute, with a grin on his face. When they tried to put the ceremonial lei of flowers over his head, he refused to even bend over, just shaking his head. Everyone in the audience yelled out to him, "Speech! Speech!"

Peterson walked over to the microphone, grabbed the check, and said, "I deserved it." Then he walked off stage, went out into the parking lot, and just took off.

The paranoia, delusions, and mental illness that had been sparked occasionally during the previous years were now raging at full blast. MP was a lost soul, barely aware of where he was at times, totally encapsulated within himself. He would no longer make eye contact with anyone and wore his trademark aviator sunglasses to shield his own eyes from anything or anyone he found intrusive. He was like a ghost, invisible most of the time until he'd come out of hiding for a few hours or days and then retreat back into his shell.

Peterson was once again trying to control his symptoms with self-administered drugs. Weed could no longer put a dent in his disturbing thoughts, so he amped up his heroin habit, snorting it more often. He was out of money and no longer had any regular source of income, especially once he stopped winning prize money. He kept borrowing from his mother and friends until those sources dried up. He resorted to stealing surfboards off cars and selling them on the black market. At one point, he hooked up with a prostitute as his girlfriend so she would share her earnings with him.

MP's biographer, Sean Doherty, describes in agonizing detail the extent of his subject's emotional deterioration. He recounts a series of incidents when Peterson would show up at a contest or just at a surf break, run out into the ocean, ride one wave, and then escape immediately afterward. MP realized he was drowning and that his excessive drug use wasn't helping matters much. He tried, and failed, multiple times to go off the heroin cold turkey. His muscular frame was now reduced to a skeleton. He knew he was sick and felt himself dying, yet he was helpless to do anything to alter the course his life was taking. About the only safe haven he had was to return home to his mother for some rest, decent food, and loving support.

Stories and Legends

It is difficult to separate the myths about Peterson's life from an approximation of truth, especially when writing about a legend, one with a mental illness in which fantasy and reality blend together. Even to this day, surfers sit around and swap stories about all the crazy things they saw MP do during his brief tenure on the scene. His friend Townsend remembers one time they were in Hawaii and MP stole Fast Eddie's girl. Eddie was the most evil enforcer on the North Shore, the one guy you'd *never* want to mess with. MP just didn't give a shit.

Townsend wondered how different things could have been for his friend if they had only had decent drugs in those days to control his symptoms. "Now they have all sorts of drugs to balance him out," he said, but then considered for a moment. "Actually, that might have hurt him. He might not have been the madman he was when it came to competition and design if he didn't have those demons."

That is indeed a common belief, if not a myth, held by many creative geniuses. I mentioned previously how writers such as Sylvia Plath and Virginia Woolf, comedian Lenny Bruce, and jazz player Charles Mingus all found their creative spirits were fueled, in part, by their extreme emotional volatility. For MP, about the only time he ever felt normal was when he was in the water, the only place he could be himself. The socially withdrawn crank transformed into a graceful ballet dancer on his board. Once he'd come ashore, he'd pull back inside himself and his eyes would glaze over.

Other surfers, the media, and the public resented that someone so outrageous and antisocial, so downright weird, was the best at his sport. "He was never going to be a role model for everyone else," observed surfer Ross Slaven. "That's the package the talent was in."

Rabbit remembers another example of a "full-drama MP" incident. They had called Peterson's name as his heat was starting, and he was still sitting on the beach rolling a joint, completely oblivious to what was going on. Rabbit walked over to him. "MP, you better get out there," he said, pointing. "Your heat already started."

Peterson looked up at him, nodding slowly. Then he casually picked up his board and started paddling out with strong, languid strokes. He won the contest, and he was only partly aware of what was going on.

Another famous incident took place during the first world championship in San Diego, one of the few times that MP ever traveled abroad. It turned out to be a magical journey for him, but not because he won the contest or even advanced past the second heat. In fact, the waves were too small for him to show his stuff. It was special because he ended up sneaking away from the team and proceedings to hop on a plane to Hawaii with Rabbit. What was supposed to be a weeklong holiday ended up lasting three months, during which he enjoyed the best surfing in his life, just for the pure joy. He was introduced to the huge pounding waves of Pipeline, among other classics. They just lived on the beach, surviving on bananas and other fruit growing on the trees.

MP did have one amazing ride in the world championship. He disappeared inside a tube for what seemed like an eternity, but only one of the judges saw him take off and gave him a perfect score. Unfortunately, it was disqualified. That was only part of his frustration. It was just a different surfing culture in the United States, dominated by what he considered washed-up longboard riders like Corky Carroll, who was an ancient 24 at the time, while the cheeky kid from Queensland was a frenetic maniac at 19.

Corky Carroll was considered the first truly professional surfer, the first one to actually make a living from the sport. He was voted by his peers as the number one surfer in the world, and he earned endorsements and appeared on national talk shows and in famous films. As an aside, he was also *my* first surfing instructor, although it's not his fault I never learned to turn. I recall one time when I was just destroyed by a wave and knocked senseless while trying to paddle out to the break. I literally crawled back onto the beach on my hands and knees, spitting sand and seawater, and I saw these spindly legs at eye level. Although my ears were clogged with water, I could still hear Corky yelling at me to never, *ever* do that again.

Like many stories that are decades old, there are different memories and multiple versions of what actually happened during the conflict between Corky and MP. What is clear is that they were competing in the same heat. Whereas Corky was a gentleman of sorts who played by the rules, MP literally tried to surf circles around him, cutting him off and dropping in front of him. It was a radical clash of style and culture, and it led to considerable drama once they were back on land, at least according to some witnesses, who alleged that Corky was so furious he reached in through the window of the car to grab MP until others intervened.

Corky remembered things quite differently when I interviewed him, although it hap-pened so long ago the details were a bit hazy. "All I know is the whole bunch of them were totally strung out and in some different universe than ours. What happened in the water was I took off on a wave and MP dropped in on me and did a big turn right into me. I straightened out in order to avoid contact, and we both ended up going straight into the whitewater."

Corky was most annoyed that he was called for interference even though MP was the one who cut him off. Whatever anger he might have felt was considerably lessened when he heard that MP was high as a kite on heroin at the time. Corky protested the interference call and was told by the judges that if MP corroborated that version of what happened, they would rescind the disqualification.

"So I went over to the car he was in to talk to him," Corky remembered. "But there was a bunch of really weird dudes there, and they wouldn't let me talk to him. They were all like 'leave him alone,' and he was hunkered down in the back seat."

Corky insisted he had no intention of hurting the guy. "I just wanted to get his take on what had happened and hoped he would back me up with the judge."

Ultimately it didn't much matter, since Corky advanced to the next heat anyway, and MP finished last. Corky was upset that the whole thing got blown way out of proportion. He even wrote MP asking him to straighten out the misrepresentation, but he never heard back from him.

Regardless of what really happened, this exemplifies the kinds of legends that have only grown over the years, usually stories that highlight the unpredictable rage MP demonstrated on the water and his obliviousness on land. He was the ultimate antihero and model for what most people hoped surfing would leave behind as it became a legitimate professional sport. It's obvious which attitude prevailed: Prize money for a major international event now exceeds half a million dollars, a figure that can easily double through endorsements.

Almost everyone agrees that MP had little use for other people, except as enemies. There were no real friends, even among those he'd known since childhood. Everyone was a potential threat. And with his propensity to entertain delusional paranoia, he really did believe that everyone in the world was out to get him. Rabbit tells the story of how their relationship abruptly changed once he turned 18 and was no longer classified as a junior. Michael believed afterwards that Rabbit was always stalking him, and one time MP even threatened to kill him if he didn't stop following him everywhere. Given that they both lived so close to one another and surfed the same breaks, it was no surprise they'd see each other every day.

Meanwhile, the voices in MP's head were getting louder and becoming more persistent. He began talking to himself or to an imaginary other. He'd carry on lengthy conversations with the phantom in ways he never would with someone in reality. If someone asked him what he was doing, he'd just deny it and then challenge the accusation angrily. At times he'd be observed just giggling to himself, completely unaware of what he was doing. It was simply agonizing for family, friends, and even acquaintances to watch, not understanding any more than he did about what was really going on. He'd become more and more isolated, going off alone for days or weeks at a time. He tried attending church to silence the voices. He experimented with cutting back on certain drugs, foods, or habits, hoping that would have some impact. No matter what he tried, his brain became increasingly scrambled. He would frequently lose track of time or even what day it was.

The Chase

MP was on his way to Noosa for a day of surfing in the winter of 1983. He wanted to stop in to see his sister, Dot, to borrow $50 because he was almost always short of funds. During the drive, he started to drift off, so he wisely pulled over to the side of the road to catch a nap. He was startled awake from a deep sleep by a frightening siren, which appeared to be coming from a Martian spacecraft. He was convinced aliens were attacking and that he could hear their voices whispering to him. Most of all, he was disturbed by the flashing lights coming toward him.

Peterson had been hearing voices in his head for many years, but they were usually friendly voices. This time they were terrifying. His first and only thought was to escape. Immediately, he slunk down behind the wheel and took off as fast as he could go in the opposite direction from the lights and noise. He was burning up the highway at speeds exceeding 80 miles per hour. Yet no matter how hard he slammed down on the accelerator, the lights were getting closer, and the deafening noise from the alien ships was driving him mad. He could see even more spaceships attacking from a distance.

It turned out that more than 35 police cars pursued him for over 100 miles (who knew that that the whole area even had that many?). He ended up running nine red lights, barreling through three roadblocks, and sideswiping two police cars before he was finally stopped and arrested. MP claimed that he thought his driving was pretty good, considering the circumstances (an alien attack). He finally gave up because he was sick of the Martians chasing him and decided to surrender. "I didn't know what I was doing. I did know what I was doing … I dunno. It was weird that night on the road." Weird indeed.

The whole thing had been filmed and broadcast on the national news, an Australian version of the famous O. J. Simpson chase in Los Angeles that occurred more than a decade later. It made headlines in the papers and earned him more fame, which he hardly needed.

The police were convinced he was on drugs, even more so when they found white powder sprinkled all over the car seats. Even though it turned out that it was just Vitamin C, they still insisted that someone who was acting that crazy *had* to be intoxicated. It never occurred to them that he really was mentally ill.

MP was convicted, sentenced to a long prison term at hard labor, and banned from driving for the rest of his life. It wasn't until months later that his mother successfully begged the minister of justice to have her son medically examined. After so many years of bizarre and erratic behavior, he was finally diagnosed as paranoid schizophrenic and put on antipsychotic medication.

Spending time in prison—an especially dangerous, violent place where riots regularly broke out—was hardly the best environment for someone suffering hallucinations and delusions. When friends and family came to visit him, they noticed MP was virtually mute. When he did mumble some response to their questions, it was to tell them he refused to pick up the phone because he believed that either he was so covered in germs he might infect them or that the phone would electrocute him.

If there was any positive result from his imprisonment, it was that MP had an epiphany: He did much better when he was alone. He realized that isolation and solitude were what he needed most. He admitted that, in some ways, he liked his time in prison. "Away from drugs, from women, away from sex, away from surfing, away from the pressure." He felt transformed. He wasn't MP anymore; he was someone or something else.

His mother was quite disturbed by her son's transformation when he was released. He was always scratching himself—a side effect of the medications. His pants kept falling down because he had lost so much weight. He wouldn't talk or respond to much, as if he had isolated himself in a shell. It was also clear to her that her unrecognizable son would never be able to hold a job or have a girlfriend and would likely never get back into the water again.

A friend remembers MP's last wave. He had been perched on the beach brooding when he slowly uncoiled and walked into the water and out to the break. After staring out at the ocean for a while, he caught the lip of a small wave, standing vertical and completely still like a statue, hands at his side. He just came in straight, unwavering, toward the shore, never once turning or moving. He rode onto the beach, stepped off onto the sand, and just walked away. That was the end.

After surviving his brief stint in prison and eventually being transferred to the mental hospital, MP was an empty shell of a human being. Nobody had ever realized he had been sick, that he had a blazing mental illness. They just assumed it was MP.

"He was a spent force after he got out of the nuthouse," his friend remembers. "He just disappeared."

Four Walls, Three Meals, Two Pills, and a Radio

The title of this final section is taken from a description of Michael Peterson's life in its last stage. He had become a recluse, locked inside a darkened room where he played the radio all day, hoping the music would drown out the voices he heard almost constantly. He had deteriorated to the point where his compulsive handwashing had expanded into an all-encompassing obsession with cleanliness. He couldn't tolerate bright lights and began to supplement his careful vegetarian diet with junk food and candy.

His mother could no longer care for him or protect his safety. She became so concerned that she had him admitted into a psychiatric facility until they could figure out a way to stabilize his medications. He would be in and out of a half dozen such facilities in the coming years. He ballooned up to almost 300 pounds, requiring his mother to get a bigger, more stable bed and replace chairs that were crushed by his bulk. He would become totally engaged in conversations with the voices speaking to him, occupied for hours at a time while sitting outside alone. The voices were as real to him as any of his family or visitors who would breeze through the house. The only consolation was that the voices were relatively friendly companions. They mostly made him laugh and seemed to be entertaining. His life become totally encapsulated in his own self-created world. In his own way, MP had found a sort of peace, seemingly content with his modest needs.

At the age of 59, Michael Peterson died of a heart attack after enduring a series of health problems, including diabetes and limited mobility. He had become morbidly obese as a result of the side effects of various antipsychotic medications, becoming unrecognizable to those who had previously known him.

MP was honored by his brethren among the surfing community. None other than Kelly Slater, 11-time world champion, paddled his board out past the break on the North Shore of Hawaii. The sun was setting, and most of the crowd had left the beach after the tournament's quarterfinal heat.

Fig. 3-2. During the height of his fame, Michael Peterson (pictured above) was a cult figure, a mysterious, alluring celebrity who brought unprecedented fame to the sport of surfing during its formative years. Eventually, schizophrenic symptoms, chronic drug abuse, and the side effects of antipsychotic medication would take a brutal toll on his mind and body.

Source: https://bit.ly/2WLo49s.

Slater is considered the greatest surfer in history, but he was on his board to acknowledge that long before him, there'd been another athlete, one from across the pond, who'd also dominated his sport. "MP and I had an unlikely friendship," Slater explained. "We were very different personalities and people, but I really enjoyed visiting him and hearing old stories." Slater had planned to visit his friend once again just the week before he died. He had once admitted to Peterson, "You are better than me."

Pipeline, with its huge, often nine-foot pounding waves, is the most hallowed place on earth for world-class surfers. A member of MP's family had flown over from Australia to deliver his ashes to Slater, who agreed to honor his friend with a ceremonial ritual out in the ocean. After first sharing some of his favorite stories about the most eccentric, unpredictable surfer he'd ever known, Slater paddled out and spread MP's ashes across the water.

Surfer magazine has named Peterson one of most influential athletes in the sport's history, and he is certainly one of those who forever changed surfing into what it has now become. Each year, the memorial Michael Peterson Classic surf tournament is held near his favorite beach. It is considered one of Australia's most prestigious events. Tens of thousands of dollars are raised each year, with much of the proceeds donated to local health facilities. MP's legacy helps so many others within his community who struggle with mental illness obtain services he was never able to access himself.

Sources

Arney, M. (2015). The enigmatic Michael Peterson. *Surf Simply*. https://surfsimply.com/surf-culture/michael-peterson/

Carroll, N. (2012, March 28). Michael Peterson: 1953–2012. *Surfline*. http://www.surfline.com/surf-news/michael-peterson-1953-2012_68441/

Carroll, N. (2012, March 28). Michael Peterson. *Surfing Life*. https://www.surfinglife.com.au/2012/03/28/9867/michael-peterson/

Childs, M. (2012, April 16). Michael Peterson: Surfer whose glittering career was ended by his troubled life. *The Independent*. http://www.independent.co.uk/news/obituaries/michael-peterson-surfer-whose-glittering-career-was-ended-by-his-troubled-life-7648153.html

Doherty, S. (2004). *MP: The life of Michael Peterson*. Harper Collins.

Gordon, M. (2012, March 29). Heart attack claims surfing great. *Sydney Morning Herald*. https://www.smh.com.au/sport/heart-attack-claims-surfing-great-20120329-1vzxu.html

Hoff, J. (Director). (2009). *Searching for Michael Peterson*. Screen Australia.

Pawlee, F. (2012, March 30). How a cheeky, troubled kid from Queensland came to personify Australian surfing. *The Australian*. https://www.theaustralian.com.au/life/how-a-cheeky-troubled-kid-from-queensalnd-came-to-personify-australian-surfing/news-story

Warshaw, M. (2005). *Encyclopedia of surfing*. Harcourt.

4

Suzy Favor Hamilton

When Athletes Fail

K elly Lundy was a drop-dead gorgeous woman in her 30s. While perhaps a bit on the older side for a top-tier Las Vegas call girl, she had an extraordinary body and a seductive, enticing personality that drove her clients absolutely crazy. At the height of her profession, Kelly earned $1,000 per hour for entertaining corporate executives, celebrities, and anyone else with money to burn.

Kelly wasn't merely a prostitute—she was the perfect model of most anyone's ideal sexual fantasy. In her profile on the agency's website, she wrote: "I try my best to bring elegance and class to the table and will dress appropriately for any occasion ... I consider dates with couples an experience to cherish. Working with couples requires special skill, and I pride myself in my ability to make a woman feel comfortable and not threatened in any way, shape, or form. A date with me will never feel rushed."

Rather than feeling exploited or demeaned by her job as a sex worker, Kelly adored what she was doing. She loved the excitement, even the risks involved. She saw herself as a sexual artist who had developed her skills to be among the best in the world. She loved the power she wielded, the attachment that some of her clients felt toward her. And she reveled in the accolades she received from her wildly satisfied customers.

On the feedback page of her agency's website, many clients described her services as transcendent. "It was the best experience of my life," one man wrote. He was so taken by the "mind-blowing" experience that he rebooked her twice within the same 24 hours. He became obsessed with her and couldn't get enough.

Fall from Grace

It was later revealed that Kelly was really none other than Suzy Favor Hamilton, America's Olympic darling and one of the most dominant amateur track stars in recent memory. She had retired from racing a decade before and was now a successful Wisconsin real estate broker, motivational speaker, mother, and local celebrity.

"Kelly" (aka Suzy) had been recognized by several of her clients, and *The Smoking Gun* website broke the story wide open. One of America's elite revered athletes was a hooker on the side. In an era when famous athletes and celebrities are routinely outed for bizarre behavior, *this* was a scandal that could never have been imagined. The publicity and outrage that followed were unprecedented.

In a profile of Hamilton after her public disgrace, writer Peter Vigneron asked the key perplexing question: "Why does an affluent, semi-recognizable, married real estate agent from Wisconsin become a sex worker in Las Vegas?" The consequential losses were catastrophic, and the accompanying shame was so powerful that her father urged her to change her name and leave the country. Sponsors such as Nike, Reebok, Disney, and Foot Locker abandoned her in droves. Race events named after her were cancelled. Speaking engagements dried up. Her legacy and reputation as one of the greatest American long-distance racers in history was tarnished. This was a woman who had won *nine* NCAA championships and participated in *three* Olympic Games.

Some clues to the mystery may relate to the reality that it was not her lack of physical ability, training, or skill as a runner that sabotaged her efforts to win an Olympic medal over an eight-year span. She even finished last and fell down during her final appearance, although hers had been among the best qualifying times. No, it was something else altogether. On a deep level, Suzy was deeply wounded, terrified of failure, and crippled by anxiety as well as a festering mental illness.

I Pretended I Was a Horse

Suzy grew up in a small town in Wisconsin with plenty of woodsy trails to explore. She would run through them on her way to collect branches and materials to build forts to hide in. Discovering that she had the capacity to run almost endlessly, she used to pretend she was a horse galloping along.

After noticing her prodigious early talent as a runner, her father began coaching her. During her first race, she finished so far ahead of the other girls that it wasn't even a real competition. Eventually she moved up to racing boys, who could also never keep up with her.

School had always been a challenge for Suzy. She felt restless and fidgety, finding it difficult to focus and concentrate. She could never sit still or empty her mind. The only thing that seemed to soothe her, calm her down, and clear her mind was running. When she was in flight, there was a purity to her feelings, and she found she could literally run off her excess energy.

Suzy always felt different as a child, not only because of her attention deficit and hyperactivity but also because of her talent. She was treated differently, too, as much a freak as a celebrity in her school. It was as if she had otherworldly powers that allowed her to move at warp speed.

Whether it was due to her inborn athletic gifts or just the desperation to survive daily life, Suzy was a phenomenon. She could outrace any girl or boy at a pace that seemed almost superhuman. By the time she was a high school freshman, she had won every single race she'd entered at the local, regional, and statewide level. She won races at almost every distance—a mile, two miles, 3,200 meters, it didn't matter. She just totally dominated the competition. When she was a junior, she won the national championship with a record time.

Fig. 4-1. Above, we see Suzy Favor Hamilton running in the world championships after a distinguished career in college as the most dominant middle-distance runner. It was her sense of perfectionism that not only pushed her to work harder and run faster than anyone else but ultimately led to her fear of failure and emotional collapse.

As much as this fame and notoriety brought approval from her parents and community, it was also a tremendous burden, which she described as the "cruel cycle of my life." She felt increasing pressure to keep winning, at whatever cost. What had once been the love of her life—running for the pure joy of movement—became a job, an obligation, an overwhelming responsibility. The more she was committed, the more rigorously she trained, the more sacrifices she made, the more obsessed she became, the faster she ran. This led to even greater obsessiveness, which, in turn, increased her performance further. And so the vicious cycle continued to the point where running devoured everything else.

At that time there was another running prodigy, Kathy Ormsby, who was just a few years older than Suzy. During one particular NCAA championship race, Ormsby fell behind the field. This was inconceivable for her, just as it was for Suzy. Neither girl had any experience dealing with what it felt like to fall behind the competition, much less actually lose a race.

Ormsby was running smoothly down the straightaway but was in fourth place. As she approached the curve, instead of staying with the field, she headed for the railing that enclosed the track. She kept going at the same speed and then ducked underneath the railing, staring straight ahead and ignoring anything and everything around her, including the confused coaches and spectators. Then she just disappeared behind the stands.

Observers—including her parents, who were in the audience—assumed she was heading to the bathroom, but even after several minutes, she never returned. She had vanished into thin air. A search began for the missing girl, but she couldn't be found anywhere. It was soon learned that Ormsby had left the track facility altogether, run across a softball field, climbed a seven-foot fence, crossed a busy highway, run onto a bridge, and jumped off the edge, plunging 35 feet to the concrete below.

Ormsby, like Suzy Favor Hamilton, was a perfectionist. She not only dominated her sport but was also valedictorian of her high school class. She had a perfect grade point average and, like Suzy, ran every race with total abandon. She managed to survive the fall but was paralyzed for the rest of her life. "It was like something snapped," she explained a decade after the incident, finding some semblance of peace, if not acceptance. Ormsby further explained that it was never really about losing a race, claiming that was not the issue: "It's like I was out of control."

Ormsby insisted that her suicide attempt was not about losing the race, but there's little doubt that this win-to-survive mentality helped define her, just as it did Suzy. In fact, Favor Hamilton was barely aware of this dramatic incident at the time because she was so focused on improving her own performance.

About that time, Suzy decided to get stronger and faster; she needed to look more like a champion runner. She had an atypical body for a track athlete, which for her was a source of shame. Whereas her large breasts might have earned her attention from boys in school—and even leering from coaches—they were embarrassing appendages in racing. She believed the extra weight slowed her down. She began binge eating and purging as a way to keep her weight down. She'd eat massive amounts of sweets, cakes, or brownies and then stick her finger down her throat to vomit. Her parents and others realized what she was doing, but it became one of many family secrets that were silenced.

Collegiate Sensation

By the time Suzy was a senior in high school, she was being recruited by some of the best college programs in the country. In spite of the opportunities available to her, she chose to stay near home and attend the University of Wisconsin, mostly because of Peter Tegan, the coach. He might have been enamored with his new prodigy's potential, but other team members felt threatened by the speedy newcomer.

Just as she had become addicted to her father's approval throughout her life, she was now totally devoted to the validation of her coach, craving any sign of his attention. And she received a lot of what she wanted from Peter after immediately dominating most of the races during her first year.

Being away from home and on her own—getting out from underneath her father's influence and the bickering with her siblings—was a relief in many ways. Yet with that freedom, some of her personal struggles became worse. She stopped eating in the cafeteria and instead would bring food back to her room, where she could stuff herself to the bursting point and then throw up in the toilet. She said she felt "clean and orderly" afterwards, a tremendous sensation of relief.

Suzy was also having great difficulty with her academic work. She had never been much of a student and was poorly prepared to succeed in college. It was discovered that in addition to her hyperactivity, she also had learning disabilities. For most students, this would be the kiss of death, but because she was a star athlete, she was provided with all kinds of allowances and resources to keep herself eligible to compete. She was assigned tutors who would write her papers or provide her with previous years' exams. Her professors, coaches, and school administrators all paved the way for her to barely pass some of the more challenging classes. Even physical education, the typical major for athletes, was too difficult for her because she couldn't handle kinesiology, so she chose art as an alternative.

Perhaps far more significant than winning races or surviving classes during her first year in college was meeting Mark Hamilton on a blind date. Suzy decided, almost immediately after meeting the scholarship baseball player, that he would someday become her husband. Indeed, throughout her life—with all its triumphs, failures, disappointments, and shameful episodes—Mark would remain her greatest cheerleader and source of support. This began soon after they started dating, when Mark would confront her about her eating issues and demand that she adopt more healthy habits. He also took on the role of surrogate coach and mentor, to the point where her dependence on him got out of control. Because their travel schedules and lifestyles sometimes conflicted, their relationship abruptly ended after a period of time. Suzy became desperate and inconsolable.

"I totally lost it," Suzy explained. "I was in pain, and the pain had to end."

She couldn't think clearly. It felt like she'd lost everything. She was drowning and unmoored. One night she carefully planned how she would end her suffering with a razor blade. She made incisions on her wrists, but once the blood started to flow, she changed her mind and called Mark to rescue her. They reconciled, and things returned to a semblance of normality.

Meanwhile, Suzy was racing. And winning. Almost every time. As her fame spread, she started getting huge endorsements and sponsors—Reebok, Clairol, Blue Cross, and others—paying six figures for her to represent their products. She was an all-American girl: gorgeous, perky, charismatic, and a sensation on the track. Her image would eventually be emblazoned on *Runner's World* as well as fashion and women's magazines such as *Vogue, Cosmopolitan, Elle,* and *Rolling Stone.*

Suzy was now training for the 1992 Olympics in Barcelona, a dream she'd had since childhood. The expectations were high, and the pressure was ramping up. Some coaches would privately take her aside and explain that to compete at this next level, she'd have to start taking steroids and other performance-enhancing drugs, but she steadily refused—then and forever after. She would only race clean and would never cross that line.

Even more exciting and nerve wracking for Suzy was that she would be racing in the qualifying heat against her idol and hero, Mary Decker Slaney, who she actually beat. She was amazed that she had fans among the other athletes in Barcelona, including the "Dream Team" of basketball All-Stars such as Magic Johnson, Charles Barkley, and David Robinson. She couldn't believe they even knew who she was!

Unfortunately, the demons inside her head sabotaged Suzy's performance, and she finished last. At times the self-talk inside her head was vicious, reminding her that she didn't belong among the elite, that she was damaged goods. Her nerves at the starting line would begin to take over, leaving her "thrumming with anxiety" to the point where she could barely focus, barely breathe. History repeated itself in her second Olympics: She once again failed to medal or even perform close to expectations.

Suzy's reputation took a huge hit after the disappointing showing. She was called a fraud and just a pretty face rather than a superstar. Then the shame and guilt would come over her, increasing her realization that her life, even her body, didn't belong to her but to all those who controlled her life, especially the coaches, her sport, and the media. She was told to wear two sports bras to keep her breasts from jiggling so much when she ran. Most of all, she was warned not to disappoint her sponsors again.

Her hero, Mary Slaney, was suspended from racing for taking drugs—another huge disappointment. Still, Suzy refused to give in to the pressure to take steroids. Instead, she had her breasts surgically reduced to streamline her body. She trained harder and worked with different coaches, and her times improved. Nike wanted on board her publicity train and further enticed her by offering her a huge bonus if she could run 1,500 meters in less than four minutes. She ran it in 3:59.

Then injuries began to take their toll. She tore her Achilles tendon—usually a career-ending disaster. Then came the worst tragedy of all: Her brother, Dan, took his own life. The signs of his deterioration were obvious to anyone who cared to notice. He had stopped taking his medication. He gave away all his things, saying he didn't need them anymore—one of the most compelling predictors that someone is going to commit suicide. His tragic death just added to Suzy's own increasing despair.

Just prior to the 2000 Sydney Olympics, Suzy made a stunning comeback, running the world's fastest time in her favorite event, the 1,500 meter. There would be several more setbacks, such as another injury (this time to her hamstring), but she managed to recover sufficiently to be ready for what would be her last chance to win a medal. She had a lot of things working against her—her age, her lingering injuries, grief and loss over her brother, the negative thoughts inside her head—but she was nothing if not persistent.

Just before her race started, she felt paralyzing anxiety and doubts about her ability to function. She sensed something terrible was going to happen and was bombarded by a "tornado of negative thoughts and doubts" spinning around inside her head. With just a hundred meters left to go, her legs started to feel heavy and listless. Her breathing became labored. All the other runners started to catch up to her and then pass her as if she was standing still. She felt such shame, helpless to do anything. She told herself she was a loser once again; she'd always be a loser. She couldn't stand the idea of finishing last in the race, so she purposely fell to the ground with what appeared to be an injury. After a few seconds, she forced herself to get up and wobble to the finish line. "I felt like I let everybody down, and it completely destroyed me." Only much later would she admit that she had deliberately collapsed in abject shame. She was "heartbroken, panicked, almost dumb with grief."

Not surprisingly, she believed that was the single worst thing that ever happened to her, the worst thing that could *ever* happen. Certainly it was a disappointment, but in the grand scheme of things, losing a race is nothing compared to all the tragic things that could befall us. But such is the distorted, exaggerated thinking of an athlete whose identity and well-being is totally contingent on winning races.

Maladjustment of Elite Athletes

After her third Olympic "failure," Suzy described herself as "psychologically debilitated." She felt so ashamed she was reluctant to leave the house. She was depressed and beaten.

It is no wonder that so many professional athletes end up in trouble. First of all, they are singularly unprepared for the constant limelight. They are bestowed riches and fame and deified as special beyond the gifts of mortal beings. Then there is the obsessive devotion to a single pursuit, sacrificing almost everything else along the way.

"No well-adjusted person will ever become an Olympic athlete," observed Brooks Johnson, who coached in five different Olympic games. While coaching Suzy, Johnson immediately recognized her insecurity and doubts and her need for constant approval and recognition. He also noticed her tendency to thrive on pushing limits just for the thrill. She was a good girl, but one who loved to take risks.

After retiring from sports and leaving behind all the attention and acclaim, the perks and screaming crowds, many athletes struggle to adjust to the normal rhythms of daily life—getting a real job, becoming anonymous and no longer special. They lose their primary identity as a runner, player, or star. In Hamilton's case, she also retired as one of the greatest runners of her time, yet she'd never won the biggest race of all.

Many athletes, Hamilton among them, nurse lingering injuries and physical limitations. Many ex-football players hobble for the rest of their lives and tolerate chronic pain. Runners such as Suzy may experience degenerative damage to joints. Certainly, much of the fun associated with sport has long passed.

People sometimes choose devotion and commitment to sport as a way to hide from their pain, soothe their anxiety, bury depression, or bolster a fragile sense of self. Female athletes often have the added pressures of being sexualized, required to wear skimpy clothing on the track or in other arenas. Consider the difference between the clothes men and women wear in a sport such as beach volleyball. The men wear baggy board shorts; the women wear miniscule bikinis. In Hamilton's case, she had been sexualized since adolescence: self-conscious about her breast size, constantly told she was hot. One of her coaches once filmed her, focusing primarily on her jiggling breasts as she ran, and shared the video with other male coaches. As she aged, she was constantly marketed for her sex appeal, even described as track and field's "pinup girl." Nike designed commercials featuring her completely naked with water sprayed all over her body. This was the beginning of Suzy feeling a sense of her power and control, not by winning races but by seducing men.

Demonstrating her incredible resilience and ability to recover from disappointments, Suzy had one more comeback left in her. Two years after the Olympics, she bounced back once again, running her best times in the 1,500 meters and ranking number three in the world. She began dreaming that perhaps she could ramp up once again for a fourth Olympics and try one more time to medal.

It was not to be. Injuries, fatigue, and wear and tear on her body started to catch up with her. She and Mark wanted to start a family and stabilize their lives instead of jet-setting all over the world for track meets. This sounded good in theory, but the reality of so-called normal life was quite a letdown for someone used to being on center stage.

Suzy tried, and failed at, a number of jobs: in an office and a sports department; as a spokesperson; then in real estate, going into business with her husband. He had the legal expertise, and she was supposed to reel in the clients. It turned out they had a good partnership for building the business, but that sort of life was not what Suzy was accustomed to. She hated the job after a while. She hated the life. There was ongoing tension in her relationship with Mark. After the birth of their daughter, the postpartum depression never seemed to go away but only take hold of her more firmly. There seemed to be no escape. She found herself driving home from an appointment with a client late one night, and her mind kept circling over and over with the thought that it might just be better to end it all, like her brother had done. She could see trees whirling past the window of the car as she picked up speed and aimed for the biggest one she could find, stepping on the gas. But then she thought about her daughter and the legacy she would leave behind. She slowed up on the gas and continued home, where she confessed to Mark that she didn't think she could go on this way. Something had to change.

Culture of Silence and Denial

In a small town in Wisconsin, mental illness was not a subject that was discussed very often. Suzy's family was no different in this respect. Ordinarily this might not have been a huge issue, except that Suzy's brother, Dan, struggled with serious emotional disturbances, depression, and an assortment of erratic behaviors. He bullied and terrorized Suzy mercilessly, way beyond what might be normal for an older brother. It was as if he thrived on his sister's misery. Dan would also take crazy risks. He had frequent outbursts of rage. He would become unaccountably sullen and withdrawn. There were all kinds of signs and symptoms that he was quite troubled, most of which were ignored, if not denied.

One time Suzy returned home with her mother to find Dan passed out on the floor, obviously drunk. Even at 16, he was medicating his extreme mood swings regularly with drugs and alcohol. His behavior became wildly unpredictable. Sometimes he would be revved up in a manic state. Other times he would slip into a deep depression, encapsulated within himself. This caused great tension within the family, coming to a crisis point when he was discovered aiming a shotgun at his head, frozen with indecision about whether to pull the trigger or not.

Suzy carried the wounds of surviving his abusive behavior, compounded by the guilt from resenting and hating him so much for the ways he consistently hurt her. Nobody within the family really understood what was going on. Even after he was clearly diagnosed with mental illness, everyone barely acknowledged the disease as anything other than his eccentricity. And yet it was pretty clear to anyone who cared to look that the boy had suffered from classic symptoms of bipolar disorder from an early age.

During the years Suzy was attending college, Dan became somewhat stabilized on medications for his bipolar disorder. He was holding a job. He had a girlfriend. He was no longer drinking excessively. It seemed that he had finally found some peace. He and Suzy also seemed to have negotiated a somewhat civilized sibling relationship as adults. The whole family breathed a sigh of relief, thinking that their problem child was finally cured of his disturbing behavior. This made his suicide all the more traumatic for those left behind.

The Fear of Failure

Reflecting on the experience of abject failure she'd felt during her last Olympic race, Suzy admitted that nobody had ever prepared her to deal with disappointment or failure. It was always about purging the very idea that she could possibly lose; that was absolutely unthinkable. Yet among the more than 10,000 athletes who participate in the Olympics, only a few hundred will ever win, and 99% will have to live with their letdowns. Most slip into obscurity, and many never recover from their lost dreams of glory.

Fig. 4-2. Although Suzy Favor Hamilton was considered one of the greatest middle-distance runners (having won an unprecedented nine NCAA championships and participated in three Olympics), she would never medal in the Games. Perhaps her greatest disappointment was during the 2000 Sydney Olympics, when she led the field in the 1,500-meter race and then fell apart toward the end, falling to the ground in despair and shame, as seen above.

Source: http://www.whatsonxiamen.com/news28708.html

Participation in sport on any level involves a certain amount of uncertainty and lack of control. Weather conditions, diet, health, family issues, and mood may affect performance on any given day. No matter how hard one trains or how much skill or ability one has, there will always be factors that are both unknowable and uncontrollable. It is enough to drive someone crazy—and it does.

Focusing on, and striving for, triumph is an important part of anyone's performance training, whether in sport or at one's job. But it's also crucial to prepare for coming up short and recalibrating one's goals afterwards. All of us can learn important lessons from our failures, treating them as opportunities for growth and further development. For instance, within the scope of my profession (training psychotherapists), the prospect of failure is a constant reminder: Some patients suffer intractable mental illnesses such as those described within this book. After interviewing famous theorists and practitioners in the field, it's become clear that those who are actually most successful don't allow themselves to become discouraged by initial failures but instead adjust their expectations and look for the gifts offered by these setbacks—ways they can use the feedback in meaningful ways.

In a classic study conducted by Daniel Wenger over 30 years ago, he discovered that it's virtually impossible to stop thinking about an intrusive thought such as "What if I lose?" In fact, trying to obsessively suppress that thought actually *increases* its power. Instead, athletes should be taught to accept the possibility of loss and failure, to confront the issue head on, to try their hardest but to also develop skills for recovery. In the context of recovery from addictions, this is called relapse prevention.

Unsurprisingly, many professional coaches in any sport would find this very idea abhorrent, if not scandalous. The pep talks they give to athletes implore them to not even consider the option of losing, believing that such doubts will lesson motivation. Part of that approach is valid in the sense that if desperation is at work, if an athlete believes his or her very life is at stake to win, perhaps there would be added incentive—but at tremendous cost. Even if such a strategy is introduced before a competition, there still needs to be considerable work completed afterwards to help athletes deal with their grief, pain, disappointment, shame, and depression. After all, they have to live with themselves and come to terms with their performance so they can recover and flourish in the future—not just in their brief careers as sports figures but also in all the other domains of their future lives: as parents, friends, role models, and employees.

The Fall From Grace

To many, Hamilton's sexual behavior seems to have overshadowed her life and career. Perhaps not surprisingly, the public and media have been focused on the most perverse and graphic descriptions of her fall from grace and her transformation from all-American girl to Las Vegas prostitute. Headlines in publications around the world displayed lurid titles promising details of her sexual exploits. It all began with *The Smoking Gun*'s revelation: "Olympian Was Premier Hooker, Clients Reported: Suzy Favor Hamilton Was Lauded by Johns."

Suzy didn't help herself much in this regard. With her characteristic honesty when under fire, she gave detailed interviews about what it was like to be ranked the best escort in Las Vegas. Her own autobiography devotes considerable space to describing the inner world of prostitution, its hardships, and especially the incredible exhilaration and pride she felt developing her seductive skills with the same commitment and discipline she'd devoted to running. In the throes of the manic stage of acute bipolar disorder, she found that nothing else, except sometimes being with her daughter, gave her the same satisfaction and thrills.

Hamilton attributes many of her problems, especially those that involved her sexual behavior, to her mental illness—particularly the symptoms that resulted from the manic stage of her bipolar disorder. Although depressive disorders may often reduce sexual drive, in some cases libido is indeed increased significantly. Certainly judgment is impaired, and risky, impulsive actions become more prevalent.

There is actually little known and understood about hypersexual acting out and risk-taking among women diagnosed with bipolar disorder. There have been just a few studies investigating the phenomenon: Basically, they validate that, indeed, there does seem to be a significant risk of such behavior. Such women are more likely to engage in unprotected sex with strangers, have multiple sexual partners, trade partners, and experiment with drugs during sex. Researchers also found that various antidepressant medications or lithium may not have much effect in moderating the symptoms. Very few follow-up studies have been undertaken to learn more about the effects, since it does not seem to be much of a priority. Perhaps Suzy's public outing and confession will lead to other women seeking help for this disorder.

During those years in her 40s, when many women still struggle with body image and declining attention to their sex appeal, Suzy (aka Kelly) was coming into her own. Just as she had thrived on the attention and approval of men throughout her life, she was now a star in her domain once again. Millionaires, celebrities, wildly successful executives, and cowboys would pay thousands of dollars just to spend a few hours with her. Yet for her, it wasn't just about the money and adulation: Her manic energy was being directed into her own libido. It was like a drug addiction: "There is always a desire—a need—to push the high to the next level."

One thing that had always ruined what she loved most about running was competition, diluting all the joy out of the experience. It was always about winning, being the best, and anything short of that made her a loser. "Now that I devoted myself to sex," she admitted, "my need to be unsurpassed in the bedroom had replaced the need to be the best on the track." The difference, however, was that there was no other competitor in the room with her; it was all about her own ability to totally control the experience.

It is well known that manic episodes lead people to engage in all sorts of dangerous behavior. They are ruled by their impulses, driven to engage in progressively more self-destructive behavior without any semblance of control. Such individuals often deliberately stay off their medications because they love the high and believe themselves to be extraordinarily productive and creative during these episodes—and in a sense, many of them are. There are, in fact, a disproportionate number of artists, writers, composers, and even advertising executives who suffer from bipolar disorder. In Suzy's case, as with her brother, the dangers and risks associated with discovery are part of the appeal.

In her book, Suzy wrote in detail and at length about the rush she felt living a secret life filled with such wanton debauchery. She talked about the intense pleasure she felt way beyond physical and sexual excitement—a feeling that exceeded winning a race or competing in the Olympics. She was no longer a depressed woman, an ex-athlete, an ex-celebrity. She was a desperately desired professional.

Recovery and Healing

Many people who are diagnosed with various forms of mental disorders must live with this reality for the rest of their lives. Whereas some types can be "cured," if not sent into remission, others must be managed carefully with medication and psychotherapy. Suzy is an example of someone who has benefited tremendously from therapy and the accompanying insights into her history, disease, and behavior. She has learned some tough lessons, most of which are the result of failures and mistakes. She has rededicated herself to maintaining a healthy lifestyle through regular moderate exercise, yoga, a good diet, and focusing on her responsibility as a mother. She has become a spokesperson and motivational speaker who speaks frankly and transparently about her troubles, what she learned from them, and how others might learn from her mistakes. She seeks to remove the stigma and shame associated with mental illness and tries to educate the public and media about the realities of such a struggle.

Suzy makes few apologies for her past. She has grown to move beyond shame and guilt. She has learned self-forgiveness, a process that was possible because of the support she felt from her husband, her friends, some family members, and a mostly understanding public. She tries to focus on the positive as much as possible, letting go of any lingering regrets and bitterness. She realizes that she always needed running, "simply for the joy of it. For my mind." It is what grounded her and helped her remain stable in the face of all her volatile mood swings. She also realizes that running provided her with the self-discipline and toughness to fight her illness, the public backlash, and shaming and to move forward in her life. "We runners are a rare breed who take on pain, who thrive on it." Maybe that's why it took so long for the pain to become intense enough to force her to reevaluate and make lasting changes.

Just imagine the things she went through that led up to—and followed—her break-down, disgrace, shaming, humiliation, and recovery. One family member completely discounted her emotional disorder, calling her a slut and a whore. One letter from an ex-fan said she should just kill herself like her brother did. Another person wrote directly to her daughter to express sympathy for having such a worthless, immoral mother. It would be hard not to take these attacks and criticism to heart. But as she said, running taught her to literally take things in stride.

Suzy Favor Hamilton is clearly a work in progress. Having reinvented herself so many times in the past, she often feels giddy with the possibilities of what she can become in the future. But she is also wise and experienced enough to hold onto a certain amount of apprehension and concern that if she isn't careful and vigilant, she could lose control—and everything she has worked so hard for—once again.

Suffering can become a kind of gift for those who know how to take meaning from the experience. Whether it's after surviving abuse, neglect, bullying, catastrophe, trauma, cancer, or mental illness, one recurrent theme associated with recovery and resilience involves finding a way to use what happened to enlighten, inform, or help others. Suzy Favor Hamilton, like others profiled in this book, became an advocate for those like her whose shame and denial made it difficult to ask for the help they most desperately needed.

Sources

Associated Press. (1996, June 5). Ex-runner finds peace 10 years after bizarre accident. *The Spokesman-Review.* http://www.spokesman.com/stories/1996/jun/05/ex-runner-finds-peace-10-years-after-bizarre/

Brewer, B. (2008). Fear of failure in the context of competitive sport. *International Journal of Sports Science and Coaching, 3*(2), 199–200.

Dutch, T. (2015, September 21). *What if Suzy Favor Hamilton had won her Olympic gold?* Flo Track. https://www.flotrack.org/articles/5045974-what-if-suzy-favor-hamilton-had-won-her-olympic-gold

Favor, S. H. (2017, January 18). *My complicated relationship with running.* http://suzyfavorhamilton.com/bipolar-disorder-sex-healthy-vs-unhealthy/

Favor, S. H. (2017, February 21). *Parenting with mental illness.* http://suzyfavorhamilton.com/parenting-mental-illness/

Favor, S. H. (2017, June 1). *Bipolar disorder and sex—healthy vs. unhealthy.* http://suzyfavorhamilton.com/bipolar-disorder-sex-healthy-vs-unhealthy/

Favor, S. H. (2018, February 5). *Shame—my intimate relationship and eventual break-up with it.* http://suzyfavorhamilton.com/shame-intimate-relationship-eventual-break-up/

Favor, S. H., & Tomlinson, S. (2015). *Fast girl: A life spent running from madness.* Harper Collins.

Favor, S. H., & Tomlinson, S. (2015, September 14). Suzy's secret life. *Sports Illustrated,* 56–62.

Gray, M. (2015, September 14). Back from the brink. *Sports Illustrated,* 61.

Hegarty, S. (2012, July 30). Should athletes prepare for defeat? *BBC Magazine.* http://www.bbc.com/news/magazine-18902643

Kamps, L. (2013, April 23). Crash of the titian. *Elle.* https://www.elle.com/culture/career-politics/a12558/olympic-runner-suzy-favor-hamilton-profile-call-girl/

Longman, J. (2012, December 20). Former Olympian cites depression for taking job as escort. *New York Times.* http://www.nytimes.com/2012/12/21/sports/former-olympian-suzy-favor-hamilton-reveals-escort-job-and-emotional-struggles.html

Marengo, E., et al. (2015). Sexual risk behaviors among women with bipolar disorder. *Psychiatry Research, 230,* 835–838.

Mazza, M., et al. (2011). Sexual behavior in women with bipolar disorder. *Journal of Affective Disorders, 131,* 364–367.

Pitoniak, S. (2016, April 8). Suzy Favor Hamilton on bipolar and hypersexuality. *BP Magazine.* https://www.bphope.com/olympic-runner-suzy-favor-hamilton-on-bipolar-hypersexuality/

Smoking Gun. (2015). Olympian was premier hooker, clients reported: Suzy Favor Hamilton was lauded by johns. http://thesmokinggun.com/file/suzy-favor-hamilton-reviews

Spain, S. (2015). Olympian-turned-escort Suzy Favor Hamilton reclaims a life rerouted by mental illness. *ESPN News.* http://www.espn.com/espnw/news-commentary/article/13656143/olympian-turned-escort-suzy-favor-hamilton-reclaims-life-rerouted-mental-illness

Stone, K. (2017, May 6). Beating bipolar: Suzy Favor Hamilton sheds "escort" stigma, plans San Diego talk. *Time of San Diego.* https://timesofsandiego.com/life/2017/05/06/beating-bipolar-suzy-favor-hamilton-sheds-escort-stigma-plans-san-diego-talk/

Vigneron, P. (2015, October 9). What made Suzy run? *The New Yorker.* https://www.newyorker.com/news/sporting-scene/what-made-suzy-run

5

Graeme Obree

Putting His Neck in a Noose

Graeme Obree was not exactly in a celebratory mood as Christmas approached in 2002. He was already regarded as one of the greatest cyclists alive, having set the world record for the one-hour distance mark. Twice. This is an absolutely brutal, grueling solo race in which a rider goes flat-out around a circular track with banked walls, called a velodrome. The bikes have no gears, no brakes; they are just designed for maximum speed. The cyclist is expected to maximize his heart rate for 60 straight minutes, riding as fast as humanly possible and covering as much distance as he can within the time limit. Obree rode at over 30 miles an hour, pumping his legs in his most unconventional machine, which was designed from washing machine parts.

On this particular day during a bike ride on the rural roads of Scotland, Obree was having a particularly tough time. A few years earlier he had been diagnosed with major depression and had been taking medication to control the depths of his despair. He was approaching the anniversary of the day his brother died in a car crash, a time that always made him feel sad and helpless. His brother was the only person during his early life who didn't make him feel worthless and inferior to everyone else; he was Obree's anchor.

In addition, his world distance record had already been surpassed several times. A recent injury made it unlikely he could ever regain his extraordinary form again. During a previous training ride, he had crashed into a concrete wall, breaking his kneecap into pieces and severely injuring his chest.

Obree doesn't remember much about this day except that he had just recovered from a stay in the hospital after a suicide attempt. He had an appointment with his psychiatrist scheduled for the afternoon, but he didn't think he could last that long. He started drinking, and in the middle of the binge, he remembered that his wife, Anne, had asked him to feed their horse, which was stored in a barn outside of town. He hopped on his bike and headed into the country, stopping at a pub along the way for another drink before he arrived at the farm.

The story of what happened after he left the pub is foggy, but reports put together from witnesses and medical personnel say that Obree pulled his bike over to the side of the road and walked into the barn.

Although Obree was married with two children, now that his cycling career seemed over, he couldn't find much reason to continue living. He described his life as purposeless, isolated, and disconnected from others and the world. "Imagine you woke up one morning," he later said as he tried to explain the feelings of hopelessness, "and every day was like that, and it took 10 times the energy to deal with every person, being happy and smiley ... and all you want to do is go to sleep, but there is no sleep, so it seems like the only option is to not be there anymore."

Obree looked around inside the barn and found a rope coiled on the ground. He threw it over the rafters, tied it carefully around his neck, and hanged himself. It was time to end the constant suffering that had been with him since childhood.

It so happened that the farmer's daughter noticed something awry and went into the barn to investigate. She discovered Obree unconscious and hanging from the rafters. He was actually clinically dead. She immediately called for help to get him down but feared they would be too late, since brain damage was likely after his oxygen had been cut off for so long. As a world-class athlete with double the lung capacity of the average human, it was his incredible fitness that saved him.

Obree was revived by paramedics, and they rushed him to the local hospital for treatment. He insisted that he remembered nothing about the incident and didn't care to talk about it further. Much later, he wanted people to understand that when someone tries to take his or her own life, it isn't personal; that mental illness, and especially depression, so clouds one's judgment that the behavior that follows is controlled by something beyond one's capability. In a sense, he felt reborn, at least for a little while: "Once you've been dead," he said, "you have to appreciate being alive more."

Just a few years earlier, after losing his world record and feeling hopeless that he could ever regain it again, he commented, "I'll do it. I'll have to do it." But he foreshadowed a creepy image that came to pass: "To try for the hour and not get it is a disaster. It's better not to attempt the record in the first place. That's why so few people do. It's like putting your neck in a noose."

Escape From Suffering

This was hardly Graeme Obree's first attempt to take his own life. When he was 20 and living at home with his parents, he felt completely isolated except when he visited the local cycling club. He had no friends. He was bullied. His policeman father was intolerably critical and judgmental of his son's behavior. It had always been that way for him, so he didn't know any better. His only respite from the loneliness and suffering was to get out on his bike. Cycling was his only escape and became an obsession until the depression became so pervasive that he could barely pedal at all.

Obree would observe "normal" people out in the world, laughing and having fun, and it only made him feel more awkward, disconnected, pathetic, and alien. He felt like a parasite or "the social equivalent of a human's appendix." He felt frozen in his condition, trapped in hell with no way out. He would spend hours sitting alone in the house staring at the fire. The thought kept coming back into his mind that he could end this suffering—if only he had the courage to do so. He later explained, "The gap between deciding, 'Okay, I'll kill myself,' to the point of killing myself was the calmest, most serene period of my life."

Finally, what at first had felt like a whim, a fantasy, finally became a compulsion. He went outside into the garden shed, where he had stored some of his bike repair equipment.

He found a canister of acetylene and sucked on the hose as he turned on the liquid gas. Tears started falling down his cheeks—tears of regret, of sadness, and of surrender. As he looked back on his life, all he could remember were the awful times, the disappointments and failures. His last thought before unconsciousness was a memory of a time when he and his brother were bullied and forced to fondle one another's genitals while the other boys held knives to their throats.

Obree eventually regained consciousness and felt sharp pain. Someone was slapping his face. He believed that even in death he would be subject to even greater suffering. He couldn't focus, couldn't concentrate. He had no idea where he was and what was happening except for the biting pain on his face. Everything was blurry and indistinct. He was so dizzy he couldn't think. He could taste vomit in his mouth. Then the image outside his body started to clear, and he saw his father kneeling over him, slapping him, his voice screaming at him to wake up.

Obree's father had unexpectedly returned early from work to find his son lying there, presumably dead. Apparently Obree hadn't been miserable enough and filled with enough shame; he had failed at even taking his own life. His father found him with vomit covering his shirt and shit and piss in his pants, and he had never felt so humiliated in his life. It seemed this suffering would never end.

Early Life

It was tough being the son of a policeman in a small rural village. Whatever resentment and fear the local boys felt toward the representative of law and order they decided to take out on Graeme and his brother. The name-calling and, especially, the violence directed toward them were relentless. But Graeme was by far the more sensitive of the two. The attacks escalated to the point where he would feel "an orgasm of fear, excitement, panic, and adrenaline." It is no wonder that by the age of seven he had already found ways to escape the torment by learning to dissociate as a defense mechanism. He no longer felt present and became an "observer" of himself and what happened around him.

There was a kind of self-protective strength in no longer caring about what happened to him or how others treated him. He began thinking about the option of suicide as a reminder that he always had a way out, one he could control on his own terms. He believed nobody could take anything more from him or hurt him any further because he was really already dead inside.

Once he reached early adolescence, Obree found solace, if not a bit of joy, riding his bike. A classmate talked him into racing in a time trial, the kind of event in which each rider goes against the clock. The idea immediately appealed to him; he wouldn't have to deal with any people but could just contain himself in the solo effort. It wasn't long before he started to show early promise as a rider.

Soon after that, he made a trip to Edinburgh to visit the velodrome, with its high, imposing, upward-sloping walls. It seemed a miracle of physics that it was possible to ride around the track so fast that you could be almost perpendicular to the floor without toppling over. Some members of the riding group who accompanied him restricted themselves to the flat surface at the bottom, but Obree immediately caught on to the trick of gaining enough speed to remain upright on the vertical wall, banking in such a way that the centrifugal force would double the speed on the way down. It was magical.

Once again, Obree appreciated that the unique culture of this sport was insular and self-contained. Each cyclist rode for himself rather than a team. There would be no complex navigation of social dynamics or risk that he would be marginalized: His standing and status would solely be determined by his individual performance. Given that he had no social life, no friends, no job, and no interest in school, for the first time in his life he had found something about which he was passionate. And he had plenty of free time to train in a way that felt like pure pleasure rather than work.

Obree began thinking that if he worked hard enough, he could win a track championship someday. To add to his interest in cycling as a possible career, he showed incredible aptitude as a mechanic. He loved to think about bike designs and ways he might improvise various parts to improve their function and speed. It was the first time in his life that he discovered he was good at something. It was also satisfying that his father was on board, supporting this interest and willing to drive him to local races and cheer him on. Obree started winning the races. Consistently. By the time he was 18, he was the Scottish national champion.

Obree's whole life has been demarcated by a series of alternating triumphs and crushing disappointments. Just when he'd achieve some semblance of pride and personal security, something would happen—either inside him or in his world—that would unravel all he had accomplished. He had been trying to support himself by running a bike repair business but was still not earning enough income to further his racing career. So he and his partner concocted a scheme to pretend their inventory of bikes had been stolen. They could collect the insurance and then also sell the "missing" bikes, doubling their cash flow. Naturally, they were arrested and convicted of fraud—another humiliating defeat, especially for the son of the local policeman. His whole world came crashing down once again. And that's when he decided to go into the shed to find the acetylene gas and finally end all the disappointments.

Ups and Downs

Graeme Obree has been described as the perfect British sports figure. "He is the underdog who took on vastly superior odds," according to journalist Nicholas Roe, "not with fancy machines and sophisticated backup but a training diet of marmalade sandwiches, a bike made of scrap parts ... and a determination to win despite obscurity and an empty bank account."

Obree has had more victories and defeats in his life than the aggregate of any dozen other people. After his recovery from the suicide attempt, he started to come out of his shell a bit more. His early 20s were chaotic years but also a time when he managed to develop some level of intimacy with a few friends and even a young woman who would become his wife.

With this newfound stability and support, he started entering races and found his form, even if it was considered more than a little eccentric. Within cycling culture, for example, riders are famously recognized for (and quite proud of) shaving their legs; in some cases, they shave their arms as well. It is kind of a rite of passage, and while women may consider this routine an annoyance, cyclists are just fine with the morning ritual in the shower. The habit is justified by the belief that smooth skin is more aerodynamic, scientifically measured as improving times by .06%, possibly "shaving" a few seconds off one's time. In addition, if you happen to take a fall, it is easier to treat wounds and "road rash" on smooth skin. Among professionals, it also makes the post-ride massage less painful. That's the theory, anyway: The reality is that it is also a way that cyclists declare their identity.

Obree would cause quite a stir at races with his refusal to shave his hairy legs—just another way he appeared strange to everyone else. His self-designed bike looked weird, with straight forks, twin down tubes, and an unusual seating position. He also held onto the unconventional belief that hair on his legs better allowed for sweat to evaporate, saving energy in his skin. Eventually, peer pressure would force him to comply with the norms, but he adamantly refused to shave his legs prior to his upcoming wedding, as there was no way he was going to stand in front of the congregation in a kilt with shaved legs.

Graeme was also quirky in other ways that only enhanced his reputation as weird. Whereas other cyclists would carry the standard high-energy foods such as chocolate to fuel their rides, Obree would bring what he called "selfish paste," a sandwich made from mustard and Marmite. He knew that nobody would ever think of stealing such a disgusting snack.

Obree was now a family man, and his business enterprises as a bike engineer, designer, and mechanic started to grow, if not flourish, during the ups and downs in this era of his life. He had now set his sights on the most unattainable goal any cyclist could possibly imagine: breaking the world track record for distance covered in an hour.

The Darkest Hour

In the world of cycling, there is no race more devastatingly difficult than the hour record. It is also the simplest event to understand: a single rider alone on a track. There is no support, no real strategy or tactics—just ride as fast and as hard as you can for an hour. Even the bike itself is just a simple contraption. The rider operates in the highest gear for 60 continuous minutes. There is no chance to make a single mistake, or the race is over. The rider holds an aerodynamic position that is so awkward and uncomfortable that cramping is a strong possibility. If the rider hopes to break the record, he must be in charge of setting a pace for each circuit, pushing beyond the barriers of fatigue and anxiety.

The race, considered the Holy Grail of cycling, first began at the end of the 19th century, when the record was first established: an average speed of 15 miles per hour. Since that time, that speed has been doubled.

Michael Hutchinson, a professor and scholar, decided in recent times that he would retire from academia and devote himself to trying to break the hour record, or at least write a book about his journey to attempt it. In so doing, he noted that what was singularly unique about this pursuit is that you are actually racing against all the greatest champions who ever lived. Eddy Merckx, perhaps the most accomplished rider in history, held the record for 28 years. Yet it was Graeme Obree who inspired Hutchinson to try because he was also a completely unknown amateur, eccentric, and maverick. He reasoned that all one needs to give it a shot is just a bike, a track, and an hour of time.

For most, attacking the hour record is an exercise in precision, technological innovation, meticulous preparation, and rigorous training. That was not Obree. He operated by instinct and impulsivity. He only trained when he felt like it, tinkered with his bike based on whims, and relied on a diet of his marmalade sandwiches.

It is perhaps not surprising that someone who experienced so much agony in his life might choose a sport in which his main job was to suffer beyond what was imagined to be possible. Obree had been fascinated with the goal and especially how it seemed like the one task that he was uniquely and singularly prepared to conquer: "It was the ultimate test—no traffic, one man in a velodrome against the clock." For a man who had so little confidence in his life, it is all the more remarkable that he felt so certain he could accomplish this: "I didn't tell myself that I will *attempt* the record, I said I would *break* it." Once he decided this, as far as he was concerned, it was a done deal.

Fig. 5-1. Graeme Obree, "The Flying Scotsman" (pictured above), looks back on the triumphs, defeats, and challenges in his life with a sense of acceptance and calm. He has grappled with a devastating mental illness, shame and guilt related to being gay, and a series of crushing disappointments from which he has emerged resilient and determined.

Source: https://bit.ly/2MSEVpf.

We are talking about an event so grueling that the human body is pushed to its absolute limits. Although Eddie Merckx, nicknamed "The Cannibal" for his single-minded ruthlessness and ability to suffer pain, had achieved more accolades that anyone before (or perhaps after) him, he described this event as the single worst hour of his life. He could barely speak, much less move, after he collapsed off his bike. After several agonizing minutes during which observers wondered if Merckx was having a heart attack, he finally whispered, "How I ache. I can hardly move. It was the longest hour of my career. It was terrible. You have no idea what kind of intense effort it is until you have done it." Forever after, he sincerely believed that that hour had taken years off his life.

While training for his own record attempt, Hutchinson consulted with Obree for some advice, finding him both gracious and helpful. But Obree also admitted during their conversation that, for him, it was a matter of life and death. "And I just don't mean that as an expression," Obree added. "I mean it absolutely literally."

Brief Triumph

Let's talk about how improbable it is that someone like Graeme Obree could have tried to break the most prestigious record in cycling. He had no pedigree, no sponsors, not even a "real" bike; he built his in his kitchen out of spare parts. He had no budget, so he was reduced to searching for abandoned or spare parts along the roadside. He borrowed the drum bearing from his washing machine to support the crank, adapted the handlebars from a kid's mountain bike, and accepted whatever donations he could from local bike shops. The result, christened "Old Faithful," was an eccentric piece of machinery. At one point, the International Cycling Union banned his creation, threatening to disqualify him until he made some adjustments that extended the handle bars. It is all the more remarkable that his cobbled-together bike had to compete against professional riders who were sponsored by the leading manufacturers and provided with technologically advanced machines that cost (in today's money) hundreds of thousands of dollars to design and build.

Obree's sole sponsor managed to have a replica of his homemade bike manufactured with more conventional materials, and that was the one he would ride in this historical event. He had flown to Norway to be the first athlete to perform in the new velodrome, which had yet to be christened for the upcoming Winter Olympics. The international track cycling officials and timekeepers had flown up to the venue to record and certify the record attempt.

On this particular morning, there were less than 100 spectators in attendance at the velodrome, some of them simply curious visitors who were taking a tour. Obree, nervous and jumpy, had not slept a wink the previous night. Soon after he finally fell asleep in the early morning hours, he was awakened by media members who wanted to interview him. He was also a little apprehensive about riding the unfamiliar replica version of his bike, no matter how pretty it looked.

When the starting gun went off, Obree felt his legs were strong, but soon his lungs were laboring. He was initially able to keep pace but could feel his exhaustion creeping in after the first half hour. Still, he pushed himself as hard as he could, but by the last 10 minutes, he knew that he would fall short. In fact, his ride was spectacular, and he missed the record time by only a single lap around the track.

As he climbed off the bike, he could hear the crowd cheering, but he felt only defeat and failure. Close wasn't good enough. He had arranged for all these officials and support team to spend the money to come to this place, and he'd let them all down. He had let himself down. Once again, he felt humiliated, this time by his own inadequacy. When some of the spectators tried to give him a bouquet of flowers to celebrate his amazing ride, he rejected them and walked away. "I should be flogged at the minimum," he declared, "and I abjectly hated myself for the disgraceful failure."

Now the story gets *really* interesting.

Normally, after such a grueling race, a cyclist will need a minimum of four days to recover from the abuse his or her body has suffered. Massages are scheduled twice daily. So many calories have been burned during the effort that nutritional needs must be carefully tended to. Most importantly, the rider needs rest and sleep—and lots of it—in order to give the system time to reset itself.

But Obree was desperate. Even though it was late in the afternoon and he knew all the officials were leaving the next day, he pleaded with them to return again the following morning. Everyone looked at him as if he was a lunatic. He had just completed a race, it was obvious he could barely walk, and now he was proposing to repeat it again within hours. It was impossible!

Obree begged. Then he insisted. He only requested that everyone show up again at 9:00 a.m.; they would be done an hour later, and then they could all go home. They just shook their heads but reluctantly agreed, mostly out of amusement.

This time Obree had a plan to break every rule that is normally followed. He would spend as much time in bed as he could during the night. He would skip warmups and show up precisely 10 minutes before the start time. There would be no further preparation. And oh yes, this time he would ride "Old Faithful," his own self-made, funky bike, the one that felt familiar and comfortable.

Next, he planned a rather unusual training and preparation method for the race, one that I'm sure has never been repeated—or even imagined—by any other athlete in the history of sport. Obree crawled into bed during the evening but decided he hated being awakened by an alarm clock, which totally disoriented him throughout the day. So instead, he decided he'd use the "bladder alarm," along with a regimen to deal with his extreme caloric deficit and strained muscles. He drank as much water as he could hold before retiring, knowing he'd have to awaken a few hours later to urinate. He would then eat a bowl of cornflakes, stretch his legs and back for a few minutes, drink glass after glass of water, and then return to bed. He repeated this process six times during the night—water, cornflakes, stretching, repeat.

Obree awoke precisely at 8:00 a.m. as he'd anticipated, and he arrived at the venue at 8:50 a.m. When he walked in the velodrome, a number of the spectators and officials were almost surprised he showed up, wondering if he was really serious and crazy enough to attempt the world record a day after his previous exhaustive effort.

As Obree lined up at the starting line, he felt a "blitzkrieg, arrogant impatience" to get rolling. He felt confident, almost certain, he could do this. For him, it was all about his mental state, not his physical conditioning. "The day before I had been a mouse. Now I was a lion."

He insulated himself inside a bubble and concentrated only on keeping his rhythm, tuning out everything else. He decided he would ride himself to death if that's what it took. He imagined himself like a horse, "galloping on and on, and entering oblivion."

Once he found a rhythm, Obree felt inspired by the cheering crowd. He could hear the announcer calling him "The Flying Scotsman" because he was going so fast, already on pace after 20 kilometers, which was more than 10 seconds better than the previous world record.

Obree was lying flat along his mismatched tubes in what became known as the "praying mantis position"—something that had never been witnessed before—with his elbows pulled up tight against chest as he leaned over the handlebars in a contorted position. He was pedaling so hard it was observed that he appeared "violent." The degree of suffering written on his face made it seem impossible that he could keep up this inhuman pace. And in truth, he did not keep that pace—he *increased* it!

Graeme was in absolute agony for the final 15 minutes. Everything ached—his hands, his feet, his crotch, every muscle in his body was on fire, screaming for relief. Even his face and scalp felt numb, and he couldn't feel his lips. But he pedaled on, faster and faster, until he heard the most beautiful sound: the pistol firing, indicating that he had just passed the previous record distance set by Francisco Moser.

Obree set a new world record that day and was now the most famous cyclist alive. Moser could only shake his head in wonder—and admiration—at the incredible feat that had been accomplished. He wrote the forward to Obree's autobiography, commenting: "So Graeme is crazy, like all of us. Maybe a little more crazy than us, a kind of peculiarity, like an artist."

Obree's triumph and satisfaction were short-lived. Just a week later, his rival and friend, Chris Boardman, broke the record again by just 600 meters, riding a bike that cost close to $1 million. There would be so many more disappointments, failures, and relapses. A testimony to Obree's courage and resilience is that, while recovering in the hospital after the suicide attempt in the barn, he decided to write a book about his experiences with depression, hoping it might help others who suffered from this illness. The subtitle of the book said it all: "Cycling to triumph through my darkest hours."

The Rainbow Jersey: Fame and Further Misfortune

Obree next set his sights on pursuit track racing, a variation of his previous achievement. In pursuit track racing, there are two riders positioned at different ends of the track. It is more of a spectator event, since the riders start at the same time and try to catch one another. In his attempt to win a world championship in the event, Obree felt his competitor closing in on him, breathing down his neck, before he took off like a rocket.

In its own way, pursuit is just as grueling as going for the hour record. In fact, Obree pushed himself so hard during the race he could actually taste the adrenaline-fueled fear in his mouth—that is, before he tasted blood. He worked so hard he blew out part of his lungs, making him cough up blood for weeks afterwards. But he set a new world record and was awarded the prestigious rainbow jersey as the prize, the multicolored hues proclaiming to all that he was the world champion.

Anyone at the award ceremony would have seen Obree in a less than celebratory mood; he appeared glum, even disinterested. He later explained that it took all his self-control not to double over in pain and collapse. He kept coughing up blood, and that was scaring him. He could barely speak at all. During the party to honor his achievement later that night, Obree managed to hobble onto the dance floor after anesthetizing himself with enough whiskey and beer. Since he could not fully straighten his body, he danced in a crouch, which others started to imitate, calling it the "Obree Dance."

What Obree wanted more than anything his whole life was to be wanted, to be admired, to prove he wasn't worthless. But now the feeling of pride was fleeting. He was only as good as his last race or world record—and those, too, were eclipsed by others. There was an impermanence to his satisfaction, and whenever he would lose a race or fail to break a record, he was filled with self-pity and self-castigation. At first he tried to soothe the self-doubts with alcohol, but the depression would return in force. He claimed to despise himself and wondered why anyone would ever choose to be around him.

Adding to his burdens of titles and records taken back by others was the cycling union, which kept altering their rules to outlaw his famous tuck position and then the designs of his handlebars, saddle, and helmet. Fatigue and burnout began to set in as the expectations for his performance continued to rise. He was beginning, once again, to lose control of himself, his life, and his sense of self. He described himself as "wallowing in self-hatred, despair, and sadness over everything he had lost." He was referring to his hour record, his world champion title, and especially the loss of his brother to the car accident that happened because his brother had fallen asleep at the wheel.

Obree was living in what he called "a black mist," a depressive state so deep and endless that even alcohol couldn't soothe the suffering. He remembered the acetylene he had used to try to kill himself when he was a young man. There were times when he would sit in his workshop getting drunk and stare at the gas canister, wondering if he had the courage to end it all. For now, he was inhaling the gas in small doses to get high. He was confused and unable to figure out what was wrong with him.

Graeme's wife, Anne, kept trying to save him in a multitude of ways. She proposed they open a coffee shop together, but that plan failed before it got beyond the planning stage. Around this time, he committed himself to riding in a few races in Europe, and while he was on the road, he became increasingly despondent. He would begin crying uncontrollably.

He wrote a final note to his wife and children apologizing for being so worthless and inadequate. He told them he loved them but that they would all be better off without him around. This time he would do the job with pills to make sure there was no screwup, but he wasn't sure which ones would be best and might be available. He purchased as much aspirin as he could from one pharmacist, then went to another one, ultimately accumulating more than a hundred tablets. He went to a bar, where he washed the pills down with beer. He felt resolved and calm, certain this was the right thing to do. He went outside to find the right spot to pass out and let the pills do their work. He walked and walked, waiting impatiently for the desired effects, but nothing much seemed to be happening except that he felt wobbly and wanted to vomit.

He felt like an idiot, thinking that mere aspirin, even in megadoses, would kill him. Then he decided to slit his wrists with his little pen knife, but that didn't work either because the blade was too dull. So next, he figured he'd jump off a building and found a suitable one that was eight stories high. He climbed up the stairs to the roof to find the service door locked. If there's one thing you could say about Graeme Obree, it's that he was relentlessly persistent, so next, he decided he'd hang himself from a tree. He broke into a car, used his dull pen knife to saw through the seatbelts to make a noose, and the next thing he knew, someone pushed him to the ground and pressed his head painfully against the street. He welcomed the pain, but in his overanesthetized condition (with four bottles of aspirin in his system), he felt nothing at all. He looked up to see a police officer sitting on top of him, who then had him escorted to a hospital, after which he was transferred to a psychiatric unit close to home.

Coming Out and Self-Acceptance

Graeme Obree enjoyed two of the most exhilarating, remarkable years an athlete could ever dream of between 1993 and 1995. He broke the world hour record—twice—and was also crowned the world individual pursuit champion. Yet it was never quite enough for him to feel successful. The fame and recognition he so desperately sought further trapped him in a downward spiral. "I was subjugated by fear of myself, because I couldn't dare be myself."

It certainly didn't help that he felt so persecuted by cycling authorities who were constantly disqualifying him from events because of adjustments he made to his bike that they considered illegal—whether the saddle position or handlebar configuration—or even his preferred riding positions, with his arms extended or held close to his body. During one race, the judges decided to ban him before he even launched himself, but Obree was determined to continue anyway. One judge, wearing his official blazer, stood on the track and attempted to stop him from competing, but Obree was so enraged he tried to run him over. Obree may be unrivaled as someone who had a revolutionizing impact on his sport, a complete amateur who stood alone against the rest of the world. The downward spiral led inevitably to a hospitalization.

During this hospitalization, he recovered some semblance of himself. He began regular psychotherapy, stopped medicating himself with alcohol, started taking lithium to help stabilize his moods, and began work on what he described as a "spiritual bankruptcy." He no longer had cycling or world records to reach for, and he felt lost.

Not to be dissuaded, Obree insisted that he would begin training to regain his hour record until he was challenged by hospital staff: If having done that already twice before didn't make much difference, why would a third attempt be any better? He had to agree.

But he still had an overpowering yearning to set a new goal, to make a comeback. He had lost the passion for racing, which had begun to feel like "bloodless mutilation." Everything was driven by the need for external validation and the trappings of achievement to prove he was worthwhile, that he had a reason to exist.

Obree tries not to hold on to regrets about the past. "You've got to break that spiral," he told me. "Talk to somebody, do something about it. Something has to change." Looking back over his life, he feels proud of what he has accomplished, something he couldn't let himself acknowledge when he was younger.

He has spent most of his adult life trying to peel away the layers: "I've got to the middle of my onion now." What he means by this is that he has come out as gay, something he had been repressing, then disguising, for most of his life. Like so many other athletes, such as tennis players Billie Jean King and Martina Navratilova, diver Greg Louganis, basketball player Jason Collins, rugby player Gareth Thomas, baseball player Billy Bean, football player Kwame Harris, and mountain climber John Menlove Edwards (see Chapter 9), he experienced shame, humiliation, and abuse after publicly acknowledging his sexual identity. In Obree's case, it was just one other way that he felt different. After all, Obree once described his relationship with the sport of cycling as equivalent to Pluto's relationship to Earth: unimaginably distant and not even recognized as a planet.

As hard as it was for Obree to talk about his depression and mental illness, he found it even more shameful and challenging to talk about his sexuality. He not only believed that his children would never speak to him again but also feared that even his psychiatrist would dismiss him.

Admitting he was gay was absolutely unthinkable in the place where he grew up, a small village in rural Scotland. He had already been teased and bullied enough just for being the policeman's child. If he had ever revealed his sexual orientation, assuming he was even aware of it at the time, he would have been murdered. It actually wasn't until 10 years ago that he admitted to himself, much less to anyone else, that he was attracted to men. He admits that he was himself extremely homophobic earlier in life, as likely as anyone else to be critical of others. It surprised him that not only did his parents come around, his sons were the ones who pushed him to come out.

Obree believes that athletes are at far greater risk for mental illness because they are constantly, compulsively, striving for perfection and success, goals that are mostly unattainable. He is convinced that this individual pursuit of recognition is dangerous and what ultimately leads to stress and depressive disorders. "Because you're a winner or a loser, with that, you're relegating 90% of the population to feel like shit." He is mostly speaking about himself, since he never found any lasting shred of happiness or well-being in his own victories. There is something terribly wrong with measuring one's value and worth by winning a race or event, and he now considers this a form of insanity. In addition, he has found that elite athletes often use their sport as a way to "medicate" themselves and hide from their troubles. The nature of the all-encompassing hours of training each day, controlling every aspect of their diet and lifestyle as well as behavior, just isn't healthy over the long run. And whatever recognition one achieves doesn't last long: People forget you, and what's left are simply memories and old injuries.

Another Comeback

If you thought Obree was going to fade into obscurity once his brief cycling career ended, you haven't been paying attention. He was, above all else, a creative engineer and tinkerer, capable of assembling machines and devices from any spare parts he could find, just as he had for "Old Faithful."

In 2013, the human-powered speed limit was 82 miles per hour. That means that someone figured out how to propel his body on a straightaway as fast as any motorized vehicle on the freeway. Although in his mid-40s, Obree set himself to the task of constructing a bike that could take him past the world record, and he would do it in his classic prone position.

Rather than using parts from a washing machine or ones abandoned on the side of the road, this time he constructed his bike in the kitchen using an old burned pot for his shoulder support and borrowing the wheels from rollerblades. His design would have him lying in a horizontal position, just knee-high, pedaling mere inches off the ground.

He would have to breathe through a snorkel within the closed space of his shell, which compressed his shoulders to a mere 34 inches.

"My life is great now," he told the media, "I haven't let my fitness go in the past few years, so the record is well within my capabilities." Considering he was approaching 50 years old, this was quite a statement of confidence. He joked that his machine would be called "Pie in the Sky," but it ended up being christened "The Beastie." And indeed it was a beast, compared to the high-tech machines constructed by engineering teams from around the world who had access to unlimited budgets.

Graeme began building his bike and training seriously on the local roads. He experimented with different positions and pushed himself to the brink of exhaustion. Just two months before the scheduled event in the U.S., he had a serious setback when a side effect of his antidepressant medication caused a priapism, which is a painful involuntary erection. "Even thinking of politicians didn't make the stiffie go away," he said with a laugh.

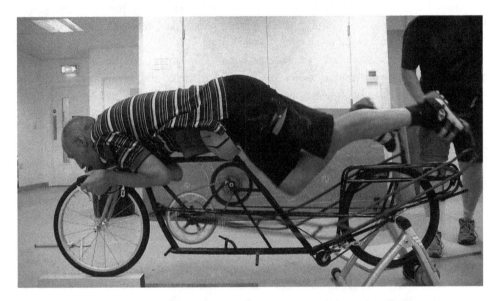

Fig. 5-2. Graeme Obree reinvented himself once again in his 50s, setting the ambitious goal of breaking the land speed record for a human-powered vehicle. Once again, he designed and constructed his bike out of spare parts he could secure with a modest budget, as seen above.

He was hospitalized for weeks. They first tried a spinal tap, followed by vascular surgery to remove a vein in his leg in order to stop the blood flow. That eventually resulted in a hematoma the size of a grapefruit, leading to more delays in his plans. But eventually, he recovered sufficiently to travel.

Obree traveled to Battle Mountain, Nevada, with one of his sons and the support of a few friends. When asked by reporters why on earth he was attempting such a thing at his advanced age, he replied: "Tigers don't change their stripes, do they?" He described himself as a tiger, even if an aging one with grey, balding hair and a wrinkled face.

During his first qualifying race, he could hit only 40 miles per hour—a terrible disappointment, considering he was hoping to double that speed. "I was riddled with doubt," he admitted, the depression hovering once again over him. He tried again and then again each day, only barely increasing his speed. Yet he refused to surrender. That's when he learned that, possibly, the world record for human power in the prone position might be within his grasp if he could eke out another 15 miles per hour.

On the very last day of the event, he was scheduled for his final attempt, and once again he failed to reach the world record. In his previous runs, the bike, so unstable to begin with, had wobbled all over the road. Within the enclosed shell and breathing through a tube, he was on the verge of passing out from asphyxiation. Remember, the guy was 47 years old trying to set a world record, and there were limits to what he could do at his age.

Obree had made a few adjustments on his bike, hoping to make Beastie a bit more aerodynamic. By this time, the machine was literally held together by duct tape along the seams. On his last ride, he hit over 50 miles per hour, but it was still not close enough. Everyone was packing up when he announced, in an almost exact reenactment of what had unfolded in Norway during his world hour-record attempt, that he was going again. He was now 25 years older than he'd been on that fateful day, but he still had the same stubborn streak and refused to give up.

Graeme Obree hit 56.62 miles per hour riding into a headwind, and he set a new world record for the prone position. He had just turned 48 years old and was cheered on by his son. In retrospect, he admits he made a serious mistake by allowing himself to be in that position of stressful emotional vulnerability, but he shrugs it off with a smile.

Just as there was a Hollywood film made about his struggle with depression and his attempt to break the hour record, there was also a documentary film made about his land speed-record attempt. Clearly he is a character who has captured tremendous public interest precisely because of his courage to overcome adversity.

Obree now tries to live a far more simple, contented life these days. He focuses more on the present and dwells much less on the past or the future. "My biggest moment," he admits, "was when I said I was done hiding: face life, straight down the line. I can't worry about pleasing people as long as I'm at one with my code of living."

What's Obree's takeaway from all he has learned in life—his triumphs and successes as well as crushing disappointments and suicidal failures? It's a lesson instructive for us all. Set our highest goals, even if they seem impossible. Try to reach them. Try again. And again. And again. And then, once it is clear that the goal is not within our current capability, then readjust the goal and reframe the failure as a different kind of success.

Epilogue

I have corresponded with Graeme about the status of his life these days. I told him how much I respected and admired his willingness and ability to bounce back from so many challenges in life. As someone who teaches psychotherapy, I was also intrigued by the role that mental health professionals had played in his recovery, at least transitionally. I wanted to understand at a deeper level the nature of his afflictions and their origins—at least his take on that—as well as what he believed has been most helpful for him. We began a dialogue about some of these issues, and I would like to share some of the most revealing highlights.

It was important to Obree that people understand that what has been most important to him is to learn to simplify life as much as possible. He doesn't care much about possessions or others' approval. He says he is done with achievements and no longer has any interest in competition; he just loves to ride his bike for the pure pleasure of it, to appreciate the gorgeous scenery and keep himself in reasonable shape.

We both agreed that we share some things in common. "At the end of the day," he said, "it's about what we did to help others who were not so lucky or enlightened." He is talking about what he has learned from his previous suffering and the gifts he received from those hard-learned lessons.

I'd been living inside his life for the previous weeks, reading his book and interviews, watching the films about him, and researching as much as I could about him from afar. I wanted him to know that he inspired me, not because of his athletic achievements but because of his courage and persistence at reinventing himself. I struggle with my own adjustments to aging, and I took some reassurance not only from his determination to keep himself going at a high level but also to let go.

I'm a psychologist by profession, and Graeme has been a patient, so it's not unexpected that we would have different thoughts on what matters most with respect to his recovery or anyone's attempt to deal with depression or mental illness. He insists that most experts often get it wrong: "Depression, abuse, substance abuse, and suicide attempts were never a problem—they were the solution." I don't much disagree with him on that.

Obree is still very much the rebel, if not the revolutionary. He has found that it is the toxic aspects of the larger culture, and especially within professional sports, that lead athletes to push themselves way too hard for their celebrity status and monetary rewards. "I feel everything in full right now," he says. "I need nothing more from the outside world to feel okay on the inside, especially the approval of other people."

He has ceased taking all medications, no longer drinks alcohol, and is somewhat cynical about the value of psychotherapy, even though it seemed to be so instrumental in his healing much earlier in life. He has developed his own style of logic and analysis to come to terms with his past. "Forgiveness is just so pithy," he told me. "It underlies the fact that something bad has really happened."

I argue with him about that because I have found that self-forgiveness for past mistakes and failures is critical for letting go, not only in my life but also with respect to those I have treated and helped in my work. Whether there is a perfectionistic streak or just a tendency toward self-punishment for one's errors, I consider forgiveness to be quite helpful. Just as important is learning to find the growth and learning from one's suffering.

Graeme was quite interested in learning more about the posttraumatic growth movement, in which it is no longer assumed that just because someone has experienced trauma, abuse, neglect, or suffering, that must mean there is lingering dysfunction. In many such cases, people simply move on with their lives. And with others, they take tremendous gifts from the events that have utterly transformed them in all kinds of positive ways. Graeme heartily agrees that this idea applies to his own life.

"I used to be so beaten down by depression," Graeme said to end our conversation, "and I thought that life was just fine but essentially pointless." He pauses for a moment. "But now I see that life is pointless but just fine."

It was time to say goodbye. Graeme was going out for a bike ride.

Sources

Baker, A. (2002, January 9). Obree suicide attempt sad news for cycling enthusiasts. *The Telegraph*. http://www.telegraph.co.uk/sport/othersports/cycling/2428294/Obree-suicide-attempt-sad-news-for-cycling-enthusiasts.html

Hicks, R. (2015, November 10). Graeme Obree: Why we need to talk about depression in sport. *Cycling Weekly*. http://www.cyclingweekly.com/fitness/depression-in-sport-45337

Hutchinson, M. (2006). *The hour: Sporting immortality the hard way*. Yellow Jersey Press.

Krabbe, T. (2002). *The rider*. Bloomsbury.

John, T. (2015, May 6). Graeme Obree interview: "My relationship to cycling is like Pluto's relationship to Earth." *Road Cycling UK*. https://roadcyclinguk.com/racing/graeme-obree-interview-relationship-cycling-like-plutos-relationship-earth.html

Kelbie, P. (2002, January 10). Champion cyclist Obree tried to hang himself after injury problems. *Independent*. http://www.independent.co.uk/news/uk/this-britain/champion-cyclist-obree-tried-to-hang-himself-after-injury-problems-9153574.html

Mackinnon, D. (Director). (2006). *The flying Scotsman*. Verve Pictures.

Moore, R. (2012, February 2). Revelation brings Graeme Obree release from torment. *The Guardian*. https://www.theguardian.com/sport/2011/feb/02/graeme-obree-cycling

Obree, G. (2005). *Flying Scotsman: Cycling to triumph through my darkest hours*. Velo.

Roe, N. (2007, June 9). Against all odds. *The Telegraph*. http://www.telegraph.co.uk/news/features/3632942/Against-all-odds.html

Scotsman Newspaper. (2011, January 21). I'm gay and it twice drove me to suicide, reveals Flying Scotsman Graeme Obree. https://www.scotsman.com/news/i-m-gay-and-it-twice-drove-me-to-attempt-suicide-reveals-flying-scotsman-graeme-obree-1-1499174

Smith, M. (2012, April 5). Graeme Obree smashes myth of sporting success. *The Herald*. http://www.heraldscotland.com/arts_ents/13099073.Graeme_Obree_smashes_the_myth_of_sporting_success/

Smith, S. (2012, May 6). Flying Scotsman Graeme Obree uses old saucepan to build world record bid bike. *Daily Record*. https://www.dailyrecord.co.uk/news/uk-world-news/flying-scotsman-graeme-obree-uses-877238

Stassin, J., & Watson, R. (1993). Appendix. Reprinted in G. Obree, *Flying Scotsman: Cycling to triumph through my darkest hours*. Velo, 238–244.

Street, D. (Director). (2016). *Battle mountain: Graeme Obree's story*. Journey Pictures.

Wilcockson, J. (2005). Foreword. In G. Obree, *Flying Scotsman: Cycling to triumph through my darkest hours*. Velo, xi–xiii.

6

Kevin Hall

He Thought He Was on Television—All the Time

Kevin Hall, Andrew Simpson, and the other eight crew members were working hard to keep their America's Cup yacht on a solid path. It was an almost perfect day on the ocean. They were sailing upwind on a starboard tack with 12 knots of strong, unstable wind. The San Francisco Bay was a bit lumpy that day. Their 72-foot experimentally designed boat, *Artemis*, was on a training run to prepare for the famous race that would begin a few months later.

Hall had been a world-class sailor since his college days and was now at the pinnacle of his sport, crewing for the most prestigious team. Simpson, an Olympic gold medalist from Britain, was just 36 and already one of the world's most accomplished sailors.

Hall had found that thus far in their practice runs, they had become very skilled at fixing poorly designed pieces of the boat that kept falling apart. He commented that it was unfortunate that the America's Cup race wasn't a boat repair contest, or they would have won easily. Thus far, the forward beam had cracked and the wing had disintegrated, leading Hall to conclude the damn boat was cursed, "that it would twist itself to death" if they didn't keep a close eye on everything.

The race was to be held in the bay where, a few months earlier, Oracle Team USA had capsized a boat of the same exact design. The crew had sustained bruises and a few minor injuries but were otherwise unharmed. It was still a bad omen.

Hall and his mates were sailing under maximum power when the bow tipped under a wave but failed to rebalance itself; it just kept going under, and then the whole boat lifted in the air. The forward beam that connected the twin hulls broke apart, leading the aft mast to collapse and the whole thing to literally split apart. Hall could hear the carbon fiber hull tearing itself to shreds. He hung on for his life before being slammed back into the water. Hard.

Andrew Simpson was trapped beneath the overturned hull, wedged between broken pieces of the carbon shell. Hall and other crew tried to free him, but he was stuck. As a last resort, they passed him bottled oxygen until rescue workers could arrive on the scene. But time ran out, and Simpson drowned.

Andrew was the kind of person, Hall recalled, "who lifts everyone in the room with his knowledge and his enthusiasm and his pure heart." Kevin helped pull his dead body out of the ocean, a horror he has never forgotten.

Hall found himself periodically uncertain whether the tragedy had actually happened in real life or was just part of a scripted show he was starring in. It was all so horrible, maybe it was just a confused memory. He had been thinking recently that perhaps the only difference between the two was that "Reality is that which, when you stop believing in it, doesn't go away." But for Kevin, that distinction was becoming increasingly blurred.

Hall began having reoccurring nightmares after the accident. During idle moments, he would hear the sounds of a boat snapping and tearing apart. He started drinking heavily immediately thereafter, even though he was already barely stabilized on various medications for his chronic mental illness: antidepressants, lithium for his bipolar disorder, antipsychotics to stop his delusions, plus injections to replace his hormone deficiencies after barely surviving cancer. Hall retreated into another tailspin. "I had nightmares for months," he reported as part of his lingering guilt, wondering if there was something he could have done differently that might have averted the disaster. He quit sailing for a while thereafter, restricting himself to supporting roles in logistics and navigation.

I Don't Feel Like Myself

Few international athletes distinguish themselves at such a young age, whether in gymnastics, snowboarding, basketball, or track. Yet by the age of 15, Kevin Hall was the youngest sailor to win the Singlehanded National Championship. And to demonstrate that was no fluke, he won again the following year. He was already being lauded as a future Olympic champion. Even more remarkably, throughout his distinguished career Hall would regularly change classes of sailing and the kinds of boats he would operate, moving from single- to double-person boats all the way up to the dozen-crew America's Cup races.

If these accomplishments weren't amazing enough, consider this: Hall was already being "visited" by "The Director": an internal voice, a "vapor of energy," that sometimes controlled his life. The Director would become increasingly influential over the course of Hall's life, but during his teenage years, Kevin seemed mostly able to moderate his volatile mood swings and delusions. He's been hospitalized a dozen different times, usually for going off his meds because "I don't feel like myself." This is not uncommon among those with bipolar disorder who, on one level, enjoy manic-fueled binges when they feel so productive.

Among creative professions, whether music, art, theatre, or even advertising, there is a disproportionate number of manic depressives, sometimes as high as five times the number among the greater population. Consider the number of artists (Vincent Van Gogh), composers (Ludwig von Beethoven), political leaders (Winston Churchill), writers (Edgar Allen Poe), poets (Sylvia Plath), actors (Robin Williams), and scientists (Isaac Newton) who are alleged to have suffered from extreme mood swings that both produced extraordinary output as well as incapacitated them. It is no wonder, then, that athletes might "benefit" in some ways from a sort of enhanced performance—golfer John Daly, basketball player Metta World Peace, tennis player Ilie Nastase, Australian rugby player Tim Smith, football player Dimitrius Underwood, boxer Frank Bruno—the list is almost endless.

People go off their meds because they believe they can perform better or access greater passion and creativity—and on one level, that is sometimes the case, even if there is ultimately a price to pay for the impulsivity and indulgence. Once, Hall stopped taking his medication and found himself dancing at a rave all night, finally climbing up cables to the top of a tent; police officers had to bring him down and have him admitted him to a psychiatric ward.

If you wonder why someone like Hall would put himself at such risk, consider the inherent danger of his chosen sport: racing 40 miles per hour in a boat turned on its side, a single error in judgment or execution possibly meaning injury or death. When asked why on earth he would deliberately stop taking drugs that help stabilize him, Hall can only shrug, explaining that "meds put a layer of gauze between you and the world." Such insulation might be comforting for someone who is plagued by despair or disturbing thoughts, but in the case of a world-class athlete like Hall, "decision making is often based on instinct and feel rather than processed thought." In other words, he needed to embrace his raw power even if it spun out of control.

In Hall's case, his courage is evidenced not only by his distinguished career and accomplishments as a sailor but also in his brutal honesty about his struggles with mental illness. In his autobiography, he writes in vivid, heartbreaking detail: "I was disintegrating, right down to my core." He talks about his arrests, the orderlies who would hold him down, gurney restraints, the antipsychotic and antidepressant drugs loaded into his body, the shame and sense of failure. He likens his inner world during some of his psychotic breaks to what it must feel like on crystal meth: the world vibrating, feelings of omnipotence and invincibility, of everything perfectly aligned. "Much of my struggle to stay on this planet is because I get those feelings. Except, I get them when I *don't* take drugs."

Hall describes in the most graphic, painful terms what delusional mania actually *feels* like—staying up all night watching movies and playing video games, reading 20 books at the same time, feeling connected to "infinite space," "jacked into the mainframe," unable to determine what is real and what is in his mind. Imagine what it's like to not be able to distinguish what is actually happening from what you imagine, to not be able to trust your perceptions, much less your judgment. Even your memories are radically distorted, if not lost altogether.

Hall's "Director" linked cameras back to the "mothership," fed him lines to say, and had strangers with secret earpieces play supporting roles in the scenes. The delusions become more embedded in his thought patterns over time, more difficult to challenge and counteract no matter how many drugs the doctors put into his system. Hall remembers one time he could hear the voice speaking to him through the tape player in his car, and the only way he could stop the escalating paranoia was to stuff tampons into the tape slot. Surprisingly, that worked pretty well.

Multiple Pressures and a Collection of Failures

While Hall was attending college at Brown University, The Director exerted increasing influence on his life, instructing him on his roles in various scenes that were to be acted out. Hall believes he needed this extreme guidance as a way to survive. This was just added pressure to the already relentless schedule that controlled his life with competitive sailing, academic study of mathematics, and earning his father's approval.

Juggling the pressures of being a world-class athlete with the rigors of attaining an Ivy League education would be enough for almost anyone. Add to the mix the onset of major depressive disorder that cycled between mania and despair, and the guy had his hands full. Then the voices appeared inside his head, ordering him to perform for a faceless audience. But that wasn't the worst of it: He was diagnosed with testicular cancer and subjected to numerous surgeries that removed his testicles and lymph glands to prevent the cancer from metastasizing any further. Is it any wonder he flipped out?

Each year during the next decade of his life, Hall was hospitalized after a psychotic break. He was arrested by police, restrained by hospital attendants on the locked psychiatric ward, and loaded with potent drugs that left him in a listless fog. Each time he recovered and regained some kind of stability—enough to resume his pursuit of an Olympic gold medal—The Director's voice would return, and he would lose his sense of self.

Ever since he was a child, Hall had felt terribly inadequate and a disappointment to those around him, especially his father. Although everyone told him he had great promise as a sailor, perhaps the best, he had yet to demonstrate that—at least according to his perfectionistic standards. By age 15, he was already a national sensation, but it was never enough for him. Those early victories and dominance in his sport were fleeting, at least according to his own expectations. He tried to qualify for the 1996 Olympics in Atlanta but came up short in several races. At one point he capsized his boat and had to be rescued, one of the most humiliating moments of his life. He felt like a failure at every level: as a sailor, as a man with no testicles, and as a sane human being.

Ironically, once he surrendered and realized it was impossible to win, he stopped caring about the results. "The remaining races I sailed with some dignity," he says. He showed better results, gained valuable experience, and learned some tough lessons that he described as character building.

Mental Disorders and Enhanced Performance?

Hall was initially diagnosed with the extreme mood swings of bipolar disorder, characterized by cycles lasting days or weeks when he might lapse into a deep funk before entering into a sustained manic state during which he'd operate at intense energy levels. Considering that he was able to write his life story in just eight days, it's clear that such a condition can lead to remarkably enhanced productivity and creativity. "It all came tumbling out," Hall explained.

Like many manic depressives, he enjoyed the hyper binges. Novelist Virginia Woolf would languish in bed for weeks in a depressed stupor before feeling an intense exhilaration that led her to complete her lengthy stream-of-consciousness novels at a racing pace. Of course, the ecstasy doesn't last long before the person comes crashing down and becomes at greatest risk for self-harm or suicide. "I had to learn," Hall shared, "that when my imagination started to percolate that probably meant I was on the road to trouble and getting sick."

It would appear that mentally ill athletes in any sport would not in any way enjoy an advantage from their mental disorder. After all, they would struggle with emotional instability and volatility. But there is also a certain uncontrolled passion that may accompany their rather unusual way of relating to the world. They reason outside the normal realm of what is expected; likewise, their behavior is entirely unpredictable. They live by different rules and are given a degree of latitude that offers a special kind of "privilege."

Those with extreme mood swings are actually quite frightening to those around them, since they seem capable of saying or doing almost anything that strikes them at the time. Indeed, they are impulsive and, at times, dangerously imprudent. This leads them to take risks that others would never consider. That's certainly true with respect to several of those profiled in this book who risked their safety and health doing things that a more rational person would never attempt. Yet it is precisely that fearlessness that allows them to test their limits beyond what most of us would ever consider.

World Cup sailors like Hall deliberately put themselves in jeopardy, not only to win a race but to become the best in the world in their sport. Mountaineers will attempt to summit a peak like K2 knowing full well that their odds of dying on the descent are one in four. You actually have better odds playing Russian roulette. And those who climb the neighboring Annapurna peak have an even higher chance of dying; they know that almost half of them will not survive.

Professional boxers have a 90% chance of suffering permanent brain damage; it destroyed the lives of Muhammad Ali, Joe Louis, and so many others. Bull riders, big-wave surfers, and base jumpers also regularly subject themselves to the risk of serious injury or death, yet they feel compelled to test themselves. Consistently, whenever athletes are asked why they do this sort of thing when they know the risks, they mostly just shrug. They insist—and many experts agree—that it is not about having a death wish but rather a desire to live their lives more intensely. It is the edge of danger that makes them feel more alive. And they are rewarded in many ways for their supposed recklessness—in some cases they earn fame and fortune, groupies and fans, admiration and respect. But it is far more than that, since nature also rewards risk-takers with endocrine reactions that produce feelings of extreme exhilaration. They consider themselves experts who can minimize risks that might apply to others. They tend to be optimistic, self-confident, and feel perfectly capable of controlling their own fate. Without such individuals who have evolved in our species—those who were willing to explore the unknown—we would have perished long ago.

Although Hall considered—or perhaps rationalized—that his manic states provided him with a turbocharged boost that was advantageous, another level of complexity to his troubles developed when the delusional fantasies began. There was, as yet, no name for one facet of his condition.

A Most Unusual Reality

A delusion is simply an unshakeable false belief that is unsupported by evidence. It often takes the form of either grandiosity (being famous or having special powers) or persecutory (being drugged, harassed, inhabited). In a milder form, a certain degree of hypervigilance is highly adaptive in that it allows us to detect and anticipate possible threats.

Whereas once upon a time during the Middle Ages, delusional sufferers believed themselves possessed by wolves, in the middle of the 20th century, visions took the form of being controlled by Japanese radio waves or Soviet satellites. During the '70s, such psychotic fantasies were transformed into beliefs that the CIA had implanted computer chips in the brain. There is little doubt that cultural forces and popular media play a role in the specific formation of the disorder. And then there is the reality that there are thousands of cameras in places like Manhattan and London filming every movement, the NSA monitoring every conversation, and the likes of Google, Facebook, Amazon, Uber, VISA, and Apple capturing data on every aspect of our lives.

Kevin Hall is surely unique in the sense that he suffered from not only an unusual mental illness but also one of the stranger psychological phenomena on the planet. The "Truman Syndrome" is a cultural variation of these themes, as evidenced by the pervasive popularity of reality TV shows like *Survivor*, *Big Brother*, and *The Bachelor*. The syndrome name is derived from the movie *The Truman Show*, which is about a man, played by Jim Carrey, whose every action is part of a reality show he only wishes to escape. He desperately wants to lead a more authentic private life, one that is uncontrolled by all-pervasive technology. This resonates quite intimately with so much of popular culture (*The Hunger Games*, YouTube, Instagram, Twitter), in which one's every thought or insignificant event is displayed for public view. Nowadays, people routinely broadcast photos, messages, and videos every day—or every few hours—about what they are doing, what they are thinking or feeling, or just what they had for lunch.

When Hall first saw the movie, he suddenly felt less alone. Someone, somewhere, imagined what he had long been experiencing—the belief that his life was a reality show. There have been other iterations of this theme prior to *Truman*, most recently in episodes of *Black Mirror* but also in a short story by Philip K. Dick and an episode of the series *The Twilight Zone* from the 1980s. Robert Heinlein wrote a science fiction story many years ago that offers one of the earliest descriptions of the disorder: "Since the world could not be as crazy as it appeared to be, it must necessarily have been arranged to appear crazy in order to deceive him as to the truth. ... Obviously the first step must be to escape from this asylum." If only escape was possible.

In today's obsessive world of social media, this fantasy is becoming even more a reality. Young people spend as much as six hours a day sending out messages or visual images of their experiences; the majority of the "iGen" age cohort actually sleep with their mobile devices under their pillows. Mary Pilon completed her biography of Kevin Hall by quoting Shakespeare: "All the world's a stage." Indeed, she concludes, "Maybe Truman Disorder isn't as rare as we think." She is referring to how commonplace it is in our virtual worlds that the boundaries between reality and artificial experiences have become blurred. Even the notion of "truth" has become diluted by some in the political arena: Multiple versions of perception and interpretation are offered as equally valid, whether there is any legitimate supportive evidence or not.

As for what it feels like to those afflicted with this disorder, Hall says, "When I'm in this delusion, I think there are cameras everywhere filming me for a TV show, and I hear the director's voice in my head telling me what I have to do for each scene." The urge to follow these directions is absolutely overwhelming, to the point where he once drove his car off a pier into the ocean because The Director told him it was required but that he shouldn't worry because there were divers who were ready to save him. His wife, who was with him in the vehicle at the time, still has posttraumatic stress symptoms as a result of their crashing into a barrier before they entered the water.

The Truman Show delusion is quite rare, with fewer than perhaps 50 documented cases since it was first identified and formalized by psychiatrist Joel Gold and his brother, Ian Gold, a professor of philosophy and psychiatry. They describe more than a dozen different patients whose delusional thinking led them to believe that certain world events were part of a plot twist in their own personal narratives, which were broadcast live to the world. While many of the more contemporary cases were influenced, in part, by the *Truman* film, Hall's own symptoms appeared years before that. When interviewed about this burgeoning mental illness, Andrew Niccol, *The Truman Show*'s screenwriter, commented, "You know you've made it when you have a disease named after you." Of course in today's instant social media world, there are thousands of people whose daily existence is broadcast to their legions of viewers.

In an article about the nature of the disorder, author Andrew Marantz noted that "the mind supplies the contours of delusions, and culture fills in details." He supplied examples of how paranoia is expressed in quite different ways in different parts of the world. In Taipei, people are more inclined to report being possessed by spirits, whereas in Christian countries, they are more likely to feel like prophets or gods. The pervasive influence of technology has pushed vulnerable people to believe that directors inside their heads are guiding their "performances" or issuing orders they should follow to entertain their audience.

Hall began doing his own research on the nature and kinds of delusions, trying to come to terms with his own personal struggles. There was voluminous research and documented descriptions of the varieties. There were people with the "Alice in Wonderland Syndrome" who distort objects they encounter in real life or "Foreign Accent Syndrome," in which they suddenly and inexplicably start speaking with a Chinese, French, or other accent. There are those who believe themselves already dead or who think they are inhabiting the body of a cow. In each case, the particular content is hardly random or universal but rather may be strongly influenced by the larger culture the person inhabits.

Ian Gold was contacted directly by Kevin after he read about the nature of the research going on. They immediately discovered a series of remarkable coincidences about their lives: It turns out they had been in the same freshman class at Brown University, but they had been only vaguely familiar to one another. In addition, it turned out their first meeting was providential, since they both just happened to be in San Francisco on the same day.

Gold discovered that Hall had many of the classic symptoms he had observed in other patients during the preceding years, although the symptoms might have been manifested in a variety of different diagnoses, such as schizophrenia, substance abuse psychoses, or bipolar disorder. Hall believed he could influence everyone around him, at least those who were watching his "show," and thereby change the world. This would be a wonderful fantasy indeed for anyone who feels powerless and inadequate and wants to feel special. Like many sufferers of the disorder, Hall had a series of rituals that would accompany any of his episodes when The Director notified him he was on camera. He would take off his shoes so he could feel closer to the earth, remove his watch (since time no longer had any particular meaning to him), and finally, throw away his wallet, since he had no use for identification or money when he was performing.

Gold explains that in many such delusional disorders, Truman Syndrome among them, the distortions of reality represent an overreaction to *perceived* threats, a sort of hyper-vigilance needed to anticipate and prepare defenses. He suggested that it's important to look beyond exclusively neural systems to explain the phenomenon because the content and nature of the delusions are strongly influenced by cultural forces.

Gold was uniquely situated and prepared for his specialty as a whisperer to Truman Show "contestants." Doing his residency at Bellevue Hospital in New York, he was at ground zero for psychoses. "I observed more delusions than I suspect many psychiatrists observe in a career." His first patient who presented Truman symptoms not only thought that everyone in his life was part of a conspiracy to disguise from him that he was on a show, but he also believed he had cameras installed in his eyes, like in the plot from the movie *Being John Malkovich*. Descriptions like this made it increasingly clear that popular culture was indeed impacting the psychotic delusions. And this was groundbreaking for Gold, not just with respect to this specific disorder but also for a deeper understanding of all mental illness.

Another realization that holds true for most of us is that Truman-like illusions and fantasies are relatively common. I remember as an early adolescent playing games on the driveway in which I imagined the whole world was watching me shoot free throws. I believed (or pretended) that if I could make five in a row, a girl I liked in school would like me back. In other words, Gold concluded, the mentally ill are different from us, but only by a matter of degree.

In addition, the experience of confusing fantasy with reality is a common phenomenon. All of us, at one time or another, imagine ourselves as the subjects of public fascination or picture how we might behave differently in the shows we watch. In a popular television show, *Westworld*, the lines between human and android become confusing and blurred.

Fig. 6-1. As seen above, Kevin Hall competed in the 2004 Olympics in Athens but finished in a disappointing 11th place. He was struggling not only with the disturbing, overpowering voice inside his head but also the lingering effects of surviving cancer.

One of the actors in the series, Rachel Wood, plays a human who is really a robot. But when the cameras aren't rolling, Wood sometimes loses track of her sense of self and imagines that she has been transported into the show itself. "I was so creeped out," she said about falling asleep in her character's bed. She woke up completely disoriented. "It was just a TV show! None of this is real!" The difference, however, is that in Hall's case, the cameras are almost *always* running.

A Body of Distinguished Work, With a Perception of Failure

Hall served in a number of different roles during his America's Cup and Olympic career. There are many specialized jobs on an America's Cup-class boat, each of which requires unique physical attributes, mental sets, and skills. The bowmen up front are like gymnasts: lithe and dexterous, since they are required to change sails. Grinders are the musclemen and engines of the operation, expected to turn the cranks of sails as fast as possible. The midbowmen and trimmers work in conjunction with the skipper to generate as much speed as possible, constantly responding to various tactical choices as the weather, seas, and competition change. Then there is a logistics expert who handles all the details to keep the crew functioning like a well-oiled machine.

Kevin was actually well suited as a navigator, a job he loved because it utilized his precise mathematical brain and competency with computers and data processing. He was especially good at making sense of all the influx of data flowing in, interpreting the most significant features, and concisely advising the skipper about how to respond at any given moment. This role required both solid left-brain analytic processing and right-brain intuition. In spite of his unique qualifications for this job, however, a few of his mates had already been witness to some of his bizarre psychotic flip-outs. With an interest in minimizing their risk as well as protecting Hall from undue stress, the team decided the best role for him was a job on land. He was thus assigned to the role of "spy."

The job of a spy is to gather data and intelligence about the competition's boats. Can you imagine anything more ironic for someone with acute paranoia? The spy's job is to snoop and to constantly look over his shoulder to prevent himself from being discovered. He is supposed to not only gather information but also spread disinformation to competitors.

Opposing crew were only permitted within 200 meters of another team's boat, which meant that Hall was required to do his job from a distance, estimating measurements and reverse engineering designs based on photos, data, and direct observations. Once the sails were packed away and he had better angles and visibility, he'd shoot photos while circling the target in a smaller skiff. Then he'd compile all the data, try to get information from anyone familiar with the boat, crunch the numbers, and prepare a detailed report for the crew about the strengths and possible weaknesses of their competition.

During training runs, he'd follow in a chase craft and track the specific techniques the crews would employ during particular conditions. He'd note any new design features and alterations and then develop a matrix that would allow them to better predict what their opponents would do in every situation.

Since Hall had always been a prodigy at math (his true love in college), this work suited him well and allowed him to contribute in a meaningful and significant way. Of course, one of the things that made his job so much harder is that he would occasionally become distracted by The Director and the delusions that followed. There was one time when he had been racing a smaller boat preparing for the Olympic trials and losing consistently. He started to believe that "they" had installed whirlpool devices that kept pushing his boat backwards, no matter what he tried to overcome with his skills. Soon after episodes like that, he might find himself on another "sabbatical" on a psych ward until adjustments in his medications would allow him to resume his duties.

In many cases, Hall attributed his recovery from the psychotic episodes as much to the other patients as to anything offered by the doctors. He felt supported and understood by others on the ward. He felt less alone. They all shared their fears, losses, and grief openly and honestly with one another. Rather than shaming and shunning him, the other patients accepted him just as he was. A week or two later, he'd be back out on the water, if not recovered, then at least stabilized.

Throughout Hall's career, there was one overriding goal that would finally validate him, earn his father's approval, and prove that he was truly special—and that was to win a gold medal in the Olympics. He had found such international competition to be quite different than the races he had won as a national champion in the U.S., races in which patience and delicacy were required to outmaneuver opponents. In the Olympic trials, it was about brute force and reckless speed, and he was not at his best in those conditions; once again, he disappointed himself. He became despondent over the losses, unforgiving, describing the experience "as tantamount to staring at the ceiling in the next room, with paper-thin walls, while your best friend fucks the brains out of the girl you've been in love with since you were 17." But Hall was so used to falling into a black hole and crawling out that he took his small victories where he could find them. This resilience and ability to bounce back was truly one of his most remarkable assets, especially when you consider all the obstacles and challenges he faced during his life. Most of us would consider ourselves fortunate to summon the strength to get out of bed in the morning, much less continue to perform at such an extraordinary level.

Hall was learning from his mistakes and lapses. After his breakdown during the 1996 Olympic trials, he had to deal with the shame and humiliation of falling apart in front of all his teammates and opponents. But he also had an epiphany regarding his sailing technique, realizing that although it seems logical and intuitive to ride upwind whenever possible on the open ocean, it was really while riding the waves downwind like a surfer that he could burst ahead. Then he added a personal trainer to his regimen and stopped all his medications, which were clouding his thinking, slowing his reflexes, narrowing his vision, and throwing his balance off kilter; he wanted to create a clear window when he could operate at his best, since time and opportunities were running out. He spent hundreds of hours in the water testing himself, building his stamina, practicing his new techniques riding waves downwind, and carving turns, and it all paid off. During the first races in the trials, he won consistently and commandingly. His confidence started to increase exponentially, to the point where he started to feel like all he had to do was follow the path that was laid out before him.

Yet there was drama going on behind the scenes. The authorities were giving him a hard time for taking a banned substance: the testosterone that his body could no longer produce. The controversy became a national story, landing him on *Good Morning America* and the front page of the *New York Times*. Though he did prevail and was chosen to represent America, but once again, he failed to medal. He tried to put the best spin on it, reminding himself what an honor it was to have been an Olympian, but alas, he labeled himself a failure once again and took another tailspin down into the black hole.

Like Graeme Obree, this was essentially the narrative of Hall's life. These dramatic ups and downs reflected not only the waves on the ocean but also the mood swings that dominated his being. Since he was now married and starting a family (eventually adopting three boys), he desperately needed a paycheck, so he joined the crew of the America's Cup team, which would experience the tragedy described earlier.

Picture what it must be like to be performing an important, crucial job, one that requires all your ability and concentration, and then in the middle of a conversation or task, something—a sound, a word, a movement—triggers you, and you realize there are a hundred cameras strategically placed all around you, recording your every word and gesture. Then you hear The Director speaking into your mind, ordering you to do or say something that is quite bizarre and out of context. This is not the sort of thing you can merely shake off and get back to work. It feels overwhelming, like something or someone else has taken over your mind and body, even your soul.

Hall was pretty much done with professional sailing after the tragedy on *Artemis* and began working as a consultant, developing software to analyze composite structures for racing boats. He used open-source codes that Pixar had developed for animation and worked at a NASA research facility to study some of their work. It was more stable, calming work that suited his family life.

Once Hall and his wife, Amanda, adopted their sons, he felt the stakes were so much higher. He and his wife started couples therapy to help them work out tensions in their relationship that resulted from his mental illness. He could no longer afford another relapse and hospitalization, so he started doing his own research and discovered that there had been dozens of other cases like his own. That's when he found the one psychiatrist, Joel Gold, who was specializing in this "Truman Disorder," so he reached out to him. When he read about the research being investigated, he felt such relief and validation: "I felt like I was looking at myself in the mirror." Forgiveness is an important part of healing.

Relatively Smooth Sailing—So Far

As with most psychotic conditions, reason, debate, and pointing out the irrationality and improbability of delusions is almost never successful; the beliefs are too entrenched and, in a sense, protective in their own bizarre way. Medications can be useful to help control the symptoms—that is, if the patient takes them on a regular basis, as Hall eventually learned. In addition, forms of cognitive therapy can help sufferers challenge their own thinking as a way to distinguish between fantasy and reality. Forms of meditation and mindfulness can also be helpful in remaining calm and clear, whether sailing on the water or sitting quietly and appreciating a sunset.

Like many athletes whose lives were defined by their performance in sport, Kevin has struggled since he gave up his training regimens and lifestyle as an elite athlete. He used to go to the gym once, even twice, each day to keep his body in top shape. He lived for the accolades and recognition as a champion. Upon retirement, it felt like everything that had been part of his identity was gone. Even the familiar visitation from The Director had been diminishing. He still goes out on the water occasionally but has given up any hope of competition. Perhaps he realizes that his system is just not built for that kind of stress.

Hall attributes his relative stability and smooth sailing to several factors, first among them his responsibilities as a father; in one sense, he believes his children saved him. He now takes his self-care very seriously. He no longer drinks wine or caffeine. He has learned to avoid triggers, recognizing the early signs that he may be losing control and getting out of touch with reality. He has also learned to prevent himself from falling into the "rabbit hole" through self-talk designed to keep him grounded. Rather than feeling regret and shame over his past mistakes and misdeeds, he feels fortunate for those experiences in some way. He has found rewards in his extreme emotional states, gifts that have resulted from the intensity of his feelings. Remember, this is a man, a world-class athlete in a dangerous sport, who thrives on risk, adventure, and pushing himself to the edge. "Maybe that's why I'm so lucky," he says. "Most people have to go pretty far out of their way to be overwhelmed like that."

Sources

Dunn, J. (2016, November 1). Twelve questions with Kevin Hall. *New Zealand Herald*. http://www.nzherald.co.nz/nz/news/article.cfm?c_id=1&objectid=11739217

Freeman, D. (2012, June 4). Truman Show delusion: Odd mental disorder makes people think they live in counterfeit world. *Huffington Post*. https://www.huffingtonpost.com/2012/06/04/truman-show-syndrome-disorder-counterfeit_n_1568159.html

Fusar-Poli, P., Howes, O., Valmaggia, L., & McGuire, P. (2008). "Truman" signs and vulnerability to psychosis. *British Journal of Psychiatry, 193*(2), 168–169.

Gold, J., & Gold, I. (2012). The "Truman Show" delusion: Psychosis in the global village. *Cognitive Neuropsychiatry, 17*(6), 455–472.

Gold, J., & Gold, I. (2014). *Suspicious minds: How culture shapes madness*. Free Press.

Griffiths, M. D. (2016, August 10). The Truman Show delusion. *Psychology Today*. https://www.psychologytoday.com/blog/in-excess/201608/the-truman-show-delusion

Hall, K. (2015). *Black sails, white rabbits*. CreateSpace.

Lecher, C. (2013, September 10). Truman Show Syndrome: Why people think they're living in a reality show. *Popular Science*. https://www.popsci.com/science/article/2013-09/truman-show-delusion-when-youre-convinced-everyones-watching-you

Manson, B. (2016, May 14). Kevin Hall: America's Cup sailor duels with bipolar. *Auckland Now*. https://www.stuff.co.nz/auckland/79184369/kevin-hall--americas-cup-sailor-duels-with-bipolar

Marantz, A. (2013, September 16). Unreality star: The paranoid used to fear the CIA. Now their delusions mirror "The Truman Show." *The New Yorker*. https://www.newyorker.com/magazine/2013/09/16/unreality-star

Mishara, A. L., & Fusar-Poli, P. (2013). The phenomenology and neurobiology of delusion formation during psychosis onset: Jaspers, Truman symptoms, and aberrant salience. *Schizophrenia Bulletin, 39*(2), 278–286.

Noble, K. B. (1996, February 15). After cancer struggle, Olympic nightmare. *New York Times*, A14.

Pilon, M. (2018). *The Kevin show: An Olympic athlete's battle with mental illness*. Bloomsbury.

Wright, S. (2008, August 6). Truman Show delusion: Real or imagined? *WebMD*. https://www.webmd.com/mental-health/features/truman-show-delusion-real-imagined#1

7

Fred Archer

A Living Myth

There is considerable debate regarding which sport has the toughest and most well-conditioned athletes. One obvious choice is the decathlon, requiring participants to complete 10 different events—running, sprinting, jumping, throwing a shot put, discus, and javelin—all squeezed into just two days. Boxing, of course, requires a high degree of fitness to survive 12 rounds in the ring being pummeled by an opponent. Then there are swimmers, gymnasts, and football players who spend hours in the gym shaping their bodies into perfect vessels for their particular events. Some would say it has to be marathon runners because of their ability to operate at top speed for over two consecutive hours, but then a counterpoint might be to mention cyclists, who ride grand tours over the course of three weeks, pushing their bodies to the absolute limit every single day. A similar grueling requirement is expected of mountain climbers, who, in addition to burning 5,000 calories a day at high altitude, also risk their lives if they make a single mistake.

Perhaps it is best to initially describe and define what ultimate athletic fitness actually encompasses. Certainly, cardiovascular endurance and stamina are crucial to the ability to function over the entire length of a game, event, or race. Body composition is crucial, including not only strength and flexibility but also, in many cases, perfect leanness. There are other traits that also come into play: mental attributes such as commitment and fearlessness as well as physical attributes such as a sense of balance, agility, coordination, and grace. Finally, ultimate speed, power, and reaction time could be important.

It may surprise you to learn that a legitimate contender for most fit athlete is one that you would likely never consider—a racing jockey. Pound for pound, no other athlete is required to function at such an optimal level, make more sacrifices, and combine power, agility, balance, and endurance while actually risking his or her life traveling at 40 miles per hour perched on top of a raging horse. Jockeys don't actually even sit on a saddle but rather crouch over it in a squat position; the only two parts of the body that are actually in continuous contact with the animal are the ankles.

In her book about Seabiscuit, the most famous racing horse of all time, Laura Hillenbrand described jockeys as the most misunderstood and underestimated of all professional athletes. "I have always watched them with awe," she wrote, "wondering what could make a person torture his body to participate in a sport that almost guarantees severe injury."

Hold your skepticism about the rigor of this sport when you realize that jockeys aren't permitted to weigh more than 115 pounds, and most have less than 2% body fat. Compare that to the average elite athlete in soccer, skiing, hockey, and most other sports; they have 10% body fat. Even the single most fit basketball or football players are in the range of 4%–5%. Then add to the picture the inherent danger of injury and fatality that comes with being a jockey; the vast majority have experienced a life-threatening accident during their career, and over 150 have been killed during a race. That's closing in on the range of people who have died climbing Mt. Everest, although many of those were hardly elite professional athletes but rather wealthy amateurs who paid exorbitant fees for the opportunity.

Horses have killed more prominent riders than you can imagine. Genghis Khan, Geronimo, William the Conqueror, King Alfonso of Portugal, and King Alexander of Scotland were all fierce warriors and successful generals, yet they all died falling off their horses. None of them were actually racing the beasts at the time.

In spite of the dangers and risks, or perhaps because of them, racehorses have captured the imagination of the populace and been revered as highly as any human being. Laura Hildebrand noted that in 1938, there were more articles written about Seabiscuit, the greatest racer of all time, than about Franklin Roosevelt, Adolf Hitler, Lou Gehrig, or the Pope. In her book about the famous thoroughbred, she presents the story of an individual that rose above his station in life and others' expectations. He was too small. He had strange-shaped legs. He had been abused and neglected. He was considered temperamental and untrainable. Actually, this is a narrative with parallels to those of many other athletes described in this book, including Fred Archer, who had his own handicap with an atypical body unsuited to the sport.

Jockeys compete at the highest level and manage to survive on less than 800 calories a day, basically a single meal or liquid supplement. Compare that to the daily diet of a tour cyclist, who consumes 10 *times* that much. Unlike boxers, who only have to hit a target weight on media day, jockeys have to maintain their ideal size and perfect physical conditioning in order to perform in *several* races each day, seven days a week, with no real off-season.

Training for modern jockeys often happens six to seven times each week and includes gym workouts, weightlifting, running, cycling, stretching, and yoga, plus riding horses for several hours each day. The goal is to build core strength in order to be able to hold the contorted position atop the horse while it is bouncing and flying along the track. In the old days, the training and preparation was both arduous and dangerous, involving an assortment of mental and physical tortures such as running endless miles in heavy sweaters to keep weight down. Celebrated jockeys like Fred Archer, perhaps the greatest in his sport who ever lived, starved himself to the point where he lived on what one rider called just "a puff of hope and a cigar."

Similar to gymnastics, horse racing requires athletes to have very specialized bodies that cannot exceed rigid weight limits. Jockeys are thus desperately and dangerously focused on dieting, often restricting themselves to less than 500 calories per day. This is in a sport that is so grueling and demanding that after a race, some jockeys have to be carried into the barn for recovery because they can barely walk.

Jockeys live in a perpetual state of starvation and dehydration. They are malnourished: The word "gaunt" doesn't do justice to the effects of the extent of their food restrictions.

As a result, they are at greater risk of developing pneumonia and a host of other diseases that can run rampant in their deprived, neglected bodies. They rely on purgatives, laxatives, diet pills, and starvation to maintain their weight.

Some jockeys would limit themselves to a single food (e.g., eggs or lettuce). They would wear rubber suits and stand by open fires to sweat off as much weight as possible. And as if that wasn't enough deprivation, water or any liquids were absolutely forbidden, leading to a state of continuous dehydration. Some of the most desperate jockeys would resort to even more extreme measures, such as swallowing small amounts of poison to kill their appetite or even ingesting a tapeworm egg or other parasite to have their body devoured from the inside.

All of these sacrifices are accepted as part of the sport.

Wonder of the World

During the 19th century, English jockey Fred Archer was a living myth, as popular during his day as Princess Diana but without any popular media to spread word of his incredible exploits. He won close to 3,000 races during a 15-year span and did that during a time when he had to travel from track to track by train and horseback. Whenever he would arrive in a town, it would be announced, "Come and see the greatest wonder of the world!" He was indeed a sensation, an athlete who so dominated his sport that he was considered the Michael Jordan of his era.

Many in his legion of fans wondered how it was possible for someone to accomplish so much with so little nourishment in his system. Archer mostly survived on a diet consisting of a single sardine, half an orange, and a sip of champagne or sherry, followed by a special purgative that came to be called "Archer's Mixture," a nasty concoction designed to induce vomiting. As he grew older, he resembled a walking skeleton, barely able to move at all because of the constant strain on his system. There were times when his strength was so drained he feared he might pass out in the middle of a race.

During his time, and most any time thereafter, Archer ruled his sport with relentless grace and precision. In 1878, he won half of all his races on two dozen different horses at Royal Ascot, an absolutely unheard-of accomplishment. He was named Champion Jockey for more than a dozen years in a row, beginning when he was just 16 years old. During his best year, 1885, he accumulated 246 victories before his tragic death.

Archer would earn a fortune during his distinguished career, often betting on himself to double his earnings. He had a reputation as being rather miserly with his money, but the truth was that he was a compulsive gambler and eventually squandered away much of what he had accumulated. His reputation also took a hit when it was alleged that at times he would deliberately bet against himself and throw a race or do so in order to help one of his friends or brothers who were training another horse. These allegations could never be proven, however, and most chose to believe it was just accusations by jealous competitors. This is a common theme in the life stories of many renowned athletes who have been accused of certain irregularities in their drive to dominate their sports. As we have seen with recent political figures, their fans tend to overlook these perceived lapses—as long as they keep winning.

Archer's racing style was often described as rather aggressive, if not vicious. He was said to be loose with an elbow on the track, willing to do almost whatever it took to gain an advantage over adversaries. In part, this is what made him so beloved among the populace, way beyond just racing fans. There came into vogue an expression, "Archer's Up," which, roughly translated, means that all is good with the world.

It's been said that the best jockey only controls about 10% of a race's outcome; the rest is up to the horse. While it is certainly true that Archer was mostly along for the ride, he also found ways to steal victories by maneuvering into optimal positions at the start, directing horses to hug the rails, and relying as much on encouraging the animal rather than dishing out punishment with a whip.

Archer's reputation and prowess as a champion eventually became so unassailable that whenever he would arrive at the track, the town crier would announce his presence at the village square. He may well have been one of the most recognizable individuals in all of England. Imagine that: A jockey from humble beginnings was treated with the respect afforded to royalty.

Fig. 7-1. Fred Archer was considered a "living myth" during his time, one of the first true sports celebrities who became a media sensation because of his unprecedented success.

Crafted and Shaped as a Jockey

Archer was never given much of a choice about whether to become a jockey. In spite of vigorous protests from his mother, his father insisted that was the only possible career path for him. William Archer had been successful in the sport for many years and decided that his sons would follow this path, whether they liked it or not. Since Fred showed such early promise, William focused most of his energy on his middle son.

At the age of 10, little Fred was shipped off by his father to apprentice with a leading horse trainer, Mat Dawson. Against his mother's strong objections, the sensitive, delicate child left home to begin the grueling preparation for a career that followed in his father's stirrups. During the preceding years, since the age of five, Fred had been pushed, scolded, and molded into the image of his father's ideal. By the age of eight, he had already been entered into donkey races.

At first, Fred was reluctant and homesick after being apprenticed to a noted trainer more than 100 miles from home, but he came to enjoy the discipline of his work. Because he was younger and so much frailer than the other boys in the stable, he was bullied and abused much of the time. Nevertheless, he redoubled his effort and commitment to show everyone, especially his father, that he could be the best among them.

There were now two authoritarian father figures controlling his life, and he spent most of his time and energy trying not to disappoint either one of them. He devoted not only his body but also his mind to mastering every nuance of the sport. He learned that what distinguished a winner from a loser was not only a fraction of a second at the finish line but also the determination to flat-out work harder than others in his preparation.

Archer was never permitted to have much of a formal education, so he remained mostly illiterate throughout his life, barely able to write a letter or read beyond a primary school level. Although he was considered quite bright and clever, all his potential was channeled into only one pursuit—riding horses around a track. Once his apprenticeship ended at the age of 15, he was immediately contracted to ride in 200 races and marked his second year with over a hundred wins. At a time when most young people were still in school, Fred Archer was already a sensation in his sport.

Sacrifices and Training

There is no other sport in which one's physical size and weight are so prescribed. A point guard in basketball, defensive back in football, or heavyweight in boxing must conform to a certain general body type, but there is still tremendous latitude allowed as long as the athlete can perform at optimal levels. For a jockey, weight and size are almost everything.

Archer had even greater challenges than most others because his height was unusual for a jockey: six inches taller than the norm. This meant that he had to resort to even more extreme measures to remain within the weight limits. When he went through an unexpected growth spurt in later adolescence, his obsession spun completely out of control. He developed a special secret elixir designed as a laxative. It was composed of prunes, grape juice, bran, and vinegar, an absolutely disgusting drink that kept Archer sitting on the toilet for much of the day.

The cumulative effect of such abuse leads not only to a series of catastrophic health problems but also to severe depression and anxiety. It is one thing to experience starvation because there is no food available and quite another to be constantly surrounded by sumptuous temptations but unable to consider even sampling them. A similar experience has been reported by women gymnasts and figure skaters who are expected to maintain a certain body type, even when it leads to serious eating disorders. All of this takes a tremendous toll on one's mental state as well as physical health. The constant diarrhea, stomach and arthritic pain, and hunger can literally drive someone crazy, as it likely did with Fred Archer.

Archer had never been used to losing many races, but as his precarious health, financial situation, and gambling problems worsened, so did his performance on the track. In his desperation, he began to initiate even more extreme measures to try and keep his weight down, even though he was already a walking corpse. He had dark rings underneath his eyes and a grey pallor to his skin. He would spend whole days in Turkish baths sweating out every drop of liquid in his body and then subject himself to more purgatives. It was no wonder he was losing his already unstable mind.

Many of the stories of fallen athletic heroes involve the toxic influences of a sport's entrenched culture. For road cyclists, it was the pressure to use steroids, growth hormones, and other performance-enhancing drugs. Certain teams develop corrosive cultures in which participants learn that in order to survive and flourish, it must be at others' expense and failure. Even the culture of Little League baseball or Pop Warner football leads parents and coaches to treat their children as commodities. Yet in horse racing, just like in gymnastics, figure skating, wrestling, or bodybuilding, weight is a crucial variable. And nowhere is the expectation more unforgivable than among jockeys, who are expected to constantly battle against their body's hunger for nutrition. Winning is everything—at whatever cost to one's health and emotional well-being. If someone like Fred Archer was worn down, depleted, and suffering from a host of nutritional deficiencies and chronic health problems, it is no wonder he was seriously emotionally disturbed as well. He had no immunity to the stresses and strains of life, much less to the catastrophic losses of his loved ones. It would not take much to push him over the edge.

Insane From Grief

One of the most stabilizing parts of Archer's life was his wife, Nellie, with whom he was deeply in love. He had literally been riding high from his consistent victories when he received the welcome news that they would have a baby. Archer became obsessed with fantasies of their future home life and dreams for his family. He would talk of nothing else. Even his race victories seemed to diminish in importance compared to what lay ahead for his growing family.

Mere hours after a very difficult delivery, the infant died. Fred and Nellie were both devastated. Even more challenging for them, Nellie suffered serious health problems afterwards and languished in bed. Neither one of them would ever be the same. While Nellie retreated within herself, nursing her failing health and mental anguish, Archer simply channeled his grief into working harder than ever.

Not too long after their tragedy, the couple learned that Nellie had become pregnant once again, although her precarious health was a bit of a worry. Archer was trying to balance his overscheduled race commitments with trying to take time to be with his wife during this difficult period in their lives. They were both still recovering from the loss of their previous child yet trying to remain upbeat about possibilities for the future. Archer was convinced they finally had luck on their side.

This was to be a roller coaster of a year for Archer. He was at the absolute pinnacle of his fame, having won more than 200 races during 1884. He was the most revered athlete in his country, and he had a lot for which to feel thankful. He was making more prize money than he could possibly spend and finally seemed to be on solid financial footing. British royalty treated him as an honored peer. He had a loving, devoted wife waiting for him at home and a baby on the way. He couldn't believe his good fortune and how full and complete his life felt. It was with such thoughts that he traveled home by train after the racing season had ended.

Archer's sister, Emily, was there to greet him at the door. She confessed her concerns that Nellie seemed so weak during the last few days before the baby was expected. Fred gave her a sympathetic smile, then returned to his room to change clothes before he greeted his wife in the outfit she loved most, his hunting attire. When he entered Nellie's room, he found her dying in convulsions after having given birth to their daughter. Nellie never regained consciousness, and Fred was never able to say goodbye to her.

Whatever reserves of strength Archer had stocked away were lost in a fit of despair. Nellie was the anchor of his life; without her, he felt lost. His depression became so severe that he admitted to being suicidal at times. Yet once again, he refocused all his despair into racing. He had first lost his son, then his wife, and he would never recover. His behavior became erratic; at first, he lost races that he would have normally dominated. Over time, he seemed to find his rhythm once again, at least on the track, and devoted himself even more compulsively to racing, sometimes riding six races in a single day. He never took a break, overscheduling himself in such a way that he had no time to think about his losses or anything else. If anything, he was winning more races than he ever had before, more races than *any* jockey had won previously.

Driving himself under these insane conditions was sure to take its toll on his health, especially with his mental state already fractured. Although, remarkably, he had never had any serious illnesses in his life—even with all his purgatives and crazy schemes to keep weight off—his immune system finally rebelled, and exhaustion set in. He described himself as "low spirited," certainly an understatement, and took to bed. Perhaps it was the anniversary of Nellie's death that seemed to take hold, or it may have been what his doctor suspected might be typhoid fever, but he seemed to lose all interest in living.

It had been two years since his beloved wife had died in childbirth. Archer was still brokenhearted, haunted, and suffering from pathological grief that had taken over his increasingly fragile sanity. Nellie "was my glory, my pride, my life, my all," he confided to a friend. His body wasting away, his energy flagging, he was also inconsolable about his recent string of losses on the track. There were even rumors that he'd been accused of throwing races. His whole life seemed like it was unraveling.

During his last few races, his strength had waned to the point where he could barely ride at all. Yet he persisted, continuing to take risks and pushing himself beyond the breaking point. He was desperate to keep winning, fearing that some unsavory characters were after him. It was unclear whether this was a paranoid delusion or based in reality, given that he was becoming increasingly muddled in his thinking.

Nobility all over England, horse owners, sponsors, and fans inquired about his health. Lord Allington expressed his sympathy and warned him to stop being foolish regarding his health: "No man can live on two oysters, one prawn, three doses of physic, and three Turkish baths daily!"

Archer languished away, slipping in and out of consciousness at times. Suddenly, almost without thought or intention, he reached into the cabinet beside his bed and pulled out the Webley revolver that had been given to him as a gift after winning the Liverpool Cup several years previously. He stuck the barrel into his face and pulled the trigger, muttering to himself but loud enough for others to hear, "Are they coming?"

These were Fred Archer's last words. Who was he expecting? Or dreading? The ghosts of his wife and infant son? A visit from creditors? Perhaps enforcers on their way to collect gambling debts?

At the inquest conducted by the coroner, it was clearly established that he had been "in a state of unsound mind." It was further determined that rather than being simply delirious from his fever, he had been clearly "disconnected in his thoughts" and insane.

After Archer's sister, Emily—the only actual witness to the shooting—was interviewed, it was discovered that she had been in the room with him, staring out the window, when she heard a noise and turned around to face the bed. She had seen her brother holding a gun in his hand, run toward him, and attempted to wrestle it away from him. But he was so much stronger than she was, even in his weakened state. A lifetime of controlling huge animals had led to inhuman power in his arms. Fred had then grabbed Emily around the neck to immobilize her, pointed the Webley revolver to his face, and pulled the trigger, blowing a hole through his cheek and into his spinal cord. Death had been instantaneous.

Emily had started shrieking after seeing the blood from her brother's head flowing onto the floor. Those who heard her said she "sounded like a wounded animal battling for its last breath." She would forever remember the sound of the pistol as the loudest noise she'd ever heard.

Fred Archer was 29 years old. He had won 170 races in the last year of his life.

Huge crowds lined the route of the funeral procession. Newspapers emblazoned his name across headlines. This was a national tragedy, and he would be honored as a head of state. Both the Prince of Wales and Duke of Westminster honored the greatest horseman of his generation with wreaths of flowers.

Fred Archer's remains lie buried in a cemetery in Newmarket alongside his wife and infant son. It is said that his ghost can sometimes be observed riding a grey horse across the nearby moor, where he first established his reputation as the greatest jockey of his generation.

Sources

Cullen, S. J., et al. (2015). Physiological demands of flat horse race jockeys. *Journal of Strength and Conditioning Research, 29*(11), 3060–3066.

Hillenbrand, L. (2002). *Seabiscuit: An American legend*. Ballentine.

Holt, S. (2013, August 15). Train like a jockey: The boot camp producing winners. *CNN*. https://www.cnn.com/2013/08/15/sport/jockey-fitness-horse-racing/index.html

Humphris, E. M. (2006). *The life of Fred Archer*. Obscure Press.

Murray, A. (2004). *Race to the finish: The life and times of Fred Archer*. Robson Books.

Reynolds, D. (2018). *Fred Archer: Just one more smile*. CreateSpace.

Stamford, B. (2016, May 5). Jockey: The most fit and toughest athlete? *Courier-Journal*. https://www.courier-journal.com/story/entertainment/events/kentucky-derby/2016/05/05/jockey---most-fit-and-toughest-athlete/83090758/

Tanner, M. (2010). *The tinman's farewell*. AuthorHouse.

Thompson, L. (2003, December 28). He won 2,748 races, with nothing but fire in his belly. *The Telegraph*. https://www.telegraph.co.uk/culture/books/3609214/He-won-2748-races-with-nothing-but-fire-in-his-belly.html

8

Christy Henrich

Consumed by Her Sport

C hristy Henrich was selected for the United States national gymnastics team at the age of 14 and placed fifth in the championships. At age 17, she won an all-around silver medal in the national championships, excelling in each of the events, including the uneven bars, vault, parallel bars, balance beam, and floor exercise. Later that year, she represented her country at the world championship, missing a medal in the uneven bars by a fraction of a single point. On the balance beam, she performed a leap so original that this distinctive skill still carries her name.

Whatever disappointment she might have felt after coming so close to winning a world medal was nothing compared to the devastation that followed afterward, when one of the judges told her she was too fat and would never amount to anything until she lost weight. Her life would never be the same after that interaction, although that comment didn't so much launch her into a nightmare of mental illness and literal self-destruction as it just reinforced the messages she had been hearing from her coaches all along.

Once Henrich felt she had a clear path to stardom and achievement, one that was measured by her attainment of the perfect body, she developed the single-minded determination to control her eating and shed pounds. After multiple hospitalizations, consultations with doctors and mental health professionals, begging and cajoling from her family, friends, fiancé, and eventually the same coach who had inspired such severe self-deprivation, she had wasted away to a shocking 47 pounds. Christy Henrich died of multiple organ failure at the age of 22, another casualty of her sport's obsessive fixation on the "pixie" body image.

Joy and Suffering

There are perhaps few experiences more satisfying or fulfilling than becoming the best in the world at some elite activity. If one was going to choose a sport that is the most glamorized and the most popular event in the Olympic Games, you could do no better than women's gymnastics. Actually, it would be far more accurate to call it a sport for girls, for children, since most of the participants have barely reached puberty.

Many of the most accomplished and successful female gymnasts become household names, celebrities, and heroines of their nations: Nadia Comaneci, Svetlana Khorkina,

Mary Lou Retton. It is staggering to consider that Comaneci, for example, was just nine years old when she won her first national championship and just 13 when she won the all-around European championship. Mary Lou Retton was just 16 years old when she won Olympic gold in the all-around event. She was the first American to do so.

Being a gymnast is just about the closest a mortal can get to experiencing what it's like to be a superhero, literally flying through the air with the greatest of ease, leaping off platforms, swinging over bars, catapulting into somersaults, and then landing with perfect grace and balance, arms extended in the air, ending with a bow. "It's a transcendent experience," confided Jennifer Sey in her exposé about the inner world of life as a gymnast. "It's beyond human."

Say, the national champion in 1986, had been a contemporary of Henrich's. Although Christy succumbed to the pressures and suffering, Say found recovery and inspiration to tell her story and talk about the hidden aspects of what she experienced and witnessed. She loved her sport. She loved the pure joy and freedom of flying through space, being the best at her craft. She loved the discipline and the work. But it wasn't until after she retired from the sport that she was able to look back at the insane world that she had been part of: a world in which coaches exploited girls physically, emotionally, and sexually; a world that almost guaranteed chronic injury and lifelong pain; a world that was so obsessive and self-sacrificing that she never menstruated until after she retired at the age of 20. Three decades later, she still has nightmares about the required daily weigh-in, a ritual that was so anxiety provoking that she would walk around all day spitting into empty cups, hoping to lose a few more ounces of water weight. Yet Say still insists that her sacrifices and suffering were worth the joy; after all these years, she still misses the sport: "I miss it every day."

Authoritarian Dominance and Exploitation

Joan Ryan describes the insidious toxic culture of sport in which young girls develop distorted body images, eating disorders, drug dependence, anxiety, depression, and other severe emotional problems as a consequence of their involvement. More recently, rampant sexual abuse has been uncovered. These are stories of abuse and exploitation in which labor laws are circumvented, childhoods are stolen away, and girls are used as vehicles of parental fantasy and coaches' ambitions.

Imagine girls as young as eight to 10 years old, required to train eight hours each day in addition to their schoolwork, other responsibilities, and tiny semblance of a normal life. Yet among the tens of thousands of children who are trained and shaped into potential Olympic stars or who seek professional careers as gymnasts, figure skaters, or track stars, only a handful will be chosen every four years to make it to the Games. In the case of female figure skaters, only six out of thousands will be selected!

The suffering, sacrifices, and pressure on young lives is both intense and unrelenting. They will give up any possibility of a well-rounded education and normal life. Their bodies will be crafted into instruments designed to do only one thing extraordinarily well. Within the sports of figure skating and gymnastics, in particular, participants are expected, if not required, to have the shape of a child's body, no matter their age and maturity level. Serious injuries are not just likely but a certainty.

Being a gymnast is essentially a life devoted to pain and agony. Beginning as toddlers, they are tracked into daily routines that will control every facet of their existence—until their careers, most likely, end in disappointment during adolescence. If they are fortunate, the bone fractures and degenerative spinal problems they encounter will mostly heal. The pressure and competition they face has been described as a "breeding ground" for eating disorders and long-term health problems that persist long after their athletic careers have ended.

In Henrich's case, she was first introduced to the famously domineering and controlling coach Al Fong when she was eight years old. He was as hard on himself as he was on any of the girls he was coaching, working insane hours seven days a week, admitting that work was his obsession. He required his athletes to follow a similar regimen, waking up at 5:00 a.m. each morning, practicing for three hours before school, then four additional hours after school until 9:00 p.m.

Fong recognized he had a gem in his midst with Henrich, whose work ethic matched his own. She trained through injuries and incredible pain, including winning her silver medal in the nationals just a few months after she fractured her neck. The two of them were a matched pair, each pushing the other to work harder. Henrich confided to friends that Fong's nickname for her was "Pillsbury Doughboy" (a reference to her weight), although he insisted later that was untrue. What he did admit is that his initial assessment of her was that she had "poor back alignment," was "a very poor athlete," had "dyslexia about instruction," and that "it was very difficult working with her." He also acknowledged that she overcame all those disadvantages by sheer force of will. It was her incredible pain tolerance and determination that so impressed him and made her so vulnerable to his criticism.

More recently, the extent of sexual abuse by coaches and staff in the gymnastics world has been discovered, with close to 400 children identified as victims. More than a dozen American Olympians, including McKayla Maroney, Aly Raisman, Gabby Douglas, and others, accused Dr. Larry Nassar of sexual assault—one of the biggest scandals in sports history. Maroney, a gold and silver medalist from the 2012 Olympics, reported that she had been abused for five years, starting at the age of 13. Nassar's method of seduction and compliance fit right into the girls' greatest weakness: bribing them with food! The girls were always starving so much that he promised to smuggle them treats if they allowed him to touch them inappropriately.

Poster Girl

Like Henrich, Julissa Gomez was coached by Al Fong. The two girls were considered the future stars of U.S. Olympics; both were precocious and hard working. They had bonded in a close friendship even though their backgrounds couldn't have been more different. Whereas Christy was from a middle-class family from the dominant culture, Julissa's parents had been migrant workers from Texas. Julissa had originally been a protégé of the notoriously abusive Bela Karolyi, but she had quit his gym to join Christy at what was considered a more "moderate" training facility.

In 1988, the same year that Christy placed in the top ten at the Olympic trials, Julissa traveled to Japan with her coach for an international event that preceded the Olympic

Games. Some of her teammates remember a conversation Julissa initiated about a Russian gymnast who had become paralyzed in an accident just prior to the Olympics several years earlier. Whether she felt a premonition or was just curious about the incident was not clear.

During the vault competition, a gymnast runs as fast as she can toward a "horse" that is positioned horizontally at the end of a runway. She then launches herself from a springboard up onto the apparatus, contorting herself into flips and twists in the air, and (hopefully) lands on the other side. It is among the most dangerous events, and injuries to the girls are not unusual.

Vaulting was not one of Julissa's best events, and she was observed as clearly uncomfortable during the months of training leading up to this competition. Many of her teammates reported that her technique was flawed and her prior performances were somewhat marginal. They were concerned that it wasn't safe for her to be attempting the routines she had been practicing.

During a warmup practice, Julissa slipped when she hit the springboard and crashed her head into the side of the horse, instantly fracturing the vertebrae in her neck. She was attached to a respirator to keep her alive after the paralysis, but she never regained consciousness during the next three years until her death. This was considered one of the most tragic accidents in the history of the sport, leading to changes in the ways vaulting is organized.

When Henrich heard about her best friend's injury, something also cracked inside her. Initially, the accident had been minimized by gymnastics authorities, but it had a profound effect on Christy, who memorialized her friend with a picture on the wall. It was a reminder of the kinds of sacrifices and risks that were part of this commitment to being a world-class gymnast.

Fong insisted that he had no idea about Julissa's fears or the extent of Christy's disordered thinking and eating patterns, which worsened afterwards. It was only after the signs and symptoms were so obvious that he could no longer ignore the seriousness of Henrich's problems. He referred her to a psychologist and nutritionist. He confided to

Fig. 8-1. Christy Henrich became a poster girl, not only for her exuberance and work ethic as a young gymnast but also as an example of the tragic collateral damage that can occur in women's sports: The athletes are at serious risk for catastrophic injury, eating disorders, and exploitation.

Source: https://www.youtube.com/watch?v=c7wG9seaFLo.

her parents that he could no longer manage her because she refused to seek help and, once referred to professionals, would not comply with their treatment nor be truthful about her secretive behavior. Eventually, he dismissed her from training and told her not to return until she was fully recovered. She was a stick figure, barely able to muster the energy to complete the basic routines.

Years later, Fong would reflect on some of his mistakes—pushing girls too fast, too hard. "I was a poster boy for everything wrong with gymnastics," he admitted years later. After two of his athletes died, he was discredited and virtually chased out of the sport, perhaps unfairly blamed for their deaths but still feeling partially responsible. He claims that he doesn't scream and yell much any longer, relying on more gentle forms of persuasion and motivation.

Sacrifices and Starvation

Henrich rarely complained about her coach's discipline and methods. In some ways she was grateful to be pushed to her limits. But something changed inside her after Julissa's death, which only added to the problems caused by the judge's fateful comment about her being overweight. She seemed to develop an almost inhuman tolerance for discomfort and pain, ignoring signals from her body and mind that she was testing their extreme limits. Hunger, for her, was just a different reminder that she was sacrificing herself for an ultimate perfectionistic goal. And she was proud that she could suffer more than anyone else.

Henrich's mother remembered one of the first things the other girls confided in her daughter after she was selected for the U.S. national team: "If there's something you want to eat, eat it, and then throw it up." Henrich began interviewing male wrestlers in her school to find out all their secrets for dropping weight before a tournament. They told her about their tricks: running in steam rooms while wearing plastic suits and using laxatives and purgatives, just as jockeys had done for centuries. She was determined to have the perfect gymnast body, just as Suzy Favor Hamilton had resculpted herself as a runner.

Henrich started regularly using laxatives and sticking her finger down her throat after she consumed any food. Purging and vomiting became her daily rituals. She was obsessed with body fat and wildly proud that she managed to reduce her weight to just 80 pounds. She may have appeared emaciated, but her coaches continuously supported and reinforced this behavior. They conducted daily weigh-ins with the team, flattering and rewarding the girls who lost the most weight. After her initial efforts at losing a few pounds, she was repeatedly complimented, which only redoubled her determination to become as thin as possible. The motto of her sport was "You have to be thin to win."

Over and over again, Henrich received messages from her coaches that she would never be good enough, no matter how hard she tried and how much adversity she faced. During her first attempt to qualify for the Olympics, she was suffering both fractured vertebrae and mononucleosis, yet she missed her spot by only one-tenth of a point. This only redoubled her determination to lose more weight and starve herself further. The culture within the sport became so incredibly dysfunctional during this time that during the 1992 Barcelona Olympics, journalists commented (and public outcry arose) about how the women gymnasts looked emaciated, like concentration camp survivors.

It was discovered that the girls were starving so severely that they were doing anything to secretly sneak food. Friends would smuggle care packages to them. When left alone without their watchers on duty, they would beg anyone for snacks and find hiding places in their rooms. But not Henrich. She was totally on board with the plan to become as lean as humanly possible.

It seems unfathomable that a child could actually starve herself to death, but keep in mind that she was outside her parents' observation and control from the time she left the house each day at 5:30 in the morning to the time she returned home at 9:30 at night. During the rare times they had family dinners, Christy would eat normally, then politely excuse herself and force herself to vomit in the toilet.

As Christy dropped more and more weight, predictably, her agility and strength were compromised. Once her peak performance eroded, the sole focus of her life was gone; the only thing left was her obsession with weight. True to the nature of Henrich's eating disorder—and common for anyone with this disease—a vicious cycle developed. She felt miserable but believed that the only thing that could improve things and make her feel better was to lose more weight. She was forced to retire from her sport, and her weight continued to drop.

A Beast Inside Me

Henrich's alarming weight loss finally convinced her family and her boyfriend to send her for psychiatric treatment at the Menninger Institute, all the way in isolated Topeka, Kansas. Her weight had been reduced to a life-threatening 60 pounds. By this point, Henrich's behavior was so disturbing and out of control that she could no longer be trusted to protect herself. When her suitcase was routinely searched prior to her admission to the psych unit, it was discovered that the bottom was lined with laxatives. Another time she had to be forcibly restrained on the unit, confined to the use of a wheelchair because she was discovered to be constantly running around the ward in order to lose more weight. She would do anything to burn more calories.

In spite of the treatment attempts and occasional stability, once she was released from medical care and constant supervision, her destructive behavior continued. The family was on the verge of financial ruin because her medical costs had skyrocketed to over $100,000, and they were not covered by insurance.

Christy's weight dropped to just 52 pounds. "My life is a horrifying nightmare," she disclosed. "It feels like there's a beast inside me, like a monster. It feels evil."

Henrich tried desperately to gain weight back, realizing her life was in jeopardy. She was readmitted into the hospital again and again and forcibly required to put on a few pounds. But internally, she had come to believe that food was "poison." Her thoughts were focused on only one goal, and that was achieving the perfect body, even if the image was so grossly distorted. She bragged that she could survive on just three apples a day, and on some level she believed that was true. There were so many other aspects of her life she couldn't control, but she could totally control what she put in her body. The "beast" had taken over.

After five years of such deprivation and abuse, Henrich's body literally consumed itself. Her liver, kidneys, and, eventually, her heart didn't have enough nutrients to keep going.

Her bones were so brittle from calcium deficiency that she could literally be blown over by a strong wind. Her organs failed, and she died a skeleton.

"They stole her soul," her mother said, "and they still have it."

Sick Sports

We are certainly well aware that every sport requires professional athletes to make huge sacrifices in order to attain their world-class performances. They earn fame, riches, notoriety, and celebrity status, but always at a cost. Regardless of the sport, many of them experience lifelong chronic pain and injuries.

Many years before Christy Henrich's tragic death, Cathy Rigby had been hospitalized repeatedly during a long struggle with bulimia that had been covered up. Once again, the United States Gymnastics Federation was disavowing Henrich's obvious problems when she was forced to retire because of "health problems." Rigby had been speaking out about the problem for over a decade, decrying the absurdity of demanding that elite female competitors fit a mold that averaged 85 pounds. "You don't want to believe something like that can still happen with all the knowledge that we have and with all the awareness that's out there," Rigby said after learning about Christy's death.

In various studies, it has been estimated that about half of all female gymnasts engaged in "disordered eating," which includes the use of diet pills, vomiting, laxatives, or self-starvation. Although it's been estimated that close to 10% of female college students have a diagnosable eating disorder, there are estimates that among female gymnasts, it may be closer to two-thirds. It may very well be that eating disorders are the most serious health risk for female athletes, whether in gymnastics, figure skating, track, or tennis (see Table 8.1).

Although eating disorders are quite common among cyclists, runners, jockeys, gymnasts, and other athletes who compete in sports in which an extra few pounds can make a difference in ultimate performance, women are especially vulnerable because of our culture's emphasis on body image and perfectionism. Female athletes who already have self-esteem issues tied to achievement—whose lives are rigidly controlled, who suffered emotional difficulties early in life—are particularly prone to developing eating disorders. The pressure is constant and unremitting. Their whole being is valued by others—and themselves—in terms of their latest performance.

TABLE 8.1 Female Athletes Who Struggled With Eating Disorders

Athlete	Sport
Nadia Comaneci	Gymnastics
Nancy Kerrigan	Figure skating
Martina Eberl	Golf
Whitney Spannuth	Track
Megan Neyer	Diving
Bahne Rabe	Rowing
Zina Garrison	Tennis
Mia St. John	Boxer
Heidi Guenther	Ballet
Angie Payne	Rock climber
Hannah Halverson	Nordic skier
Mara Abbot	Cycling
Hollie Avil	Triathlete

Another challenge girls face is that although they naturally develop more body fat than men, they are forced to artificially maintain a weight and shape that are unhealthy even though they may be better suited for increased performance. Another difficulty is related to the secret world that many such athletes inhabit, hiding their self-destructive habits in a multitude of ways. Whereas anorexia, or self-starvation, is somewhat obvious to diagnose because of the wasted appearance, bulimia allows a sufferer to pretend to eat normally, purging the contents of her stomach afterwards. She may even appear to be of relatively normal body size, and she may consume huge amounts of calories each day, but then she'll use laxatives, diuretics, or vomiting to rid herself of the indulgence. The result is a metabolic disruption within the body, placing added stress on the digestive, cardiac, and nervous systems.

It isn't just the genuine risk of death from starvation in extreme cases but also the collateral damage that occurs as a result of restricting needed nutrition. Osteoporosis and low bone mass, infertility, gastrointestinal diseases, cardiac irregularities, and neurological irregularities are all common side effects. These debilitating chronic conditions are made much worse by the ambivalent emotional reactions that accompany them. At first there are feelings of pride and satisfaction, but they are usually followed by cycles of deep depression and anxiety.

Among all sports, it has been found that eating disorders are most common among female gymnasts. This is true not only because of the ideal standard of a small, slim body but also because the athletes themselves were often robbed of their own childhoods, groomed and trained since kindergarten to excel in their sport. Add to the picture the presence of authoritarian, abusive male coaches who demand absolute obedience, and one can see that it is a miracle that anyone survives reasonably well adjusted and healthy. They are told what they are allowed to wear, what they can think and say, what they are permitted to do—and not do—and, of course, what they can and cannot eat. As they age, they are still required to present themselves as prepubescent, not only in their physical appearance but also in the artificial effervescent, childlike joy they pretend to radiate when they stick the landing at the end of their routine. Their development is stunted at every level of personal functioning, so they are uniquely unprepared to deal with the emotional problems they face outside the gym.

Athletes are starting to become more emboldened to speak out about the abusive culture that elite athletes often work in. Gymnast Jennifer Sey recounted once having the audacity to eat a bagel that was given to her by her mother after a practice session. She looked around the gym and noticed everyone staring at her and shaking their heads in disappointment. She wondered what was wrong until she was informed that this was just not done, even after an intense seven-hour workout. Her coach intervened immediately, suggesting that it might be best if she didn't finish the forbidden food, even though she was starving. She got the message loud and clear. Controlling her weight was just as important as anything she did in front of the judges. In no time, she was addicted to laxatives, sneaking around to different pharmacies in order to stock up on supplies because she was consuming a whole package of pills every day. It was a hopeless struggle for a growing adolescent girl.

Even after she had reduced her body fat to less than 3% and her weight to under 100 pounds, Sey still felt like a "beast." And it wasn't just her self-perception. Her coach constantly scolded her, telling her she was obese. "I can see the fat on you!" she would scream. "Can't you see yourself? After all this. All we've done. You're gonna give it all away. You're nothing!" After the abuse, threats, sacrifices, and suffering, she felt like nothing. The coach then threw her out of the gym and would not let her return until she lost three more pounds—another 3% of her body weight.

Katelyn Ohashi, a former national champion, also disclosed the ways she had been body shamed by her coach, beginning when she was 13 and weighed just 70 pounds. She was told she looked like she had swallowed an elephant. "I was compared to a bird that was too fat to lift itself off the ground." She was even asked to sign a contract stating clearly that she would be dismissed from training if she failed to lose more weight.

Distorted Thinking, Disordered Eating

Among the general population, the likelihood of body image and eating problems is usually directly related to underlying family conflicts and issues related to self-esteem and feelings of helplessness. When such concerns are exacerbated by the culture of a sport that requires single-minded devotion and obsessive commitment, it is no surprise that so many female athletes struggle with eating disorders. They are teased, bullied, and humiliated for the shape and size of their bodies, since aesthetics and visual appeal are so much a part of their performances. Internalized thinking patterns develop that are often variations of the following themes:

1. *It's all or nothing:* "If I eat this one chocolate chip cookie, I'll have to eat the whole bag of them. I won't be able to stop."

2. *Perfectionism:* "One single lapse, and I'll lose everything I've worked so hard for."

3. *Extreme exaggerations:* "If I allow myself to enjoy this meal or treat, it will ruin everything."

4. *Distortions:* "This meal will disqualify me from the next training competition."

5. *Impaired reasoning:* "I feel fat no matter what others tell me, so they must be wrong."

6. *Disasterizing:* "If I slip up even one time, it will lead to ultimate failure."

7. *Overpersonalizing:* "My coach gave me a look because he thinks I'm too fat."

8. *Comparisons:* "I'll never be as thin as her unless I try harder."

9. *Internalized cultural/gender scripts:* "Everyone knows that girls must be thin to be admired."

The cognitive styles most often associated with developing eating disorders—perfectionism and obsessive commitment—are also virtually required to succeed in gymnastics. Almost by definition, gymnasts are extraordinarily disciplined and self-controlled. They are experts at denying pain and suffering. They have developed internalized rationalizations to justify the changes to their bodies that delay menstruation and physical maturity. They associate joy and satisfaction with sacrifices they make in other areas of life. These are precisely the sorts of thinking patterns that lead to disordered eating. These athletes tell themselves that they are not sick or suffering from a mental illness—one that has one of the highest mortality rates—but that they are making a conscious choice. There are even websites devoted to helping sufferers trade tips and secrets for how to lose more weight as well as deceive parents and health professionals so they may continue the downward, life-threatening spiral.

Athletes have an insatiable need to succeed, to become better, to score a perfect 10 in an event. They almost always come up a little short and are dissatisfied, as are their coaches, who push them harder. On one level, becoming lighter and leaner can help them improve performance—to a point. But sometimes extraordinary self-discipline becomes internalized to such a degree that all control is lost. Understandably, this is a formative and impressionable time for young girls, who are often unable to resist the pressure they feel from authority figures in their lives. They have virtually surrendered their own autonomy.

Within many sports, such as gymnastics, figure skating, and women's track, it is about the pursuit of perfection, as we explored with Suzy Favor Hamilton. It was a few years before Hamilton's era that Mary Wazeter had developed such a perfectionist belief, entrenched in her eating disorder. She was convinced that if she could just lose more weight, she'd crush the competition. When that didn't work as well as she hoped, she jumped off a bridge while walking her dog. She survived the fall but was left paralyzed from the neck down with shattered vertebrae. She later wrote about her experiences and began research on the phenomenon, hypothesizing that biochemical changes take place in an athlete's brain that disconnect self-preservation safety switches. How else to explain an extraordinarily gifted physical specimen that starves herself to death and, when that fails, throws herself off a bridge?

In a study of this pathological disorder and its accompanying self-defeating cognitive style among female gymnasts, Andrew Bloodworth and his colleagues explored the nature of the distortion and denial that permit the behavior to continue. Just as the athlete has such incredible self-discipline in her sport, she also applies this to the illusion that she is in control. One girl admits she doesn't eat much at all but says it is for the "right reasons" and that it never affected her in negative ways. Another girl believes that her restriction of food intake reflects a "strength of character." It's also clear that because these girls have given up so much in the quality of their education and preparation for success in the wider world, succeeding in gymnastics is all they have. They are desperate to do anything within that single domain.

It's clear from these examples that such cognitive patterns can lead to highly self-destructive behavior that is impervious to reasoning. That is one reason why the prognosis for eating disorders is so guarded and why the illness can become so intractable and eventually life-threatening. It also doesn't help that the coaches are so insistent that athletes fit the mold of an idealized body image. One study from Henrich's era in the sport found that fully two-thirds of female gymnasts had been repeatedly told by their coaches that they were too fat. As a result of these internalized messages, almost all of them engaged in some pathological behavior related to eating, whether it was vomiting, purging, fasting, restricting fluids, or using laxatives, diuretics, or diet pills.

The dysfunctional thinking related to serious eating disorders is part of a larger pattern that develops from the extraordinary influence of coaches. Within gymnastics, historically, most of the coaches have been dominant, authoritarian, controlling older men who wield power over young girls, telling them what to do and what to think. The girls are in no position to challenge such authorities, even if they are capable of doing so at such a young age. In one study of how current and retired gymnasts view their experiences, there are startling differences in their perceptions. Although the current athletes, with an average age of 14, did not generally see themselves as having disordered eating behaviors (18%) and certainly did not acknowledge full-blown eating disorders (less than 3%), three-quarters of retired athletes believed they had problems, mostly as a result of disparaging comments made about their bodies by their coaches.

It should be mentioned as well that although participation in gymnastics—or, for that matter, any sport—has some negative side effects and personal sacrifices, such devotion is also associated with tremendous benefits beyond mere physical fitness. As we have seen in other stories, distinguished and successful athletes have discovered ways to manage their anxiety and depression in adaptive ways. They have significantly higher self-esteem and, in many cases, reduced psychological distress. There is also considerable evidence that within the general population, even amateur athletes, such as girls who participate in varsity sports in high school, are less likely to engage in drug or alcohol abuse and tend to be less sexually promiscuous. Team sports, in particular, create intimate bonds that are known to last a lifetime.

In her book about the poisonous culture of gymnastics for children who are forced to give up their childhoods in pursuit of their dreams of athletic achievement, former National Champion Jennifer Sey acknowledges how much she still misses those days training and performing. To some extent, she has felt like her life has been a failure ever since, having been the very best at something at such a very young age. "How can I ever be the best at anything ever again?"

That is indeed the question that every elite athlete must consider, whether an Olympian or even a varsity player in high school. Once you have experienced the incredible elation of winning at such a high level, ordinary life may never feel the same again. As we've seen in so many of the other stories in this book, adjustment to life after one's athletic career becomes the greatest challenge.

Sources

Amdur, N. (1994, August 1). When thin is in, disaster can strike. *New York Times*. https://www.nytimes.com/1994/08/01/sports/when-thin-is-in-disaster-can-strike.html

Bernstein, S. J. (2008). Starving to win: An exploration of eating disorders in female athletes. *Graduate Student Journal in Psychology, 10*, 64–68.

Bloodworth, A., McNamee, M., & Tan, J. (2017). Autonomy, eating disorders, and elite gymnasts: Ethical and conceptual issues. *Sport, Education, and Society, 22*(8), 878–889.

Kerr, G., Berman, E., & De Souza, M. J. (2006). Disordered eating in women's gymnastics: Perspectives of athletes, coaches, parents, and judges. *Journal of Applied Sport Psychology, 18*, 28–43.

Klinkowski, N., Korte, A., Pfeiffer, E., Lehmkuhl, U., & Salbach-Andrae, H. (2008). Psychopathology in elite rhythmic gymnasts and anorexia patients. *European Child and Adolescent Psychiatry, 17*, 108–113.

Meyers, D. (2017, September 1). Abused gymnasts' voices are finally being heard. *Deadspin*. https://deadspin.com/abused-gymnasts-voices-are-finally-being-heard-1798687945

Noden, M. (1994, August 8). Dying to win. *Sports Illustrated.* https://www.si.com/vault/1994/08/08/131742/dying-to-win-for-many-women-athletes-the-toughest-foe-is-anorexia-gymnist-christy-henrich-lost-her-battle

Park, A. (2018, April 22). McKayla Maroney says she reported Larry Nassar sex abuse to coach in 2011—and nothing happened. *Time.* http://time.com/5249833/mckayla-maroney-reported-larry-nassar-abuse/

Plummer, W. (1994, August 22). Dying for a medal. *People, 42*(8).

Ryan, J. (1995). *Little girls in pretty boxes.* Doubleday.

Sey, J. (2008). *Chalked up: My life in elite gymnastics.* Harper.

Tan, J., Bloodworth, A., McNamee, M., & Hewitt, J. (2014). Investigating eating disorders in elite gymnasts: Conceptual, ethical, and methodological issues. *European Journal of Sport Science, 14*(1), 60–68.

Tan, J., Calitri, R., Bloodworth, A., & McNamee, M. (2016). Understanding eating disorders in elite gymnastics: Ethical and conceptual challenges. *Clinical Sports Medicine, 35*(2), 275–292.

Wilstein, S. (1994, August 21). Beasts of anorexia nervosa, bulimia ravaged gymnast's body. *Los Angeles Times.* http://articles.latimes.com/1994-08-21/news/mn-29434_1_christy-henrich

Witherstein, W. (1994, July 28). Disorder consumed her life. *Los Angeles Times.* http://articles.latimes.com/1994-07-28/sports/sp-20762_1_christy-henrich

Zucker, N. L., Womble, L. G., Williamson, D. A. (1999). Protective factors for eating disorder in female college athletes. *Eating Disorders, 7,* 207–218.

9

John Menlove Edwards

A Nervy, Craving Mind

John Menlove Edwards is both a fascinating and curious figure, not only within the climbing community but among all elite athletes. He was considered the greatest climber in Britain in the 1930s. Before he was 21, he had already completed new routes to some of the most difficult climbs in the United Kingdom. As accomplished as he was as a climber, he also excelled in swimming, rowing, and sailing. In addition, he left behind a legacy of essays, musings, and poetry that revealed both his spiritual ecstasy and adoration of the mountains as well as his tortured suffering.

Edwards is unusually articulate among our subjects because he was not only a world-class athlete but also a poet, essayist, physician, and psychiatrist, an expert on healing mental illness—except in himself. One of his climbing partners and former patients perhaps best summarized his mentor: "He was a very difficult man for the ordinary mortal to understand."

Another fellow climber, Kevin Fitzgerald, described Edward's life as "proceeding with the inevitability of a Greek tragedy." In that sense, Edwards's life and diverse career held all the elements of such a mythical epic by evoking both fear and pity among the audience over the hero's demise, which resulted from hubris, insolent pride, and self-destructive, fateful choices. And like all such stories, the narrative unravels at the end to a spectacular climax. In Fitzgerald's conclusion, "Everything that happened to him appalled him; everything which he cherished and touched fell to pieces in his hand."

In Spite of His Achievements, He Was a Dismal Failure

Menlove Edwards was truly a Renaissance man in that he combined his commitment to mountaineering and love of sport with other achievements as a physician, scholar, and researcher. He wrote a guidebook to the British hills and edited the *British Mountaineering Journal* as well as contributing numerous essays on the subject of climbing. In each of his subsequent guidebooks for climbers, he combined his sense as a poet with clear technical descriptions. In one passage, for example, he wrote: "Numerous scratches lead easily up and round the main corner and onto and up a little subsidiary slab on the edge of all things."

As if his life was not interesting and varied enough, practicing as a psychiatrist during the week and then struggling with his own personal demons while climbing on the weekends and during sabbaticals, his tragic death has been enshrined forever in mountaineering lore. Although he accomplished more than anyone could expect in a lifetime—as an athlete, healer, and intellectual—he ultimately considered himself a dismal failure.

Edwards certainly faced more than his fair share of troubles and obstacles, feeling marginalized in almost every domain of his varied life. His iconic climbs were denigrated and criticized because he chose unconventional routes and adopted an "inelegant" style. He appeared clumsy, awkward, and fidgety on the rock, abruptly halting and starting again, always improvising—yet he could go places that others would never consider. He made up for a lack of grace with reckless courage.

Menlove Edwards was revolutionary in his thinking about emotional disorders, both curious and challenging of standard treatments and conceptual models of his time. He was a pacifist and conscientious objector during the time when his nation was gearing up for war with Nazi Germany; for this, he was branded a coward. He joined the Communist Party, as much out of attraction to radicalism as any allegiance to its core beliefs. His rather unusual psychiatric theories and research were ridiculed by colleagues. And then there was the repressed secret of his homosexuality during a time when that was hardly accepted. It is no wonder that he attempted suicide several times and landed himself in a mental hospital, where he was subjected to the further indignity of electroshock treatments. He was deemed by many among his profession as having a brilliant but unstable mind. By his own account, he felt like a failure at everything he attempted.

Eccentric, Weird, or Revolutionary

Edwards was born during the first decade of the 20th century in a small village in Northern England, a fishing and farming region since medieval times. He was a rather shy, withdrawn, and oversensitive child, the youngest of three brothers who were always squabbling. He found the conflicts in his family intolerable and did his best from an early age to serve as a compromiser and peacemaker. It was as if, like many who enter the mental health profession, he was conscripted and fated to become a healer.

Solitude and privacy were especially important to young Menlove, especially with his many shameful secrets. He was an avid reader and thinker as well as a talented writer, earning himself scholarships to prestigious schools. Remarkably, he also showed early promise in sports, excelling in cricket, hockey, and swimming. It was as if there was almost nothing he couldn't do.

His love of solitude and physical challenges led him to climbing during his adolescence. It was in the mountains that he could be alone with his thoughts and away from the critical scrutiny he felt all around him. Before he was 21, he'd already completed more than a dozen first ascents, earning him a reputation as one of the most fearless, accomplished British climbers. He relied on his brute strength, rather than careful delicacy, to find routes that others would never attempt. Yet his volatile mood swings dramatically affected his abilities. There were some days when lethargy and despair would so overtake him that he would fail to complete the most simple climbs. Needless to say, he fell a lot.

Edwards was a charismatic and passionate figure who would mentor many others within the climbing community. Among them was a young, impressionable climber by the name of Wilfrid Noyce, who would someday become a member of the 1953 Everest expedition that made the first ascent with Edmund Hillary. During those early days of Edwards's life, Noyce was both a dear friend and climbing partner. Noyce remarked, "Under his eye I was made to lead climbs I had not dreamed of, but to profit even more from the experience of his mature and affectionate loyalty than from that of leading." It is no wonder there is such reverence in these words, since Edwards confessed later that Noyce was the singular love of his life.

Noyce's gratitude was earned, in part, because during one climb in 1937, Noyce fell 180 feet off the side of a wall and was only saved from hitting the ground by Edwards's skill and experience at belay. Noyce remained unconscious for three days after the accident while Edwards remained at his bedside on vigil.

Over time, Edwards became bored with climbing if there was not some novel goal to be attained. Perhaps that is what led him to revolutionize climbing technique as it was practiced at the time, attempting walls in which he relied on loose rocks and vegetation for handholds and shimmying up cliff faces that were previously believed to be impossible to scale. Once again, he seemed to live in a different world than others, wondering why, with so many unclimbed walls "still staring down upon a pretty stiff-necked veneration. What is the fascination of young climbers in the old Slabs … ?"

His peers considered him eccentric, if not downright weird. But he was used to that. Although a psychiatrist, he misdiagnosed himself as schizophrenic; he most likely had the characteristic dramatic mood swings of bipolar disorder, which was yet to be understood

Fig. 9-1. John Menlove Edwards, seen above, exemplified the spirit of courage and adventure within the climbing community, achieving a number of first ascents. Yet he was a misunderstood, tortured figure who struggled with depression and suicidal impulses throughout much of his life.

during that time. Throughout his life, he did appear to alternate between episodes of despair, inertia, and deep depression and weeks of manic energy in which he would undertake ridiculous feats of athletic performance.

Extraordinary Physical Feats

Edwards tested himself in a series of courageous—or perhaps reckless—ways. Was it a death wish that drove him or the need to test the limits of his capability? He launched a binge of adventures during his 20s, first rowing a boat to the Isle of Skye—in a raging storm. Next, he went for a swim through a narrow gorge—of course, during maximum snow melt in the spring, when the runoff was at its peak. Then he paddled a canoe in the sea for 16 straight hours, followed by another effort to row across the Irish Sea—naturally, during a storm. Next on his list of endurance sports was to row a boat for 28 straight hours to an island and then make the return journey in 24 hours. This was followed by more swimming feats during which he taught himself to ride huge waves that would lift him high into the sky and drop him onto the next trough. A few British commandos who were watching this craziness from shore decided to follow his lead but drowned during the effort.

When asked why he subjected himself to these dangers and discomforts, Edwards would shrug, claiming it was all part of his research into self-discipline, fatigue, and self-analysis. When pressed, however, he described his addiction to the kind of "strong fragments of feeling" that accompanied dangerous activities. He seemed to be addicted to the rush of adrenaline that would accompany his death-defying feats.

Keep in mind that climbing during the first half of the 20th century was considerably more challenging and dangerous than it is today. They had no reliable weather reports. No climbing gyms for training. No helicopters for transportation. There were no GPS positioning systems, satellite phones, accurate altimeters, smartwatches, or even walkie-talkies. If they needed assistance, the only option was to scream loudly.

Climbers carried 50% more weight than those today and were significantly less protected from the elements. They wore wool clothing instead of Gore-Tex, down, and high-tech fabrics. They carried hemp rope instead of reinforced nylon. They wore heavy crampons tied on their leather boots with string. They carried heavy oxygen tanks weighing more than 50 pounds instead of the eight-pound canisters that are used today on big mountain climbs. There were no expansion bolts or spring-loaded devices for anchors on the ice or rock. They survived with the most basic tools that existed during the time, making climbs we might consider routine today singularly extraordinary efforts during that era.

There's something intrinsically masochistic for those involved in climbing and mountaineering—and I speak from personal experience, having spent more than my fair share of time trapped in freezing tents during windstorms, drudging up volcanoes gasping for breath, lost and isolated in blizzards, wondering whether I would survive another night with supplies having long run out.

David Roberts, a climber and journalist, explored the drive and motivation of those who risk their lives to scale such inhospitable, dangerous mountains, all for some prideful ego and perhaps fleeting notoriety. He confesses that "some of the worst moments of my life have taken place in the mountains." He is referring to the misery of being stuck in a tent for days at a time, the terror of finding himself in a predicament that makes it seem doubtful he can escape, and the lifelong grief of having witnessed a handful of his climbing partners fall to their deaths off a rock wall. Even with these tragedies and challenges, he discloses that, like for Menlove Edwards, "... nowhere else on earth, not even in the harbors of reciprocal love, have I felt pure happiness take hold of me and shake me like a puppy ..."

Climbers like Roberts and Edwards speak consistently about never feeling more alive and about the spiritual transcendence they experience during a climb. Psychologist Mihaly Csikszentmihalyi first coined the term "flow" to describe this effortless concentration after he interviewed climbers who talked about losing themselves in the moment without thought or will. They felt transported and operated at their peak performance.

For Edwards and many climbers like him, normal life paled in comparison.

So, to answer Roberts's question about why climbers risk their lives, he concluded that it is really about being "launched on the flight that turned neurotic thrum of ordinary life into a staccato pulse of purpose ... a blissful escape from the petty pace of normal life."

In his own words, Menlove Edwards described the feeling this way: "So as you would imagine, I grew up exuberant in body but with a nervy, craving mind. It was wanting something more, something tangible. It sought for reality intensely, always if it were not there. ... But you see at once what I do. I climb."

In a previous book, I wrote about a friend and colleague who decided she wanted to become the first of her nation and gender to climb the "Seven Summits," consisting of the highest peak on each of the continents. Sara described the horrific experiences that accompanied her expeditions, the suffering and agony of life in the Death Zone above 8,000 meters. Sleep is virtually impossible at that altitude. Lost digits are a real possibility. There is a decent chance that death will result—from hypothermia, falling into a crevasse, getting caught in an avalanche, cerebral edema, heart attacks, strokes, even a loss of concentration or lapse in judgment. Yet this is a sport in which athletes routinely risk their health, parts of their bodies, and their lives in order to reach the top of a mountain. In one sense, you have to be a little insane.

An Agonizing End

Menlove Edwards could never come to terms with his own emotional suffering, even though he devoted his life to helping others with these problems. Over time, he felt increasingly misunderstood and marginalized, an outlier who would always be alone. At one point, he wrote, "It has been said that the secret of life is detachment from it." He added, "Good."

Was this detachment for self-protection? Did this tormented man seek to insulate himself from emotional fears that crippled him? It is so interesting that such a fearless risk-taker with respect to physical and athletic challenges was so incapable of managing those related to his intense feelings. He actually studied this as his profession yet still felt paralyzed by the destructive emotions that consumed him.

Regardless of his intention, it is clear that the pain became too much for him to endure. And this was a man who had among the highest pain tolerances known to humankind—someone who could tolerate freezing temperatures, muscles screaming for hours on end while he remained in contorted positions, and dealing with physical challenges for days on end without complaint.

In the end, he decided to take his own life, but certainly not by any ordinary, practical, relatively painless means. Imagine how insane he must have been to choose potassium cyanide as the way he wanted to die. This may be one of the most excruciating choices possible. Just five minutes after ingestion, oxygen is cut off at a cellular level, leading to slow suffocation. Victims of such poisoning are seen grimacing, convulsing, thrashing around, gasping for breath. Prior to seizures beginning, there are first headaches, nausea, muscle contractions, sweating, and increased agitation as the victim struggles for breath. Eventually, there is intense, throbbing pain like that of a heart attack prior to merciful unconsciousness.

In the very end, Menlove Edwards not only wanted to die, but he wanted to do so in the most tortuous way possible. Jon Krakauer, chronicler of many adventurers and mountaineers, observed about Edwards that "he climbed not for sport but to find refuge from the inner torment that framed his existence."

Sources

Csikszentmihalyi, M. (2008). *Flow: The psychology of optimal experience.* Harper.

Curran, J. (2016). *A great effort.* YouTube. https://wn.com/john_menlove_edwards

Fitzgerald, K. (1961). Reviews. *Climbers Club Journal,* p. 259.

Hargreaves, A. B. (1958). In memoriam: John Menlove Edwards. *Climbers Club Journal,* 259–260.

Kottler, J., & Safari, S. (2018). *Above the mountain's shadow: A journey of hope and adventure inspired by the forgotten.* Cognella.

Krakauer, J. (1997). *Into the wild.* Anchor.

Lewis-Jones, H. (2011). *Mountain heroes: Portraits of adventure.* Bloomsbury.

Noyce, W. (1958). In memoriam: John Menlove Edwards. *Climbers Club Journal,* 360–362.

Noyce, W. (2004). *South Col: One man's adventure on the ascent of Everest 1953.* Birlinn Publishers.

Perrin, J. (1993). *Menlove: Life of John Menlove Edwards.* Ernest Press.

Roberts, D. (2006). *On the ridge between life and death: A climbing life reexamined.* Simon & Schuster.

Smith, K. (2015, November 21). A black rainbow: The life and times of Menlove Edwards. *Footless Crow.* http://footlesscrow.blogspot.com/2015/11/a-black-rainbow-life-and-times-of.html

10

Donnie Moore

An Unforgivable Mistake

According to sports announcer Al Michaels, it was the single most exciting hour in sports history, or at least the most engaging he'd ever seen in his lifetime. It was the fifth game of the 1986 American League Championship Series. The California Angels, owned by famed movie star Gene Autry and managed by Gene Mauch, had never made it to the World Series. This was to become their first pennant, and it seemed to be in the bag. The crowd was going wild in anticipation, revving up for a well-deserved celebration after so many years of frustration.

The Angels were just one strike away from the World Series. They held the lead 5–4 over the Boston Red Sox, with Dave Henderson at the plate. It was the last of the ninth inning. They were leading the series 3–1. The tying run was on first base. All Moore had to do was shut down the inning with a final pitch, and it was all over. Head to the locker room for champagne.

Al Michaels was beside himself with excitement about how entertaining the game had been. Now the tension was ratcheted up. Henderson at the plate, premier reliever Donnie Moore on the mound warming up. You could barely hear yourself think, the crowd was screaming so loud. Policemen had started to line up along the sideline and dugout, prepared to handle crowd control when the game was completed and the celebratory fans streamed onto the field.

The first pitch was a ball. The next two fastballs flew by in a blur. It was obvious to everyone that Henderson was overmatched by the pitcher. One more pitch, and the game—the series—was over. The Angels players in the dugout readied themselves on the steps to leap out onto the field in celebration, to hoist Moore onto their shoulders for saving another game with everything on the line.

The next pitch was another fastball, but low in the dirt. The catcher scooped it up and looked the runner on first back to the bag.

And so the tense battle continued. Moore started throwing off-speed pitches, since he sensed that Henderson was waiting for a fastball. A couple of foul balls. He threw a forkball that was intended to drop precipitously as it approached the batter, but it just hung there in front of Henderson, who slammed it over the left field wall.

"To left field and deep," Michaels yelled into the microphone. "Downing goes back, and it's gone! Unbelievable!"

Henderson danced around the bases, jubilant. Moore looked dazed.

The Red Sox now had the lead. Moore finally managed to get the last out, but as he walked off the field, the chorus of boos started.

The game would continue to shift back and forth and go into extra innings. The Angels bounced back and managed to tie the game again, then lost the lead. Then Moore—tired, dispirited, shoulder and back aching—gave up hits to load the bases. The manager pulled Moore out of the game, and the boos started up once again.

There were all kinds of reasons why the Angels eventually lost that game and the rest of the series in which they had held such a commanding lead. But it was Moore and that one fateful pitch that everyone would remember. "I'll think about that until the day I die," he admitted.

And how could he not? Nobody would let him forget it. The following year, fans and media wouldn't stop asking him about The Pitch. They called him an "alleged" closer, a fraud, a bum, a loser.

GOAT (Greatest of All Time)?

Although Moore's shoulder was sore from a nagging injury earlier in the season as well as pitching the previous day, he had jumped at the chance to enter the game with everything on the line. He thrived on that kind of situation, lived for it, even when he was in pain and worn out. It was later discovered that he had serious injuries to his rib cage and shoulder as well as a bone spur in his back.

The previous season, Donnie Moore had, by all accounts, been the best stopper in the game. He had an unhittable 98-mile-per-hour fastball and a split-fingered pitch that looked like it was coming in to the plate straight and juicy until it just fell into the dirt. Hitters looked ridiculous sometimes, trying to flail at the ball. He saved 31 games, breaking a team record. He had been an All-Star with the grit, attitude, and dominance to close down any game. He had been voted by his fellow teammates as their most valuable player. He was adored by everyone, not just for his performance on the field but also for his engaging personality and spirit.

Moore's life couldn't have been any sweeter. He had been signed to a three-year contract. He had a million-dollar home with a swimming pool and a pond in a beautiful neighborhood. He had a Mercedes, a loving, devoted wife, and three beautiful children. All that seemed to change with one errant pitch, one swing of the bat.

As the story goes, that single unforgivable mistake drove the man insane. Some say it was the single most notorious athletic mistake of all time. It went down in history alongside Columbian soccer player Andres Escobar's accidentally scoring a goal against his own team during the World Cup. Bill Buckner, who played first base for the Boston Red Sox, only ended up playing in the World Series because of Moore's misguided pitch that lost the championship. Ironically, Buckner is also nominated for the most notorious GOAT of all time for when he let a ball roll through his legs, thus losing the World Series.

Mistakes like this on the world stage can indeed by humiliating—or worse. In Andres Escobar's case, it actually led to his murder as retaliation for the mistake. Buckner was hounded for years, with some Boston fans never forgiving him. In Moore's case, many were convinced it was baseball that led to his shocking deterioration—the enraged and disappointed fans, the media that endlessly relived the episode, his teammates and management that couldn't seem to let it go. Most of all, Moore couldn't let it go. It seemed like his whole life, his whole distinguished career, was reduced to a single pitch.

One of Moore's teammates, Brian Downing, insisted that it was the fans and media who put that albatross around his neck. "You buried the guy," he lashed out at reporters after news of Moore's suicide. "You destroyed a man's life over one pitch."

It's Part of the Job

The motive for his eventual self-destruction is all the more peculiar, considering that even with his brimming confidence and achievements, Moore seemed readily able to accept the realities of his position. "The job I do is not easy," he admitted in an interview just

Fig. 10-1. Donnie Moore, seen above pitching for the St. Louis Cardinals, was often unhittable when his 98-mph fastball and split-fingered pitch were working their magic throughout his 13-year career. Yet his life took a tragic turn when disappointments and depression incapacitated him to the point of violence and self-destruction.

Source: https://www.findagrave.com/memorial/95735428/donnie-ray-moore.

prior to the fateful game, "but I thrive on it. I can handle failure. That's one thing most people have a hard time doing. If you can go out and take the glory, then the days you're a goat, you've got to handle that, too."

It's not like he hadn't done this sort of thing before in his life. In fact, it is the nature of baseball that even the best hitters will fail to get on base seven out of ten times or that a pitcher will routinely give up hits on the mound with runners on base or miss the sweet spot on the plate a tiny bit high and watch the ball sail into the stands. When Moore played for his Lubbock high school in the Texas State Championship, pitching and batting cleanup, he once gave up a hit that cost them the game. But he recovered nicely and had a stellar season the following year. In his return to the state tournament, he was once again on the mound with the game on the line—and that time, he closed it down.

Once Moore made it to the major leagues, his career had its inevitable ups and downs until he ended up with the Angels as their premier relief pitcher. It's understood that this is one of the most stressful jobs in all of sports. This is the guy they bring into the game only when it's all on the line—runners on base, a tenuous lead, everything at stake. One error in judgment or execution, and it's all over. The great Hank Aaron once remarked about the incredible pressure his pitching adversaries faced: "The pitcher has got only a ball. I've got a bat. So the percentage in weapons is in my favor, and I let the fellow with the ball do the fretting."

According to Moore's agent, Dave Pinter, Donnie could never let that home run go. "He blamed himself for the Angels not going to the World Series," Pinter explained. "He constantly talked about the Henderson home run." The agent explained that Moore was never the same after that. He was obsessed with the mistake, so much so that Pinter urged him to seek psychological help for what was spinning out of control. "That home run killed him." It also killed Pinter's career. He lost his job as an agent after that.

Haunted by the Past

Donnie Moore searched hard for some sort of reconciliation of the past, some kind of forgiveness. Whether his imagination or not, he felt ostracized and isolated. Nobody could really understand what he had gone through and what it felt like to feel such remorse for a little mistake that ended up with disastrous consequences. It turns out that there was one person in the world who could understand this predicament: Bill Buckner. It's interesting that Moore struck up a friendship after the season with Buckner, someone who was intimately familiar with the wrath of disappointed fans and teammates because of his famous bobble during the 1986 World Series, which some say cost the Red Sox the championship. Nobody seemed to remember that over the course of 22 seasons, Buckner accumulated close to 300 hits and drove in over 100 runs in several seasons. All they remember is The Error.

These two critical mistakes, made during the same season, condemned both men to eternal hell. They went hunting together to talk things through and offer mutual support. After the trip, they wouldn't disclose what they had shared with one another, but they did admit they hadn't shot many birds.

Moore never seemed to recover after that season ended. It wasn't just his injuries that crippled him and caused his loss of confidence; the fans never let up on him, booing him constantly. He pretended the attacks didn't bother him. He was a survivor, a tough guy, but his teammates disclosed it was all a façade. They could tell how upset he was about letting them down even though, they realized, he had no business even accepting that fateful assignment with his injury and compromised throwing motion.

Moore was on and off the disabled list the following year. He was called a malingerer, supposedly unable to deal with a little pain, especially after being paid over $1 million for his services. He only saved a total of five games that year. He was released by the Angels at the end of the season, his career unceremoniously over.

Something Broke Inside Him

His home life offered him no respite. Donnie and his wife, Tonya, had always had a very tumultuous relationship, one in which Donnie exerted fierce control. There had been passion between them ever since they'd met as kids, but there had also been volatility and violence. She was described as rather free-spirited and sometimes did not take well to having herself constantly criticized and dominated. She was frequently seen with bruises on her body or face, which she explained away as accidents. He told her what clothes she was allowed to wear and was constantly fearful she might attract undue attention. Yet he was also proud that she was so gorgeous.

Their three children had long observed the ongoing warfare in their home. Friends and teammates were also familiar with their squabbling. They had known each other for so long that their fighting was just viewed as their normal form of communication.

Once he was out of baseball, something inside Donnie Moore seemed to crack and crumble. He became more impatient and irritable. He snapped at his kids and, most of all, at Tonya. They started to argue more violently. He started to beat her mercilessly, taking out his rage and frustration at life, his disappointments, and failures on her. Eventually they separated and Tonya got her own apartment, although she would frequently return to their home to help with housework, laundry, and cooking.

People have asked Tonya why she hadn't left her husband earlier, why she didn't protect herself, knowing he was so out of control. But those people didn't understand that they had been together since they were children in Lubbock. After everything that happened, she insisted they loved one another deeply. There could be nobody else. Even years later, Tonya would be torn about their relationship, at times calling him a miserable husband and father, a "selfish asshole," and at other times singing his praises and talking about how deeply they adored one another.

Whatever problems they had became so much worse once he realized his baseball career was over and he had nothing left. His finances were abysmal. He was overdue on his taxes. The house, like his life, was falling apart. He no longer had any prospect of a job or future. He was so depressed he could barely function. Out of desperation, he called his friend, Reggie Jackson (of New York Yankees fame), for advice and to borrow money. The request was declined. Much later, Jackson would second-guess himself about that decision and wonder if that rejection sealed his friend's fate, making him feel abandoned by everyone.

Messages Left Behind

It was in mid-July, 1989, when the couple realized they had no choice but to sell their house to try to reduce their debt. They were both on-site waiting for their realtor when another fight broke out—a vicious one this time, a screaming match of epic proportions.

"Oh fucking no," Tonya yelled, "you said you weren't gonna hit me no more." She then went out to their pool in the backyard to get the kids.

"I'm leaving here and I'm never coming back," she told him. Then to the children: "Get out of the pool."

Tonya then called her daughter to come and get her. While she waited, she tried to keep her distance from her husband, remembering that one time he'd said he'd drown her in their pond. She took swimming lessons after that, just to prepare for that possibility.

"Come back here," Donnie yelled back. "I said come back here right now!" Then he walked away.

Things seem to settle down. She was about to leave the house with her daughter when she turned around and saw Donnie pointing a .45 caliber semiautomatic pistol at her. She had given it to him as a Christmas present.

"Put that damn thing away," she taunted him. "You're not going to do that." But Moore believed that this time Tonya wouldn't be coming back. Maybe she had someone else. Maybe she'd given up on him. But whatever the reason, he believed that if he lost her after everything else, then nobody else could have her either. All hope was now lost.

Tonya started running, but not before he fired a shot that penetrated her neck. He caught up to her again in the laundry room like a hunter stalking his prey and fired two more shots, both to the chest. Somehow, miraculously, none of the bullets had been fatal even though they had gone straight through her body, leaving six bleeding holes. She managed to crawl through the door out to the driveway, where their teenage daughter was waiting with the car, and the girl sped to the hospital to try and save her mother's life. Improbably, each of the bullets missed a major organ or artery, so Tonya actually recovered from her wounds.

Meanwhile, the two young boys, aged 7 and 10, were left inside, where they watched in horror as their father turned the gun on himself. When the police arrived, they discovered no evidence of drug use or alcohol consumption. This in itself was surprising, considering Moore's addiction to Jack Daniels. To this day, none of his kids will allow the whiskey inside their homes.

There was no suicide note. The only signs of what he might have been thinking prior to the incident were two baseballs sitting on his bed. One was from the 1985 All-Star game, and the other was signed by Reggie Jackson. There was also a single sheet of paper on which he'd written "Comfort in the time of loneliness" and "Guidance in the time of decision." There were some psalms listed underneath each of the headings as well as a single statement at the bottom of the page: "Let go, Let God."

The Pressure on Pitchers

In studies of athletes in general, and baseball players in particular, who've committed suicide, it's been found that the special pressure on pitchers doubles their chances of self-destruction. They have *way* too much time to think while they are on the mound trying to figure out what will fool their opponent standing there with a club in his hands. Everyone depends on them. Nothing else happens until they do their thing. And for a relief pitcher like Moore, they are only called into action when the game depends on their performance.

Moore's death called into memory another dramatic suicide of a ballplayer. In 1940, Willard Hershberger, a catcher, was called into action to replace the regular starter. This is a position that, along with the pitcher, touches the ball every play. The catcher has the most responsibility for calling the game, selecting the pitches—literally running whatever is happening on the field. In addition, it is the most physically grueling job, sitting in a squat position and having balls thrown at you at close to 100 miles per hour. You have to have legs like steel and an arm like a cannon to make the throw all the way to second base when a runner is trying to steal. And when someone is running full speed toward home plate, you have to position yourself to block him from touching it. It is brutal. And for Hershberger, the pressure was apparently too much. He went hitless in the game. He made some mistakes calling bad pitches, so he was partially responsible for losing the game.

Hershberger went back to his hotel room, carefully spread towels on the floor of the bathroom to avoid making a mess, leaned over the tub, and slit his own throat.

The pressure of pitching has taken a toll on other players over time. Mike Flanagan lasted for 17 seasons in the major leagues, where he won both a Cy Young Award and a World Series with the Baltimore Orioles. After retirement, he was one of the fortunate ones who secured a job as a baseball executive. Yet the depression he'd been dealing with throughout his life became much worse when he felt like he failed at that job. He hadn't met his own exacting expectations. To a pitcher accustomed to perfection, that means missing the sweet spot by a few millimeters. Eventually, he blew his head off with a shotgun.

Mysterious Motives

It's easy to cite failure or a mistake as the reason for such inexplicable behavior—ending one's life because of a single disappointment. In Hershberger's case, things were far more complicated than that, an accumulation of life difficulties. It turns out that as a child he had been the one to discover his father's body after he had taken his life in the exact same manner. There were many other stressors in his life, just as there were for Donnie Moore. It's just too simple to blame one thing for such an act of madness.

Later, his friend and hunting partner, Bill Buckner, admitted that in the grand scheme of things, handling that bad pitch and home run would have not been a big deal if Moore hadn't been emotionally vulnerable deep inside. He was a lonely, isolated man and always had been. At times he tried to talk to Tonya about things, but there were limits to what she could do for him.

The narrative about his death was reduced to a bad pitch, but he had been miserable on some level throughout his life. It came out later that neighbors would see him crying in the backyard at times. His body was failing him, and he was losing the only skill he had in life. He knew it and wondered when others would finally discover his secret. This is consistent with what one researcher, Loren Coleman, discovered in her study of over 70 suicides among baseball players. Inexplicably, 45% of them were all right-handed pitchers (no left-handers among them!). Her best explanation is that "They get to the big leagues, something happens—an injury or a bad season—their career ends, and they have no safety net, no way of coping."

Tonya didn't get out of the hospital in time to attend her husband's funeral. Some of the attendees went so far as to blame her for pushing him over the edge. Others insisted her version of what happened couldn't have been the whole story. For her and the children, the legacy only continued. Tonya ended up in a psychiatric unit for months after her physical injuries healed. The boys also required intensive therapy after seeing their mother almost murdered and watching their father kill himself. It takes a special brand of madness to take things that far in front of the people you love most. For years afterward, many reporters, experts, and fans chimed in about the impact of that one bad throw.

But of course it wasn't that one mistake that doomed Donnie Moore. It was a lifetime of not ever feeling understood. For years after his death, Tonya visited her husband's grave—the grave of the man who tried to kill her—and just asked him one simple question: "Why?"

Sources

Almond, E., & Penner, M. (1989, July 19). Donnie Moore dies in apparent suicide: Home run pitch in 1986 haunted Moore, says his agent. *Los Angeles Times*. http://articles.latimes.com/1989-07-19/sports/sp-3894_1_donnie-moore

Berkow, I. (1989, July 30). Donnie Moore and the burdens of baseball. *New York Times*. https://www.nytimes.com/1989/07/30/sports/sports-of-the-times-donnie-moore-and-the-burdens-of-baseball.html

Feldman, L. (2017, May 31). What broke Donnie Moore? *The Stacks*. https://thestacks.deadspin.com/what-broke-donnie-moore-1795651449

McKnight, M. (2014, October 5). The split. *Sports Illustrated*. http://www.si.com/longform/donnie-moore/index.html

Neff, C. (1989, July 31). Scorecard: The Moore tragedy. *Sports Illustrated*, p. 7.

11

Jimmy Piersall

Clown, Lunatic, and Advocate

Let's begin with the admission that Jimmy Piersall was a complicated human being and controversial athletic figure. During his almost 90 years on this planet, he was revered as perhaps the greatest defensive outfielder in the history of baseball and one of the most entertaining "performers" in the sport; he was also one of the most notorious players in the game—in every sense of the word. His antics on the field, and in the dugout, were both celebrated as hilarious and amusing by his fans and reviled by his peers and managers. He was incorrigible, unpredictable, and sometimes downright cruel. He was also seriously mentally ill, at times disturbingly out of control. Yet his life stands as an example of how someone with serious emotional problems can use that experience to fight against the shame, stigma, and marginalization that is so often targeted against those who suffer from mental illness.

Piersall's story as a fallen hero is remarkable as a detailed narrative of what it *feels* like to have one's mind disintegrate, to be unable to distinguish between fantasy and reality. Whereas we must often rely on the reports of others or the observations of family members and doctors in order to reconstruct someone's deteriorating mental condition, in this case our subject left behind two very personal memoirs, written decades apart, describing the most intimate and personal experience of the internal process with his characteristic brutal honesty. Piersall's life stands as an open book about his struggles, revealed in such a way that one cannot help but feel some deep understanding and compassion.

Who Could Survive Such an Early Life Without Collateral Damage?

There has long been a debate as to whether emotional disorders, as well as more severe mental illness, result from genetic factors and biological disposition or from environmental influences and early trauma. Of course, the answer is either—or both. In Piersall's case, he was subjected to almost every possible influence and cause that could lead to future problems. He certainly inherited a predisposition to major difficulties from his mother, who was repeatedly hospitalized for "mental exhaustion." He lived in poverty and deprivation during childhood, and he was subjected to major abuse at the hands of his father.

It is actually a wonder that he functioned as well as he did throughout his life, a testimony perhaps to his own resilience as well as to effective medical and psychological care and support from family and friends.

Looking back on his life, Piersall insisted that being "crazy" was the best thing that ever happened to him. It not only earned him notoriety but also brought fans out to see him. He once admitted, "I'm the gooney bird that walked to the bank," referring to how his craziness was found to be entertaining, if not endearing, by fans who would come to the park just to see what outrageous thing he might do next. Piersall rarely took himself seriously, but it's also evident that his personal struggles taught him some important lessons that became the source of his strength and resilience.

James Piersall was born during the Great Depression in a small town in Connecticut. Although he had an older brother, their 20-year difference in age essentially made him an only child. To say that his early life was challenging would be a significant understatement. The family lived on the edge of poverty. They had no hot water and barely enough to eat. Piersall's earliest memory was crying from hunger at the age of three. His father could barely support the family, in and out of work during times of great economic hardship.

As mentioned, it is now understood that mental illness results primarily from two main factors. The first is genetic, especially in the cases of major psychosis, bipolar disorder, and schizophrenia. The second major precipitator includes environmental stressors within the family. While it is difficult to separate the two variables, it is probably not necessary to do so, especially when there are many elements at play.

Throughout most of Piersall's early life, his mother was often so depressed and incapacitated she would cycle in and out of the hospital for six-month stays, returning in a state of temporary stability until the next "spell" would come upon her. Piersall remembers that whenever he would return from school to find his father preparing a meal in the kitchen, he knew his mother was gone again for "some rest."

To add to the burdens, Jimmy's father was hardly a model of comfort and support during these difficult times. His sole obsession and purpose in life was to shape and mold his son into a professional baseball player. As soon as Jimmy was born, his father taught him to play with a ball. As he grew older, the boy's primary job in life beyond school was practicing the requisite skills. He was told that "fun" had nothing to do with the sport; this was work.

If playing baseball with his father had been perceived as a bonding experience, perhaps there could have been some intimacy, some loving connection between them. Although Piersall would insist throughout his life that he adored his father and appreciated all that he had done for him, his memoir tells a different story altogether. He mentioned repeatedly the constant fear of disappointing his father and the absolute terror of his raging temper. Both verbal and physical abuse were a daily occurrence. If for some reason Jimmy failed to slide properly when they practiced base running in the backyard for hours, his father would kick him: "I wouldn't be able to sit down for a week."

Piersall describes how his father's bellows and screams would literally rattle the windows and shake the pantry dishes. "I lived in fear of his wrath," he admitted. So, apparently, did his mother, who would need "to go away for a while" every few years. Frequently, Piersall would return home to find his mother sobbing in the kitchen, muttering to herself, "I can't stand it. I've got to get away from here." One time she tried to escape by walking into traffic to kill herself but somehow escaped injury.

Piersall tried to protect his mother as much as he could, but he had a hard enough time trying to survive without his own injuries. It was therefore not surprising that Jimmy grew to become a very anxious child, agitated about nearly everything. He worried about school, money, the weather, being late, making mistakes, his mother's sanity, and most of all, his father's incandescent and unpredictable rages. He also lived for his father's praise.

Every action Piersall took—every choice he made, every small decision—was weighed carefully by his father in terms of risk or reward: would it jeopardize or enhance his future baseball career? He was not permitted to do anything that might in any way potentially distract him from that ultimate goal. Even when the family was so desperate for basic necessities, Jimmy had to beg his father to allow him to get a job, first as a paper boy and later assisting with milk deliveries. This early experience—rising in the dark for his part-time jobs, attending school, then going through all the required baseball practices until he fell into exhaustion—helped him develop the amazing work ethic and self-discipline he carried throughout his life.

To make matters still more overwhelming for the overstressed child, he constantly had to hide his family secrets: that his mother was "crazy" and his father overly "strict." It is no wonder that he had trouble concentrating and sitting still, and he struggled in school. He described himself as a "perpetual motion machine" and like a spring that was "never able to uncoil completely." He complained of headaches. Sleep disorders would become a lifelong problem.

Once Piersall entered high school, it was apparent to everyone, including pro scouts, that he did indeed have some special talent for the game. Although he was an accomplished hitter, it's interesting that his extraordinary skill as a defensive fielder came from his ability to anticipate where a ball would land once it left the bat. Like the child of any abusive or mentally ill parent, he learned to survive by becoming an expert at predicting others' behavior. He developed literally the perfect confidence to catch anything that was ever hit to him, rarely making an error in judgment or execution.

An Inhabiting Force

All of Piersall's talent and hard work, not to mention his father's coaching and pressure, paid off in measurable results: He clearly showed all the signs of a baseball phenomenon, dominating the games he played in. Scouts began showing up at his games during his senior year in high school, but he had his heart set on attending an Ivy League university on a baseball scholarship. It was not to be: His father's precarious health and mother's instability virtually required that he try to secure a professional contract to support his family.

Even though he was offered huge signing bonuses and salaries by both the Yankees and the Braves, his father, operating as his agent and manager, insisted that he only play for their beloved Red Sox, even if it meant significantly less compensation. During negotiations, the one condition that was a deal breaker for Jimmy was that the team provide arrangements for his father to receive medical testing and treatment for his heart condition.

It could reasonably be assumed that once he had attained his family's (or at least his father's) lifelong dream that he play professional baseball, Piersall would finally give himself a break. If anything, the pressure he felt was even more unrelenting. He described feeling paralyzed by anxiety during this stage of his life, his worries redoubling with added responsibilities. The one comforting influence was meeting Mary Teevan, who would soon become his wife. She was studying to become a nurse, a job that would eventually involve the primary task of trying to keep Jimmy on a more even keel. She was the only person in the world to whom he ever felt comfortable confessing the extent of his desperate internal struggles.

Mary was indeed the ideal companion for such an insecure, troubled young man. She was endlessly patient and comforting, if not indulgent of his neurotic whims. As he prepared to report to his first spring training as a professional ballplayer, Jimmy was also working shifts in a factory and taking care of both of his parents. Mary had suffered a miscarriage early in their marriage, and her health was precarious. Despite all this tumult, in early 1950, Piersall was called up from the minor leagues to the Red Sox for a trial period to see if he might have the right stuff. On the very first pitch he swung at, he not only missed the ball but sent his bat flying into the stands. He just stood at the plate looking helpless, wondering what the hell he should do next, until the player on deck loaned him another bat so he could try again. He promptly hit the next pitch safely to right field, earning a hit during his very first at-bat. While he was soon sent back down to the minors for more seasoning, his career outlook was promising.

Things calmed down for a brief period during his first few years as a pro. He was blissfully happy with Mary. The couple bought a home and became pregnant again, and both of Piersall's parents remained relatively healthy. He enjoyed what he considered the most productive playing season of his career in 1951, not only continuing his stellar defensive record but also becoming one of the best hitters in the minor leagues.

Rookie Season

The year was 1952, and Jimmy Piersall had just been signed to his first major league season with the Boston Red Sox after playing three years in the minors. Ever since childhood, he had been conditioned to believe the Red Sox was the one and only team he would ever be willing to play for. He was positioned in the outfield next to his childhood idol, Ted Williams, who became a mentor and reinforced the strong work ethic first introduced by Piersall's father. He learned that greatness doesn't merely come to those with talent but through fierce effort and determination. Piersall was one of the first hitters to keep detailed records on every pitcher he ever faced; during his career, he filled up 18 notebooks with specific information about opposing players' tendencies and weaknesses.

During his first season, Piersall was playing in a game at Yankee Stadium when he objected to a call made by the umpire and raced across the field, protesting violently. He was immediately ejected from the game. That was just the beginning of a trend.

Just two weeks later, he was playing the Yankees once again when he got into a fistfight with Billy Martin, a notoriously feisty and impulsive individual in his own right. Then later, in the locker room, he got into another physical altercation with one of his own teammates during an argument about what had happened earlier. The manager intervened and determined that Piersall needed to rest for a week to cool off. That did not sit well with him either, and he became increasingly restless and agitated, at one point swinging from the dugout like an ape.

Piersall begged his manager to put him back into a game; he'd play any position, even the infield. When the manager hesitated and then told him no, Piersall broke out sobbing. By the time he earned a spot back in the rotation, his behavior had become increasingly bizarre. He started doing calisthenics at his position in the outfield, taking exaggerated mock bows after the most routine plays. The last straw was when he started mocking his teammate, Joe DiMaggio, the most acclaimed player on the team. Every time DiMaggio would run out to his position in center field, Piersall would run after him, imitating his distinctive stride.

The great Satchell Paige, who played for an opposing team, was considered the best pitcher in history. Paige was one of the first African American players to break the color barrier after playing for years in the Negro League. He was so dominant during his era that his infielders would simply sit down on the grass because they weren't needed: Paige would routinely strike out all the batters. By this time, he was an "old man," well into his 40s and not nearly as effective. Piersall taunted him, yelled out to him that he was going to bunt, and then beat out the throw as he'd predicted. Once on first base, he started making noises like a pig, distracting the great pitcher to the point where he subsequently gave up six runs and a grand slam home run. This was disrespect at a whole other level.

The only reason Piersall wasn't benched is that they needed his defensive abilities on the field. So the team put up with his antics even as they accelerated. He'd run around the field whispering into other players' ears and scream out sometimes nonsensical instructions to everyone. One time he fired a throw to his pitcher at close range. Angered, the pitcher threw it back as hard as he could. The throw sailed over Piersall's head, and Piersall just shrugged and stared him down. When the umpire ordered him to retrieve the ball so they could resume play, Piersall pretended he was a dog and crept up to it on all fours, kicking it further and further away until it reached the fence. At that point, the umpire ordered him to leave the field.

Piersall became a disruptive force that could no longer be ignored. He was sent back to the minor leagues for "rehabilitation" and to get his head straight. Nevertheless, he kept heckling umpires, giving his manager a hard time, and generally driving his teammates crazy. The absolute last straw was during a game when the plate umpire called a last strike and Piersall completely lost his composure. After arguing the call, the umpire ejected him from the game, after which Piersall pulled a squirt gun out of his pocket and shot water all over home plate, as if to say to the umpire, "Can you see it *now*?"

Later, Piersall would have absolutely no memory of any of these incidents, as if they involved somebody else who resembled him. He would feel tremendous shame about these acts of disrespect toward umpires and his teammates, not to mention his outbursts toward fans, but he had no recollection whatsoever that *he* was the one who'd committed them.

Piersall continued to feel painfully insecure, worrying about everything that could possibly go wrong and interpreting everything that happened as a sign of impending doom. What could have been called restless, excessive energy was now transforming into signs of mania, which commonly first make their appearance during early adulthood. His tenuous hold on any semblance of control began to fall apart, in particular after the Red Sox wanted him to change position from outfield to infield because they needed a shortstop. Although anyone else would have been flattered at such an opportunity, Piersall interpreted the decision as an attempt to sabotage him. Ruminations continued to plague him to the point where he would spend whole days sitting in a movie theater trying to quiet his chattering mind.

Mary became so concerned that she insisted he see a doctor for his insomnia and "restlessness," but when the physician refused to give him sleeping pills until he answered a few basic questions, Piersall stormed out of the office. Once again, it was only the movie theater that seemed to still his mind.

When it was time to report for spring training again, as well as special sessions to prepare him for his new position, he started engaging in magical thinking, believing he could will himself to disappear. He deliberately "forgot" to pack his baseball glove, thinking that would somehow get him out of the predicament of having to learn a new position. When that didn't work, he escalated his campaign to avoid the duty. But even that statement implies some intention on his part when, in fact, there was some other force that was now inhabiting his body and mind.

Once he boarded the plane for spring training, Piersall began to notice that his manic symptoms were becoming far worse. His heart was pounding, and sweat was pooling along his back. His hands felt clammy, and he could barely keep himself from falling over as dizziness became the norm. He hadn't had a decent night's sleep or a peaceful hour in weeks. He felt like he was going to jump out of his skin.

Then he felt nothing at all. Just darkness.

The Looney Bin

No matter how one felt about Jimmy Piersall, with all of his antics and abilities, one had to admire his brutal honesty. He was frank, not only about his opinions regarding others but most of all about himself. In both of his autobiographies, he was completely transparent and disturbingly candid about his own disruptive behavior as well as its impact on others who may have been offended or wounded along the way.

In an initial excerpt from his confession that was first published in the local newspaper, he explained, "I want the world to know that people like me who have returned from the half-world of mental oblivion are not forever contaminated." He was tired of feeling pushed into the shadows, ashamed of a condition, if not a disease, that was beyond his control. He offered an impassioned plea: "There is no better therapy than understanding."

Jimmy Piersall actually lost a year of his life during that rookie year. One minute he was on a plane to begin spring training, and the next moment he woke up in a hospital bed with no recollection of how that abrupt change in locale had taken place. His next awareness was of being strapped to a bed, wondering where he was and how he got there. Two weeks had elapsed, and he had no memory of what had occurred. In addition, most of the memories from the whole previous year had been wiped out. Later he would review scrapbooks of news stories saved by his father to piece together what had transpired during the preceding months.

The attendant for violent patients in the psychiatric ward explained to him that he had undergone electroshock therapy in order to help control his outbursts and bizarre behavior. In those days, that meant he was strapped to a table with restraints to prevent convulsions that might fracture his bones or spine. This was a controversial treatment at the time, just as it has been throughout its history until present times. The only defense for subjecting patients to such brain stimulation, which is still poorly understood, is that it sometimes works when nothing else will.

After administering anesthesia and a mouth guard (so the patient doesn't bite off his tongue), electrodes are attached to the skull. A couple hundred volts of electricity are then shot through the brain to induce seizures, sort of like doing a hard "reset" on a computer or mobile device that has frozen. There are several theories to explain how and why this might be helpful to those with depressive or other psychotic symptoms, but in Piersall's case, it was hoped that it might shake something loose inside his brain. It actually worked pretty well for him, at least in the short run, but with significant side effects: He lost a year of memories.

His wife, Mary, spent hours with Jimmy, helping him reconstruct many of his lost experiences. He had no recollection of his friendships or teammates, believing visitors to be complete strangers. At first he didn't even recognize his wife, nor did he recall that he had two daughters. His last clear image from before ending up in the hospital was arriving at spring training with a suitcase. He awoke in his hospital bed to the terrifying screams of the psychotic patients on his ward.

His doctor and the nursing staff attempted to carefully screen the information he received about his condition and what had caused him to land on the psychiatric ward. They censored his letters and controlled who could see him and what they could say. One time, a newspaper article slipped through. It described some of his bizarre "mad antics" and said that as a "hopeless mental case," he would likely never play baseball again and would spend the rest of his days institutionalized. This was an example of the public perception of mental illness at the time and why Piersall's own account of his illness and recovery became such an important statement that counteracted the myths and misconceptions.

Not surprisingly, the doctors and staff were required to offer their patient constant reassurance that he could fully recover and continue a productive life, if not regain his previous form. But this would require vigilance and the sort of self-care that might reduce the stressors in his life. The good news is that for the first time since the age of 15, he no longer felt a crushing headache. He was released six weeks later.

Piersall pronounced himself cured, for now and forever. He believed that his prior altercations with teammates were all just a misunderstanding and that all would be forgiven. He claimed that nobody he had offended or humiliated held any grudges or resentment, demonstrating either incredible denial or naivete. He also insisted that he would never have a relapse, closing his first memoir in 1953 with a happy ending, saying that the prior year had been the best of his life, since it was the year he was cured.

But that wasn't quite the end of the story.

A Staggering Array of Disruptive Behavior

Looking back, it is hard to imagine how Piersall actually got away with his extraordinarily "eccentric" behavior. He managed to antagonize and alienate every one of his teammates, terrorize umpires with his raging tirades, and even insult and threaten his managers. The umpires started to take vengeance against this player who was so disrespectful, challenging their calls; Piersall once joked that he paid so many fines he was subsidizing their salaries. Opposing pitchers began deliberately trying to hit him with pitches in retribution for his disrespect. He had become despised and ridiculed, not only by other teams but also by those on his own team. Many of the fans might have found him to be comically endearing, but most players believed he was, at best, an annoying nuisance. Some journalists found his behavior so disruptive and disturbing they refused to write about him at all.

Piersall became noticed as much for the stupid things he did to delay games as for his performance on the field. He ran into the dugout in the middle of a game or refused to return the ball after a stellar catch in order to take his bows. It was no wonder he was so often thrown out of games or sent packing to other teams.

Fig. 11-1. Jimmy Piersall's antics were legendary. He was both a great source of entertainment for fans and a disruptive influence on the sport because of his struggles with emotional control and mental illness. Here he is pictured throwing a tantrum after once again being ejected from a game, this time for dancing and doing calisthenics in the outfield, trying to distract other players.

For the first few years, fans and other players thought it was all an act. Sportswriters called him quirky, zany, impish, clownish, nuts: It was all in jest and for attention, if not entertainment value. Perhaps most generously, he was described as "charismatic." But then the interpretations began to change as he became increasingly annoying and disrespectful. It was only later that the public realized what was really going on: They were seeing evidence of full-blown psychosis.

It is no wonder that Piersall played for so many different teams during his distinguished career. As much as his playing skill was valued, he would constantly wear out his welcome, if not with his fellow players, then certainly with his managers. There were so many notorious altercations that it is amazing that he was "allowed" to carry on with such abusive behavior, especially toward fans. There was one incident when two guys in the stands were yelling at him the whole game until he turned around, approached their seats, and spit in their faces.

In 1961, one of the greatest battles in the history of baseball was taking place between two Yankee sluggers, Mickey Mantle and Roger Maris, who were vying for the home run title. The media and fans were riveted by these two storied players who happened to be on the same team. Yet attention was diverted from their battle when two fans interrupted the game to run into the outfield and deliver angry punches at Piersall, who punched one guy and kicked the other. He later refused to press charges against the offenders because "that's the first time I've ever won."

Managers and teammates perhaps made allowances for his eccentricities because he was a defensive savant, catching anything that was hit anywhere near him. During one stellar season, he robbed some of the greatest players in the game—Mickey Mantle, Mickey Vernon, Bob Lemon, Al Rosen—of certain hits. The legendary Yankee manager Casey Stengel called him the greatest right fielder he'd ever seen and selected him to play in the 1954 All-Star Game. It was precisely his extraordinary talent and value that gave him a pass and continued to enable his outrageous behavior.

Sportswriters were so blown away by the sheer number and variety of antics displayed by Piersall that they started to catalogue them. You can decide for yourself whether they are evidence of impulsivity, clowning, a "colorful" personality, or mental illness. He enacted hula dances while standing in the outfield, sprayed insect repellant all over the outfield, choked a reporter who asked an offensive question, and walked off the field in a huff before a game was over.

During one particular game in 1960, he was already feeling resentful because he hadn't been selected for the previous year's All-Star team even though he was averaging .340 and had a 15-game hitting streak going. He was standing on second base right next to the infield umpire, and he didn't like the way the home plate umpire was calling strikes on his teammate. He started screaming after each pitch and was told to knock it off. When his disruptive behavior continued, the umpire justifiably threw him out of the game. But that wasn't all. He was so furious and out of control he went into the dugout and started throwing anything he could find onto the field—bats, balls, mitts, whatever he could find. Then, while walking past the opposing team's dugout, he started throwing garbage from their side onto the field.

I'm certain this was amusing to those who were watching, but Piersall's behavior was clearly out of control. His conduct that year escalated to the point where umpires would get up close and stare into his eyes to see if he was in the midst of a crazed state. Finally, the team had enough and required him to once again seek psychiatric care. He still refused to acknowledge he had a problem, explaining that others were just jealous of all the attention he was getting.

Piersall admitted that he was a little "high-strung" but felt his performance on the field and celebrity status off the field entitled him to special treatment. Whereas the psychiatrist didn't help him much, except to reassure him he was fine, it was a new manager who helped calm him down. This was a guy he respected who told him right away, "Don't worry about the umpires. I'll take care of them." Piersall was persuaded the manager had his back and would protect him. It was such relational support that made all the difference.

The year that Piersall played in Washington was pivotal for him in many ways. Greatest among them was his first introduction to President Kennedy, who knew something about emotional difficulties from his own bouts of depression and chronic pain after serving in World War II. Kennedy, a baseball fan, asked to meet Piersall, and they had several interactions during that fateful year prior to the president's assassination.

Eventually, Piersall's exceptional performance on the field was not enough. Even after his single best year as a player—hitting a phenomenal .322, scoring 81 runs, and playing perfect defense—he was traded to another team when the season ended. He was traded three more times the following year.

Piersall had been nursing a number of physical injuries to his shoulder, leg, and wrist, and his whole body was falling apart after 17 years in Major League Baseball. Fans started to get on his case more enthusiastically, calling him all kinds of names—"nut job," "lunatic"— but when someone yelled out to him, "You're a nut, and so is your mother," that sent him into a fury. Piersall raced into the stands and started beating on the poor guy until the fight was broken up by the police and ushers. Both of the combatants were arrested, and Piersall only escaped conviction for assault because nobody would press charges.

A Morning at the White House, Afternoon in Jail, Evening in a Hospital

It was after his playing days were winding down that Piersall was finding it increasingly difficult to locate teams that would sign him to contracts. One year he was traded to four different teams, after which he bounced around year after year. After the incident in which he ran around the bases backwards—a stunt he actually practiced ahead of time—he was released, and nobody else would touch him. It didn't help that he appeared on a variety of late-night talk shows bragging about the stunt. The team didn't even bother to trade him; they just released him outright, believing nobody else would want such a hapless clown who no longer had the speed, strength, and ability that had granted him allowances earlier.

Finally, he headed west to play in Los Angeles, his last chance. Although he was immediately injured and his baseball career was about over, he was now making the rounds as a celebrity entertainer, appearing on talk shows, hobnobbing with the rich and famous in Hollywood. He even took acting lessons to develop his "schtick."

Piersall wrote a second memoir, *The Truth Hurts*, mostly to settle scores after his retirement. He wanted to seek revenge against the writers, players, umpires, managers, and owners who he believed had treated him unfairly. If the truth "hurts," then it must be said that Jimmy earned a lot of his poor treatment from others: He was incorrigible and unpredictable as well as both self-centered and self-promoting.

Just as Jimmy had been fearless when talking about his mental illness, he also regaled audiences with his "bad boy" disruptive behavior. Indeed, on one single day, he visited the President at the White House, got into a fight with fans during a game that ended up with his being arrested for assault, and then got injured that same night. He never seemed to feel any shame about these incidents, instead bragging about them as notable accomplishments.

After the Playing Days Were Over

The first few years after retiring from baseball in 1968, Piersall struggled both financially and emotionally. He felt increasingly lost, pressured to take jobs that increased the stress on his already fragile stability. His marriage ended. He described 1972 as the most difficult and depressing year of his volatile life. Although he blamed the recurrence of his depression on his boss, who he called a "rotten bastard," it was also the result of his inability to adjust to life after being a celebrity and important person. Now he was just a washed-up player who had been forgotten.

His family was so concerned about his emotional fragility that they had him committed to a psychiatric facility for observation and treatment. Piersall insisted that the doctors and staff did nothing for him. During his therapy sessions, he made up a bunch of garbage just to keep himself entertained and play games with his therapist. He refused to take his medications. He was as infuriatingly resistant and noncompliant as a patient as he ever had been as an athlete. Yet he managed to recover pretty much through his own determination, finally convincing his doctor to release him after a month because he had a new job opportunity managing a minor league team. This would keep him in the sport that he loved.

Piersall found meaning again working with young players in the minor leagues. He loved passing along a lifetime of wisdom and experience about baseball, the only thing he'd ever known. The problem, however, was that some things never changed for him: He set a record for being thrown out of 23 games for arguing with umpires. He was repeatedly fired by a half dozen employers, and each time, he blamed others for his problems. He was actually fired twice—by the same owner—before the season ever began. What's most remarkable was his resilience, or perhaps stubbornness, that allowed him to keep putting himself out there after losing so many jobs year after year.

One team owner finally drew a line in the sand and insisted the only condition under which Piersall could be hired was if he agreed to ongoing psychiatric care. Once again, he just went through the motions, hated the doctor, and played games with him, refusing to acknowledge he had any problems. The only real lasting benefit came because there had been new advances in psychopharmacology since his initial diagnosis of bipolar disorder. He was prescribed lithium as a mood stabilizer and pretty much stayed on the drug for the rest of his life.

Piersall entered the field of broadcasting and became one of the most famous commentators of all time. He teamed with Harry Caray as a radio announcer for the Chicago White Sox, and fans listened to the games as much to hear them talk as to follow the action. The two of them had what was often called a "vaudeville act," designed to take the attention away from the bad baseball the team was playing in those days. Caray, who would go on to earn a stellar reputation as the distinctive voice of the Chicago Cubs, was then tethered to Piersall and often teased his partner after some bizarre or inappropriate statement, asking, "Hey, did you take your pills today?"

During his career, first as a player and later as a broadcaster, Piersall feuded with some of the biggest names in the game, many of whom would become managers: Billy Martin, Tony La Russa, and Jim Leyland, to name a few. Piersall would find ways to get his licks in, attacking them mercilessly for some imagined slight from their past.

Fig. 11-2. After he made the transition from player to television announcer, Piersall, pictured above, never tempered his propensity for controversy, insulting players, owners, and even the team he represented with outrageous and inflammatory remarks.

He was initially suspended from broadcasting because of one of his most inappropriate outbursts: He remarked that baseball wives were generally all "horny broads." Not too long afterwards, he was fired permanently by the White Sox for being incessantly critical of the team he was hired to promote. He spent the next 15 years jumping from one minor league team to another in various capacities, usually as an instructor. Inevitably, he'd be dismissed for behavior that was considered unbecoming of a professional.

Eventually Piersall found the perfect job: hosting a sports radio talk show in Chicago. He could rant and scream to his heart's content. Listeners tuned in less for his deep insights into baseball analysis than for the unpredictable and unscripted tirades that paralleled the bigoted and sexist tweets of a future president. Piersall would attack anyone who crossed his radar: the team owner, the owner's wife, the general manager, or the team manager. And the more outlandish he became, the more his fans loved it.

Influential and Fearless Mental Health Advocate

Upon Jimmy Piersall's death in 2015 at the age of 87, there was an outpouring of support on his behalf. Hundreds of articles were published, not only reliving some of his most notorious behavior but also offering acclaim for his courage and honesty.

One article in the *New York Times* by a noted psychiatrist claimed that Piersall was one of the earliest and most influential figures who brought attention to the plight of the mentally ill. He used all his status and prestige, his fame and media leverage, to bring the diseases of the mentally afflicted out of the shadows and into a far more compassionate light. We might take this for granted today, but almost 70 years ago, this was absolutely groundbreaking.

When Piersall confessed his condition in an article he cowrote with a sportswriter, the reaction from readers was mostly sympathetic. It was not just the severity of his illness and its consequences that had been on such public display but also that he had been able to recover from his illness after psychiatric help. He would always live with his bipolar disease, but most of the time he could remain reasonably in control, at least as long as he took his medication and practiced self-care. He would have occasional relapses but mostly lived a reasonably normal life—at least normal compared to what had occurred previously.

His memoir, *Fear Strikes Out*, was made into a well-regarded Hollywood film starring Anthony Perkins and Karl Malden. Although Piersall claimed he hated the movie, especially the way Perkins "pitched like a girl" and "danced around the outfield like a ballerina," the popular film offered a sensitive portrayal of mental illness in such a way that it influenced public opinion about such disorders. Piersall also disputed many of the incidents in the film as exaggerations, if not fiction, claiming that the conflicts with his father were blown out of proportion.

After his release from the hospital following a major psychotic break, Piersall was recruited as a spokesperson for Fight Against Fears, a mental illness advocacy group. He was described as "the most famous former mental patient in the country," and his visibility and fame were valuable to changing public opinion about diseases of the mind.

Piersall became overconfident, if not misguided, in his later years. He claimed that medical or psychological professionals never really helped him; they were just a "crutch" that people relied on. He professed himself to be "cured" of his manic and depressive symptoms, denying their reoccurrence even in their most florid states. He remained convinced that all it took to cure such problems was self-discipline and a few simple habits that he claimed to follow. He was skeptical that psychotherapy, or even talking about problems, had any real value. He insisted that "going nuts" was the best thing that ever happened to him, "a blessing" that allowed him to be the individualist and nonconformist he always wanted to be.

The main problem, as Piersall defined it, is that he called things the way they were; he was a truth teller. Of course, "truth" is a relative concept, and many others didn't much appreciate his vindictive attacks against players' wives or even the owner.

One controversy after another followed soon after he started attacking players on the team he was hired to support as well as managers, owners, and anyone else who didn't meet his standards. Afterwards, he seemed surprised that others were so upset and retaliated against him, sometimes leading to physical altercations and screaming matches. Another marriage ended. Friendships were fractured. The press jumped all over him. It was no surprise that his self-inflicted damage led to physical ailments and anxiety attacks. Once again, he was required to seek psychiatric care, and again he resisted and played games, insisting he was fine—it was the rest of the world that was crazy.

Nevertheless, in spite of his continued erratic behavior, his was one very loud voice that brought increased attention to the plight of those suffering from mental disorders that were poorly understood and accepted even less. He is considered a significant influence that helped change the public perception toward these problems, especially those experienced by athletes.

Sources

Dolgan, B. (2001). Jimmy Piersall's antics overshadowed his talent. *Baseball Digest, 60*(12), 4.

Goldstein, R. (2017, June 4). Jimmy Piersall, whose mental illness was portrayed in "Fear Strikes Out," dies at 87. *New York Times*. https://www.nytimes.com/2017/06/04/sports/baseball/jimmy-piersall-died-mental-illness.html

Lerner, B. H. (2015, April 9). Fighting mental illness on the ballfield. *New York Times*. https://well.blogs.nytimes.com/2015/04/09/fighting-mental-illness-on-the-ball-field/

Piersall, J., & Hirshberg, A. (1955). *Fear strikes out*. University of Nebraska Press.

Piersall, J. (1955, January 29). They called me crazy—and I was! *Saturday Evening Post, 27,* 69–71.

Piersall, J., & Whittingham, P. (1985). *The truth hurts*. Contemporary Books.

Puma, M. (n.d.) A hall of fame personality. ESPN Classic. http://www.espn.com/classic/biography/s/Piersall_Jim.html

Roscher, L. (2017, June 5). Jimmy Piersall, former MLB player, and mental health pioneer, dead at 87. *Yahoo Sports*. https://sports.yahoo.com/news/jimmy-piersall-former-player-author-fear-strikes-dies-87-173807822.html

12

Marco Pantani

Compulsive Perfectionist

I included two cycling stories in the book for several reasons. First of all, the two individuals profiled, among the most accomplished athletes in their specialty, couldn't have been more different in their personalities, values, styles, and the nature of their emotional problems and self-destructive behavior. Whereas Graeme Obree was focused on conquering the hour record—essentially an all-out sprint on a track—Marco Pantani was perhaps the greatest mountain climber in history. He excelled during the three-week endurance races like the Tour de France or Giro d'Italia, whereas Obree operated as a solo athlete, racing against the clock.

Pantani's arena was a multifaceted team sport that involved a myriad of complex strategic and interpersonal dynamics as well as mastery of the unpredictable weather, terrain, and mechanical issues. The wear and tear on one's body, spending more than six hours in the saddle, day after day, was also a factor in just surviving the grueling grand tour events. Road cycling is alleged to be the most challenging of all sports, with races lasting so long that you need a haircut before it's over. With 23 days in the saddle—the equivalent of racing a marathon every day—it's all about stockpiling and preserving energy and then carefully expending it at the most opportune moments.

Still one other huge difference between Obree and Pantani was their attitudes toward performance-enhancing drugs (PEDs). Obree was among the most vocal and passionate critics of the widespread practice (that still continues), while Pantani was perhaps the most avid user of PEDs. Although there have been a handful of biographies written about the Italian national hero, most of them were less than truthful about the realities of Pantani's inner life because of the Italian vow of silence (*omertà*), which is an integral part of Mafia culture as well.

Lastly, the final reason I included this story is because road cycling is the sport that I know and love the most. It is also among the most popular sporting events in the world, putting the Super Bowl or Wimbledon to shame. The Tour de France is watched by more people in the world than any other spectacle: four billion people in 190 countries, including 15 million spectators who line the roads to watch it in person!

As much as I've watched the classic tours and races, I still can't fathom the complexity of strategy, hierarchy within a team, and the unique rules and conventions of the sport that emphasize fair play. When a race leader slows down because of a mechanical malfunction or "call of nature," the whole peloton will stall its progress to wait for the rider to catch up.

I suppose I also just admire the sheer grit and insane conditioning it takes to ride 120 miles a day at maximum effort and then repeat that six out of seven days for three weeks. Pro cyclists are often so exhausted after a day's grueling ride that they are carried onto the team bus for a massage, consume 5,000 calories for dinner, and then fall into bed until the next morning, when it begins again.

I appreciate the amount of suffering involved in pedaling up a steep slope, heart and lungs at the bursting point, gasping for breath, fighting for position against competitors. In his classic ode to cycling enthusiasts, Tim Krabbe describes the sort of honorable suffering that Marco Pantani exemplified. He vividly describes what it's like to climb up and then descend Mont Ventoux in France, the brutal mountain that solidified Pantani's fame during his most significant race in the Tour de France. "Halfway down the snowy moonscape," Krabbe writes, "I was able to use the only unfrozen muscle I had left to break." He was so cold he had to get off the bike and walk to get his circulation going again, "... but after I'd been rolling downhill a bit my forehead and hands began to freeze." Yet, he insists, "the best part was the suffering." Indeed it is the suffering etched on Pantani's face when he climbed up those slopes, neck and neck with Lance Armstrong, that will forever be remembered.

This anguish and self-inflicted pain—over so many hours, so many days and weeks— are what make the sport the most beloved. There is a catalogue of martyrs whose names have been etched into history. During one of the first "day classic" races in Italy, the winning cyclist had to take shelter in a mountain hut during a blizzard. Another race a few years later was won by a guy who rode over 30 miles on a flat tire, arriving at the finish line close to midnight. Few suffered at the level that Pantani could endure: He thrived on the pain, taking small comfort from the voice he heard inside his head urging him, over and over, "Attack! Attack!" He seemed to want to get to the top as quickly as possible to reduce the agony—and escape himself. These are the legendary figures who are celebrated—precisely because they suffered so mightily. And perhaps nobody ever suffered more than Pantani, not only on the slopes of the Alps, Pyrenees, and Dolomites but also inside his own mind and heart.

Angel of the Mountains

There has never been a cyclist with faster acceleration up a steep mountainside. I am talking about someone with a resting heart rate of 32 beats per minute, a lung capacity that was otherworldly, a featherweight physique that seemed to float uphill, and a competitive spirit that drove him to the brink of madness and beyond. With his shaved pate covered by a skull-and-crossbones bandana, oversized ears adorned with rings, mascara tattoos under his eyes, and a vicious, swashbuckling style, he was known as "The Pirate." Once Marco Pantani approached the beginning of an ascent, he would rip the skull-and-crossbones kerchief off and ceremoniously throw it to the ground, as if to announce that he was now the one in control.

He was the first Italian in almost three decades to win the Tour de France; this only added to his mystique and legend when he also won the Giro d'Italia the same year. He also won 14 other races that year. Even during those times when he wasn't a threat to win the general classification, he was still always a presence on any mountain stage.

Prior to Pantani's arrival on the international scene, it was the time trial specialists like Miguel Induráin who won the grand tours. They could rack up maximum time bonuses during the short, flat prologues that were almost impossible for others to overcome. In addition, cycling was relying more than ever on scientific breakthroughs: wind tunnels that tested optimal aerodynamic positioning, low-friction racing jerseys, and bikes that cost as much as a Ferrari to design and build. Once Pantani entered the scene, he changed cycling forever from a more tactical, cerebral, team-oriented sport to one in which a single rider could apply intermittent, unpredictable brute force to shake up the whole race.

Spectators and fans were smitten with this brash "Angel of the Mountains," a rider who didn't play by the rules. For audiences, the drama of racing on the slopes of the highest mountains in Europe attracted the most attention. There was gorgeous scenery, and lines of spectators snaked along the narrow, steep roads, standing so close they could touch the riders as they passed, often running alongside their favorite heroes in weird costumes to encourage them. It was in the mountains that breakaways occurred, lone riders attacking with a vengeance. Then after cresting the summits, they would throw themselves down the descents, exceeding 60 miles per hour around treacherous turns with steep drop-offs, sometimes on slick, rainy surfaces. More than a few have plummeted to their deaths.

Fig. 12-1. Marco Pantani, seen above, was one of the most aggressive and combative climbers in the history of cycling. Small in stature and fragile emotionally, he nevertheless became an icon of his nation. Eventually, the unrelenting pressure, exacerbated by drug abuse, led to unbearable depression and despair.

During his early years, Marco was making steady progress: He was awarded "Best Young Rider" in the 1995 Tour de France, winning stages and a third-place finish two years later. But then he believed himself to be the victim of repeated bad luck in his life, confirmed when a black cat literally crossed his path, running in front of him during the 1997 Giro and causing him to fall and injure his leg. These sort of ups and downs would remain the story of his life and cycling career.

It was the following year after his recovery from the accident that he would set records, absolutely trouncing the competition in the most prestigious races. As usual, he had fallen behind in the Giro during the time trial prologue and lost further precious minutes during the ensuing stages, clearly out of the race. But then once in the mountains, he knocked everyone else out of the race with his characteristic flair.

The same plot would be repeated during the Tour: He was virtually in last place after the time trial, more than four minutes behind the dominant German, Jan Ullrich. Yet once again he caught, and passed, Ulrich, and everyone else, to triumph with almost impossible climbing skills. Alas, this was followed by a series of devastating humiliations when he was accused of doping and expelled from racing. Pantani insisted—and stuck to this story throughout the rest of his life—that he had been framed by the Italian Mafia, who had placed bets on a competitor. This explanation really wasn't as outlandish as it may seem.

Crippled by Self-Doubt

With any legend in sports, journalists often dig deep into an athlete's history for anecdotes that reveal their early promise, if not the first recognition of their extraordinary gifts. Little Marco was a restless child, a bit strange looking, with overgrown ears on his tiny frame. He spent much of his childhood as a loner, inclined to suck his thumb until he was eight years old. Although he enjoyed playing soccer, most of the other boys wouldn't let him in the games because he was so skinny and small. He tried to be patient and wait his turn, but it never came, so he eventually reconciled himself to being a loner. Whatever self-consciousness he felt about his small size was only compounded once he hit adolescence and started going prematurely bald.

Pantani was also a fidgety kid, unable to sit still, perhaps displaying symptoms of hyperactivity. His parents encouraged him to ride a bike, hoping he could burn off some excess energy. At first he borrowed his mother's bike to ride with older boys, who ridiculed him—at least until he showed he could keep up with their fancy racing bikes and then leave them behind once they hit the mountains. Once his grandfather purchased him his first proper bike, his fate was sealed.

Pantani was a whirlwind once he was mobile on wheels, and he displayed a certain early recklessness. He ended up being hit by cars a handful of times, among his other accidents. He became so attached to his bike that he insisted on washing it in the bathtub and sleeping with it next to his bed. It was his escape from his otherwise insecure, shy, and withdrawn demeanor. And it worked well for him because it was something he could do on his own. He also realized he would never be handsome, virile, and attractive to women in any conventional sense, so he felt a desperate urge to compensate through his athletic achievements. In Italy at the time, there was no greater hero than a cycling star.

Like so many famous athletes, Marco showed immediate and early promise, stealing victories from boys much older than him. He already had a fan club and considerable notoriety by the time he turned 20. Unfortunately, similar to other superstars in sport, his life was one-dimensional—almost all his time and energy was devoted to the singular task of riding a bike as fast as possible. As such, he never developed much emotional maturity or the capacity for handling many of the normal disappointments in life. Although he had incredible determination and resilience to recover from physical setbacks, numerous accidents, and broken bones, he remained muted in his ability to deal with negative feelings. This would haunt him.

A Climbing Specialist

During a time when cyclists were expected to be generalists—accomplished in time trials and flat stages as well as the mountains—Marco Pantani was an anomaly, even among his breed. Climbers are usually small and light, with an inhuman lung capacity that allows them to fly up steep roads while others falter. They are considered fearless, if not reckless, attacking slopes during times when everyone else is trying to catch their breath and recover. Lance Armstrong called Pantani "the best climber in the history of the sport," no small claim from his nemesis.

It was on Alpe d'Huez, the most mystical, iconic of all stages in the Tour de France, that Pantani truly established himself as a force. The stage is eight miles long, with 21 hairpin turns and an average gradient of 8%. Some sections are so steep that recreational riders would have difficulty even moving forward without falling. After his win there during the 1995 Tour, it was recognized by fans and competitors alike that he was a phenomenon unlike anything they'd ever seen before.

If his future as a leader of the pack seemed assured, he also experienced some devastating accidents that threatened to end his career. The same year he came out, he was hit head-on by a car during a fast descent, shattering his leg. After numerous surgeries and the installation of a metal splint, the doctors informed him he might never walk again. He took a full year to recover and came back stronger than ever—with a new, refashioned image, wearing earrings, a nose stud, and a shaved head, resembling a pirate.

He had an unprecedented banner year in 1998 when he won both the Tour and the Giro, an accomplishment that has never been repeated since, considering there is only a month between the two races during which to recover and train. To make his Tour win all the more dramatic and inspiring, he fell impossibly far behind the leader as the race went into its third week in the Alps before he made his move. There was driving rain in the cold, wet conditions on the steep road when he attacked. Initially none of the other leaders followed him, since they were so far ahead of him in the standings and they believed his gesture was misguided, if not insane. After he hit the summit, he actually stopped to put on a rain jacket and then descended like a madman on the slick surface. He gained 10 minutes on the leaders, enough to win the race.

In spite of his prowess and confidence as a climber, he had a strange habit of riding at the very back of the peloton, keeping hundreds of riders in front of him and requiring him to weave through the tight pack to get anywhere near striking distance to the front.

When asked why he chose to position himself as the last rider in the peloton, he smiled, revealing an essential core aspect of his personality: "You don't know how good it feels to see my friends suffer on the climbs." Here was a terribly insecure young man who had finally found a place where he could be dominant, even with his small stature, big ears, and bald head.

Perhaps because of his insistent need to be adored by his fans, he was different from most other athletes on the course. He made every effort to talk to spectators before and after the races. He played marbles with children. He donated both time and money to charitable causes. His interviews with the media were raucous, unscripted, and endlessly entertaining. He loved the attention, adulation, and all that went with them, including the wealth he accumulated, which was estimated to exceed $20 million. He also started to believe in his own infallibility, speaking about himself during interviews in the third person, as if his public personality was a completely different identity.

The Giant of Provence

If the Tour de France is cycling's most famous race, then Mont Ventoux is its most import-ant stage. Nicknamed the "Giant of Provence," it is a mythical mountain soaring high above southeastern France in a series of switchbacks snaking 12 miles up the slopes. It seems so much higher than its 6,273 feet because it rises vertically above the virtually flat countryside around it. Although the average pitch is about 8% (sufficient to make it difficult for any amateur rider to remain upright), there are sections that rise to an angle of 15%!

The first part winds through somewhat shaded vineyards, but then the road steepens for endless miles thereafter. The summit is utterly barren, swept by ferocious winds often measured above 50 miles an hour. They have been known to be so strong they've blown cars off the cliffs. The temperatures can rise into the 90s during the summer, even at that rarified, oxygen-deprived altitude. Riders are completely exposed, facing mile after mile of bleached white rock and scree.

A French philosopher, Roland Barthes, once described the mountain as "a god of evil to whom sacrifice must be paid." He further added that for cyclists of any and all abilities, "it exacts an unjust tribute of suffering." Close to the summit, British cyclist Tom Simp-son, one of the greatest British champions, collapsed into a mortal coma, a victim of the unrelenting heat and steep ascent (plus, likely, the drugs in his body.)

Among Pantani's most legendary victories, his battle against Lance Armstrong in the 2000 Tour is considered one of the most memorable. The two were evenly matched, not only in their climbing capabilities but also in their mastery of the chemistry involved in maximizing energy output through performance-enhancing drugs. This was a time when virtually everyone was relying on various substances to increase their ability to recover from the grueling stage rides. There has been a long history of doping within cycling, just as there has been in other sports. In the old days, riders would use cocaine to keep them-selves going. Amphetamines had been used by the military to counteract combat fatigue or keep pilots alert; cyclists used them quite legally to enhance their own performance. It wasn't until the 1990s that such drugs were banned, but there were always ways to get around the testing. Both Pantani and Armstrong—and, to be fair, the majority of other top riders—became increasingly creative at developing new ways to seek an advantage, or at least keep up with everyone else. But the main point is that the two competitors were on an equal footing as they began the ascent of Ventoux.

Lance Armstrong held the yellow jersey, the race leader. His only goal was to win the whole Tour de France. Pantani, on the other hand, was the climbing specialist, interested in stage wins. Although Pantani had already been one of the few cyclists in history to win both the Tour and the Giro in the same year (1998), Armstrong had won the Tour the previous year and was the favorite to win again.

Fig. 12-2. As seen above, the duel between Lance Armstrong and Marco Pantani was both spectacular and fraught with drama. Although eventually they reconciled, Pantani felt disrespected and ridiculed, leading him to retaliate against Armstrong whenever he could.

Source: http://capovelo.com/lance-armstrong-invited-ride-pantani-gran-fondo/.

Pantani's reputation as a reckless "slasher" was never on display more than when the peloton hit the bottom slopes of Ventoux. The Pirate took off immediately, leaving everyone else in his wake. Armstrong had no choice but to follow the attack. Winning the stage was less important to him than staying close enough to minimize the loss of time in the general classification. The two went head to head in a duel that was one for the ages.

Pantani launched a vicious attack, opening a gap on the steepest part of the ascent. Armstrong followed again, and the two worked in concert to keep their collective lead, taking turns drafting one another. They opened up a 25-second lead on the other riders as they approached the finish line on the summit. Pantani took off again in a final sprint, and Armstrong hung back, either satisfied with the time he gained against everyone else or just out of energy.

Pantani eventually prevailed, but Armstrong was less than gracious afterwards, saying he let Marco win—which may have been the case. This was seen as both humiliating and disrespectful, so much so that Pantani spent the rest of the race launching crazy, erratic attacks just to punish Armstrong for the perceived slight. He wanted revenge big time, so he won another mountain stage a few days later to make his point. It would be a long time before he forgave Armstrong for what he perceived as contempt and insolence.

"If Armstrong thinks the tour is over, he's wrong," Pantani announced to the French press after the award ceremony. Then, in his pique, he referred to himself in the third person: "Pantani does not need Armstrong to give him a victory."

In spite of his accomplishments, Pantani was notoriously insecure and thin-skinned, and this is what motivated him to make a point against his adversary. And his strategy did indeed succeed to a certain point, especially on the very last mountain stage, when Armstrong completely "bonked," meaning that his stores of energy were completely depleted, and he lost the stage by a huge margin to Jan Ulrich. "It was the hardest day of my life on a bike," Armstrong admitted. He did indeed look vulnerable, largely the result of Pantani's accumulative damage to him.

The drama of the day's events at Ventoux was so exciting it was considered by some the greatest stage race in the history of cycling. A theater company even produced and performed a play, *Ventoux*, based on the story as it unfolded. Much of the dialogue in the play was taken directly from all the interviews and news reports that followed the drama.

The whole story of that stage and its aftermath contained many of the themes prevalent in Marco Pantani's life, including his passion, dignity, paranoia, and emotional vulnerability. Although he had taken on the nickname "The Pirate," reveling in the image of a swashbuckler, Lance Armstrong called him *Elefantino*," translated from Italian as "Dumbo."

Several years later, Pantani, Armstrong, Ulrich, Eddy Mercykx, Francisco Moser, and Alberto Contador—so many of the biggest names in the sport—would eventually be discredited for doping. In one sense they were all operating on a level playing field and drugs became just another training variable, along with bike construction, nutrition, massages, testing equipment, and all the other things they did to improve their performance.

A series of accusations, then investigations, were launched against Pantani. More than seven different judicial inquiries accused him of crimes, including "sporting fraud." It was clear his blood levels were abnormal. While technically there were no traces of drugs in his system, it was also apparent that he was doing something that was illegal and prohibited by the sport. He was found guilty and sanctioned with a suspension.

"My life is already over," he announced afterwards. "The thing that matters in life is to feel death. I'm left all alone." Even cycling was taken away from him.

Deep Depression

Cycling, of course, has a long, checkered history of performance-enhancing, pain-numbing drugs being used by the athletes. During the early days, riders would stop to guzzle brandy as they passed through villages—or, more secretly, ingest heroin or strychnine. Then riders started dying; the most famous was the great British racer Tom Simpson. As mentioned earlier, he had been climbing Mount Ventoux during the 1967 Tour when he collapsed with heart failure. It was later determined that his blood contained massive amounts of amphetamines, alcohol, and diuretics.

Cycling authorities ever since then have tried to put a brake on the most obvious signs of PEDs, and some would say Marco Pantani became their sacrificial lamb. Perhaps his constant boasting that he was clean and his ridiculously improbable public denials made things so much worse. He also refused to accept any sanction or punishment, once again going on the attack, just as he had in the mountains. He claimed there was a conspiracy among the cycling authorities to stop him from winning so much because other teams and sponsors were upset because they were becoming increasingly marginalized. Why was *he* being singled out?

It turns out that Pantani—and later, Lance Armstrong—were not that wrong when they claimed that since everyone was doing it, it was just a way to remain competitive. It was later discovered that, in fact, 18 of the top riders during that era had evidence of blood doping in their systems. The dark side of the sport was busted wide open, and the widespread culture of drugs was exposed. One physician alone was found to have been distributing illegal drugs to over 60 different riders.

Marco Pantani's life began to crumble, one piece after another. "I've been leaned on and humiliated, and I haven't really known how to cope," he confessed after the investigations into his extracurricular activities. After all his sacrifices—all he'd done for the sport, his country, his fans—he felt disrespected. And respect was *everything* to him.

During one of his last interviews, he announced, "The champion I was exists no more; he is far from the man that I have become." Then he dismissed his legion of admirers as fickle and disloyal, only interested in him as a personality.

He could handle much of the pressure of the public stage, the stress of a three-week race, and the challenge of a mountain climb, but the one thing he could not endure was disgrace. His reputation and achievements were being called into question. He pouted. He withdrew. Always temperamental and moody, he slipped into a state of chronic depression and despair. He claimed he was done with the sport of cycling altogether. He was even quoted as saying that if everyone thought he was a drug addict, he'd show them what a real drug addict was like: In a fit of pique, he start snorting cocaine, eventually smoking it as crack.

Pantani's relationship with his girlfriend, Christina, had finally ended. He was accused of cheating, fraud, and using performance-enhancing drugs, even though he had never tested positive. He claimed that all the evidence was circumstantial even though authorities discovered syringes, insulin, and small traces of other drugs in his room. He was insistent he hadn't even stayed in that room the night before and there was a conspiracy against him directed by outside forces. Whether he believed this was the Mafia or some rival, he refused to say, but he felt he was being singled out for special prosecution and believed the world was out to get him. He was convinced there were video cameras installed in his rooms to record his behavior. "How could you not hurt yourself after that?" he wondered.

Hurt himself, indeed. Pantani's use of cocaine and other drugs grew far worse. He made frequent trips to Cuba, ostensibly for treatment but actually to indulge in binges with drugs and prostitutes. He isolated himself more and more from friends and family. His previous displays of charm during interviews with media became embittered rants. He gained weight. He started talking about himself more often in the third person as if he had lost his sense of self. He ended up in a series of car crashes.

A psychiatrist was eventually consulted about Pantani's deteriorating mental condition and drug addiction. There are several possible ways that a health professional might have conceptualized and diagnosed what was essentially wrong with him. The most obvious cause for his problems would be his series of career setbacks and the assault on his reputation. That would be identified as "reactive depression" and generally treated with psychotherapy, plus an inpatient drug rehabilitation intervention to get him clean and sober. There is some question as to whether all the drugs he took were a form of self-medication to deal with the deeper psychic pain (and thus the primary issue) or the addiction itself was the cause of all his other misery. Naturally, the best interpretation is that both factors were at play.

The good doctor, however, decided to do a full psychiatric workup on his patient, diagnosing him with just about anything and everything imaginable. At least we can say he was thorough.

Journalist Matt Rendell located a copy of Pantani's medical records. It won't surprise you to learn there are some doctors and mental health professionals who tend to over-pathologize people, diagnosing and naming all sorts of different conditions, supposedly to contribute to a greater understanding of their predicament. In this case, Pantani was diagnosed with bipolar disorder, just as several of the other athletes in this book have been. It was also determined he had a "nonspecific" personality disorder, meaning that the doctor identified features of someone who was narcissistic, antisocial, and obsessive. Of course, we could say that about almost any famous athlete, given the privileges and adulation they are allowed as a function of being "genetic celebrities."

Then there were descriptions of his florid addictions to multiple substances that played a role in his erratic behavior. In addition, he was identified as having paranoid delusions related to being watched at all times and fearing his food might be poisoned. And if that doesn't cover everything, it was also suspected that several head injuries might have caused organic damage of the brain. In other words, regardless of what might be described as the central problem, it was clear to everyone that Pantani was not in his right mind and no longer functional.

Because of the doping allegations, Pantani was disqualified from riding in the Giro d'Italia. The media and public jumped on the bandwagon, skewering him mercilessly. He felt humiliated beyond anything he could tolerate and began to isolate himself, hiding from the world. He lapsed into a deep depression from which he would never recover in spite of what anyone attempted. And so many of his friends, teammates, and fellow cyclists tried to reach out to him.

Pantani and Armstrong eventually reconciled their differences, especially after Marco was one of the few cyclists who contacted Lance after his cancer diagnosis to offer his concern. They agreed to meet in a bar prior to a race in Spain, and Armstrong was more than conciliatory: He was downright supportive of Pantani's legal troubles and urged him to put the past behind him so they might renew their rivalry in the mountains with mutual respect and even affection. "Don't withdraw with your bad thoughts," Lance advised. "Think about winning."

Among all those who were interviewed after Pantani's downfall, Armstrong remarked that cycling had lost a great champion, then added that the sport had also lost an indomitable personality. He could, of course, relate to the image of Marco Pantani as a fallen hero, since they both shared a hit to their reputations as a result of doping accusations. Ironically, both never tested positive in urine or blood samples, even though many witnesses and team members testified to their behavior.

Armstrong learned some hard lessons in his own life after cycling, feeling regretful and nostalgic about the plight of his lost rival. He insisted that the greatest danger in any sport is when the athlete retires: "Fame is fleeting, and life after being at the top is never the same." Reflecting on Pantani's suffering, he observed, "He went from being a god in Italy to being someone who lost so much." Armstrong noted how important it is to be "prepared for the day when you're just a dude walking down the street and no longer the star." He said he thought about that reality a lot related to his own public humiliation and involuntary retirement. He also realized that Marco Pantani could never make that adjustment, just as he never fully dealt with his fame as the hero of his country.

Pantani eventually entered a mental health facility at the urging of his manager. It was time to deal with his depression and chronic drug addictions. On several previous occasions, he tried drug rehabilitation programs but only lasted a few days before bolting; he even smuggled drugs into the facility during his stay! He added 30 pounds to his tiny frame and became even more discouraged about his prospects for the future. He genuinely believed himself to be a scapegoat for all that was wrong with the sport of cycling, claiming that drugs had always been a part of the scene and always would be. There are some who would claim that even today the practice continues, only in ways that have yet to be identified.

On Pantani's 34th birthday, his friends organized a party for him at a local disco, hoping to boost his spirts and show their support. This was to be his "last supper," one of his final appearances in public. They had all been sitting around the tables drinking and eating when suddenly, and without warning, Pantani abruptly stood up. Everyone was startled and turned to watch him reach into his pocket and pull out a packet of cocaine. He stumbled toward the bathroom; a friend tried to stop him but was pushed away angrily. Onlookers could only shrug helplessly, whispering to one another that they wondered if this was the last time they'd ever see him.

During his last few days locked in a hotel room, his madness continued to spiral out of control. He began mutilating himself. Other guests on the floor described him as confused, rambling, incoherent, and disoriented. At one point, he was heard crying out, "I'm mad!" He had tied a bedsheet to a railing, possibly in an attempt to hang himself.

Death Scene

Pantani remained in his hotel room for a week, ordering carryout pizza deliveries but otherwise remaining locked inside. The delivery man noticed immediately that "There was no light in his eyes." He added, "This is going to end badly."

Other guests on his floor started complaining to management about the lunatic who was screaming all the time, throwing furniture around the room, and making loud noises that were disturbing everyone. When the maid knocked on the door to clean the room, he just yelled at her to go away.

Hotel staff became increasingly concerned about their famous guest when he ceased to answer the phone or even turn on the lights. The receptionist was sufficiently worried to go and check on him, but when he tried the key in the door, he discovered it was blockaded with furniture. When he finally managed to squeeze into the room, he found Marco Pantani's body on the floor. He saw medicine bottles strewn across the room and a pool of blood near the body. It was Valentine's Day, 2004.

The police and coroner eventually determined that his cause of death was a drug overdose, as yet undetermined whether accidental or suicide. One decisive factor that would soon be discovered is that he had somehow managed to ingest six times the lethal dose of cocaine and was even found to have residue in his mouth. The only initial clues about what first appeared to be a heart attack were 10 different containers of tranquilizers and antidepressants scattered around the room, along with some remnants of cocaine.

John Wilcockson, one of his intimate confidantes, wondered if his friend actually died of loneliness: "I believe he was alone at the very time he was most in need of help." There was evidence of his warped mind everywhere. The room had been dismantled. The microwave oven and bathroom mirror had been unbolted from the walls; perhaps he had imagined they were used to monitor his activities. He had been raving at other guests, at one point screaming, "I know who you are!"

Pantani had left a series of notes with scribbled thoughts. One of the notes read, "Nobody has managed to understand me, not even my family. I am alone." He had clearly felt betrayed and abandoned, with no hope that things could ever be otherwise.

On a recent trip to Cuba, he had scribbled notes all over his passport pages. He was bitter, angry, lashing out at his critics, increasingly convinced everyone was out to destroy him and ruin his life. "I was humiliated for nothing," he scrawled on the pages, "and I was in the courts for 4 years. ... The sport of cycling paid and lost. I'm suffering with this letter."

Nine blank pages of his passport were covered with his self-pitying ramblings, summarized by the statement: "I'm left all alone. No one managed to understand me. Even the cycling world and even my own family."

With this defaced document, the only reason he managed to get through passport control was because the officer had been a cycling fan.

Circle of Blame

Considering Pantani's status and fame in Italy—rivaling that of the Pope—there was endless speculation about what led to his death. In one article, there was finger-pointing from anyone and everyone involved in the cyclist's life. Pantani's parents blamed his girlfriend, Christina, who abandoned him after allegedly introducing him to the drug scene.

Christina was with Pantani during his most raw, vulnerable moments during their years together; they each described the other as the only true love of their lives. He was absolutely obsessive about every aspect of his sport, taking his bike apart and reassembling it every day, making the tiniest adjustments to his saddle or the compression of his shoes. She believed, ultimately, that all this discipline and attention to detail was the means by which he fought the chronic depression that had plagued him since childhood. He was so self-conscious about his appearance, especially his small size, that he eventually had surgery to reduce the size of his ears and even had tattoos added underneath his eyes to emphasize his look as a "pirate."

Many years after his death, Christina finally consented to an interview. She confessed to still feeling guilty, seeing her role as a savior who had failed in her responsibility. "My life with Marco was a perpetual cycle of hope and despair, coming together and breaking apart." Finally, the partying, drugging, and erratic behavior had become too much for her. She had wanted them to settle down and start a family, but he had refused, eventually forcing her to save herself and escape the constant debauchery and destructive behavior.

Christina also provided insight into Marco's gifts and burdens. She confirmed, once and for all, that he had doped, in spite of his denials. She saw the products he kept in the refrigerator and witnessed him injecting himself; at times, she assisted him by holding his arm. Yet she forgives and excuses the practice because of the pressure he felt to satisfy his fans and stay competitive with his rivals.

Pantani's friends blamed his parents for exploiting their son's fame for their own lucrative gains. His friends were blamed for not intervening in his life and allowing his self-destructive behavior to continue. The media was blamed for hounding the man relentlessly and treating him as a scapegoat for all that was wrong with the sport. Pantani himself blamed these and an assortment of other reasons but would never accept responsibility for his own behavior. If he had only been willing to accept a brief suspension or own up to his use of performance-enhancing drugs, he would have been forgiven and allowed to ride again.

In retrospect, there are many possible sources of blame for Pantani's death. The culture of sport in general, and cycling in particular, certainly played a role. The races are essentially designed as opportunities for sponsors to display their products and disseminate indelible images. The virtually universal doping within the sport significantly increased the risk of emotional disorders, health problems, and death. More than a dozen cyclists employing blood doping have died of heart failure. The culture of deceit and subsequent cover-ups mean that there is little oversight or even competent medical supervision. Finally, cycling has its own strange hierarchy of power and status in which the team leader is permitted to do whatever he wishes, and everyone else exists to serve him. They are even called *domestiques* (domestic servants) whose jobs involve retrieving water bottles and snacks for the leader, riding in front of him to break the wind, and even scoring drugs and women for him on demand.

Yet reputation and status were *everything* to Marco Pantani; when those were tarnished, it felt like his life had already ended. He had been on the verge of being named cycling's greatest champion ever, having won both the Tour and Giro in 1998. Since that time, no winner of the Tour has managed to excel at the Giro at the highest level, and likely never will. John Gleaves, an expert on doping in cycling, remarked in an interview with me: "It is now a feat that cannot be done anymore. Anti-doping rules and talent make it too difficult to be at a high enough level in May and July to win both the Giro and the Tour. It also may be that too few athletes can live on that extreme razor's edge of training/

diet over that length of time. Pantani may have been the only one with the 'right' mix of personality traits to do it."

Whatever fame and respect that Pantani felt he rightly earned, the scandals that followed sent him into despair. "He was completely paralyzed," Christina remembered, describing how he refused to leave the house after that, lying in bed sobbing in misery, lamenting that his whole life had been destroyed.

Whatever insecurities Pantani had always carried with him became much worse once he lost his mooring as his nation's champion. The depression and mood swings worsened, exacerbated by the cocaine binges he used to medicate himself. His paranoia and feelings that people were out to destroy him were not necessarily all delusional, especially considering that authorities did actually raid his hotel rooms and closely monitor his goings-on.

Most of his relationships with managers, team members, marketing experts, politicians, celebrities, and hangers-on felt exploitive to him; he knew he was a meal ticket for dozens of others who depended on him to keep winning. The only person in his life he truly trusted and depended on was Christina—and when that fell apart, he had nothing or nobody left to help stabilize him.

At the time of his death, Marco Pantani's reputation and standing in Italy were still intact. He was The Pirate. Of course, he could be wicked at times, but that's what made him so successful and loved. He was a flawed human being, certainly self-destructive at times, but who wasn't? Yet the nature of his insecurities and emotional vulnerability made him an easy mark for others to exploit. He carried a whole nation on his small shoulders. As such, they overlooked the recklessness and irrational behavior off the bike that mirrored his style during a race.

During his funeral, tens of thousands of people lined the streets to honor their hero. Walking six abreast, mourners formed a line over two miles long. His grave has since become a shrine, as if Marco Pantani has been relegated to sainthood by his millions of fans and countrymen. Just as Americans may remember exactly where they were and what they were doing when President Kennedy was assassinated or when 9/11 occurred, many Italians and cycling fans recall the moment when they learned The Pirate was dead.

What Killed Marco Pantani?

The coroner determined that Marco Pantani, the hero of Italy, the wayward son, The Pirate, died of an accidental cocaine overdose. But the circumstances of his death and his previous state of mind were much more complicated.

It's pretty evident that Pantani was not in his right mind, so to speak, during his last months. His thinking was highly irrational, and his behavior was highly self-destructive. He was clearly paranoid and believed the world was out to destroy him. He was a raging, chronic drug addict and had been for the previous few years. What had begun as a dependence on performance-enhancing drugs that were common in his sport eventually accelerated to include a variety of recreational substances. After his various injuries, he was also prescribed highly addictive painkillers that did far more than just mute his physical suffering.

Pantani did not adapt well to disappointments, especially those he believed were not within his power to fix. He couldn't just accelerate and drop his enemies behind him on a mountain slope. His dignity took a hit from which he couldn't recover. His reservoir of ability to suffer physical pain was limitless. After all, the main talent of a cyclist, and especially a climber, is to suffer beyond the capacity of any normal being, beyond even the tolerance of the most experienced and hardened competitors. Yet dealing with the emotional pain was beyond him.

Many of the mental disorders covered in the stories of athletes in this book involve insidious biologically based diseases of the mind. Schizophrenia, bipolar disorder, and endogenous depression are not only caused by chemical imbalances in the neurological system but also usually inherited. A host of other emotional problems are developed situationally as a result of some misfortune, tragedy, trauma, or life condition. These adjustment reactions can be just as devastating as any chronic mental illness; in some ways, the individual is even less prepared to manage the symptoms because they feel intolerable. The onset is swift and sudden, the result sometimes debilitating.

Most of us have experienced moderate symptoms of such an adjustment reaction in our lives. We encounter losses, grieve loved ones, have financial or family problems. We lose jobs or friendships, survive crushing disappointments, or are just caught by life's surprises in ways for which we were unprepared. Such emotional struggles are usually time limited, and most people recover within a few months without any professional help required. Time does indeed heal many wounds.

Marco Pantani suffered these sorts of disappointments and perceived failures. He felt abandoned by his friends, family, and the sport to which he had devoted his life. He believed himself to be unfairly persecuted. Rather than sucking it up and facing his problems, accepting responsibility for his mistakes and miscalculations, and seeking some kind of redemption, he pouted and simmered in anger, eventually turning it inward toward himself.

Among all the stories presented in the book, Pantani's troubles are among the ones we can perhaps most easily identify. He was not chronically mentally ill, even if he did eventually succumb to deep depression. He had found ways to cope with his insecurities and mood swings through devotion to his sport. We can all relate to what it feels like to be misunderstood, to feel like we have been treated unjustly. Most of us can remember times in our lives when we felt lost, with no easy way back to a semblance of normality. We surrendered hope, at least for a while, until we could recover and heal ourselves.

Whether Pantani's overdose was intentional or accidental, he had died of lost hope. He died completely alone. Misunderstood. The sport that had brought him such joy, achievement, pride, fame, and wealth eventually destroyed him in the end.

Sources

Armstrong, L. (2014, February 13). If I was a carpenter, Pantani was an artist. *Cycling News*. http://www.cyclingnews.com/features/armstrong-if-i-was-the-carpenter-pantani-was-the-artist/

Erskine, J. (Director). (2014). *The accidental death of a cyclist*. PBS.

Friedman, S. (2004, February 13). The tragedy of Marco Pantani. *Bicycling*. https://www.bicycling.com/culture/people/tragedy

Fotheringham, W. (2004, February 15). Pantani dies broken and alone. *The Guardian*. https://www.theguardian.com/sport/2004/feb/16/cycling.cycling

Gladstone, G., & Brown, G. (2017, October 16). The giant of Provence: The magic and mystique of Mont Ventoux. *Cycling Weekly*. http://www.cyclingweekly.com/news/racing/tour-de-france/tour-de-france-preview-mont-ventoux-256751

Kelso, P. (2004, February 18). Pantani's revelation of torment. *The Guardian*. https://www.theguardian.com/sport/2004/feb/19/cycling.cycling

Krabbe, T. (2002). *The rider*. Bloomsbury.

Rendell, M. (2004, March 6). The long lonely road to oblivion. *The Guardian*. https://www.theguardian.com/sport/2004/mar/07/cycling.features

Rendell, M. (2015). *The death of Marco Pantani*. Weidenfeld & Nicolson.

Ronchi, M., & Josti, G. (2005). *Man on the run: The life and death of Marco Pantani*. Robson Books.

Wilcockson, J. (2004, February 15). Marco Pantani: A tragic figure. *Velo News*. http://www.velonews.com/2004/02/news/marco-pantani-a-tragic-figure_5563

Wilcockson, J. (2005). *Marco Pantani: The legend of a tragic champion*. Velo Books.

13

Theoren Fleury

Fury Incarnate

In a sport like hockey, in which size matters a lot, Theo Fleury was an anomaly, just five and a half feet tall, almost lost in a crowd of giants. If his diminutive appearance didn't put a chip on his shoulder, then being bullied and shamed for being a Cree Indian didn't help matters. As a child, he was teased constantly because of his size and heritage, leading to a level of counteraggression and retaliation that got him constantly in trouble, not only in school but also in the penalty boxes of hockey arenas. He had developed a way to protect himself and prevent himself from being pushed around by retaliating first, hitting others before they knew what had happened. He was provocative, intense, argumentative, and wildly aggressive in a sport in which those traits were tolerated to a certain extent. He usually went beyond those limits.

It had long been assumed that Fleury's uncontrolled rage and propensity toward violence was just a component of his mean spirit. It is also often a part of the game that those who may not have sufficient talent to score goals take on the role of enforcers. They create a different sort of spectacle on the ice, starting fistfights, which are encouraged by fans and temporarily indulged by the referees. But in Fleury's case, there was a darker force at work, a deep-seated emotional disorder that was embedded in a closely guarded secret.

Betrayal of Trust

Like so many of our subjects, Fleury first discovered the joy of his sport in preschool and never looked back. He was determined to not allow his small size to limit his potential, setting records for penalty minutes as a result of the fights he started, some without apparent provocation. There were many reasons for this seemingly erratic behavior, the most obvious of which was that he had so little adult supervision in his life. He had been left to his own devices most of the time because his parents were both addicted to alcohol and drugs, doing their best to keep their own lives under control. Fleury was left in the care of his hockey coach, Graham James, the only adult he truly trusted. But this relationship was also the source of many of the most severe problems he would have for the rest of his life.

Fleury had been recruited at the age of 13 to play for a minor league hockey team in Winnipeg, Canada. This required him to move away from home, a predicament he was more than willing to accept, given the chaos and deprivations of his daily life. He was offered sleeping accommodations with a local family in the new town, but James insisted that the young boy spend at least a few nights each week at James's home, ostensibly so they could spend more time together for instruction and mentoring.

Fleury would sleep on the couch and then be awakened in the middle of the night to find his coach masturbating over him. Eventually this escalated to the point where James pressured the boy to have oral sex with him. At first Fleury would ignore James, wrapping himself tightly in his blanket as a form of protection. He would find excuses to stay away from the coach's house, offering reasons why he wasn't available and even hiding from him. But James was relentless, and his threats became more urgent. He told the boy that unless he agreed to have sex with him, he would never play professional hockey; he would never have any support or endorsement to make it to the next level. He demanded that Fleury cooperate with the sexual abuse or his career was over. This would continue two to three times each week for two years during the most vulnerable time of the boy's adolescence.

The Secrets Were Killing Him

Although wounded by this early trauma, crippled by guilt and shame, Fleury quickly rose to the top of the sport in hockey-crazed Canada. Almost anyone could see he had a chip on his shoulder, a simmering passion for the sport that seemed almost a life-or-death struggle for him, and perhaps it was. He played for his country in the Junior World Championships and later the Olympics, winning a gold medal. But it was within the pros that he most distinguished himself as a force, not only with his consistency scoring goals but also his fierceness on the ice. He was the rare player who could stand up for himself and teammates not only with his fists but also as a scoring threat and competent defenseman. He was selected as an NHL All-Star seven times and won both the Stanley Cup and the Canada Cup. It is for that reason that some of his antics were tolerated. And some of them were doozies.

Fleury was frequently fined for making obscene gestures toward fans. He was repeatedly suspended from teams for violating their substance abuse policies. He was involved in drunken brawls in strip clubs. He went on drinking sprees until the wee hours of the morning. He overdosed on crystal meth. He was constantly penalized for starting fights during games and then sometimes refused to sit in the penalty box, instead skating off the ice to disappear. And then there was the time he attacked the San Jose Sharks' mascot, S. J. Sharkie, in the hallway of the arena, breaking the poor guy's ribs.

At one point, things got so bad he went on month-long benders fueled by alcohol and cocaine. Finally, he couldn't take it any longer. He stopped at a pawn shop, put $5,000 on the counter, and convinced the owner to sell him a gun and just one bullet, figuring that's all he'd need for what he had on his mind to end his pain. He went home and started guzzling a bottle of vodka until he could find the courage to put the barrel of the automatic in his mouth. He flipped off the safety, put his finger on the trigger—and then threw the weapon on the floor in anger.

Fleury sat stewing for several more minutes, reviewing the wreck of his life. He could never get the vivid scenes of sexual abuse out of his head. He considered all the neglect and prejudice he had suffered in his life, not only because of his Native heritage but also because of his size. With his short stature and background, nobody had ever given him a chance. And even now, after everything he'd done for the team, all the coach and team officials gave him such grief. There seemed to be no hope, no way he could redeem his sullied reputation. He just shook his head in despair, then laid out a few more lines of coke. He took more swigs of vodka, once again trying to work up the gumption to end it all. But something stopped him; some small remnant of sanity reminded him that it was his secrets that were killing him. He wondered if releasing those secrets might be the only thing that could save him.

Fleury spent the next few years in and out of rehab programs, ostensibly for drug and alcohol abuse but actually to deal with the burgeoning emotional difficulties that stemmed from his early childhood experiences as well as sexual abuse. All he remembered about his family during childhood was that the interactions at home were rather "volatile." This wasn't particularly surprising, considering that his parents had usually been high or drunk. There had been nobody he could confide in, nobody he could talk to about his family troubles, except Coach James. That came with a price he would pay for the rest of his life.

It is hardly surprising that throughout adulthood, Fleury had a hard time maintaining a stable family of his own. He had four children with three different mothers, finding it difficult to remain committed to a relationship or, for that matter, really trust anyone.

Fleury's temper had become legendary, even among a herd of angry men with short fuses. It is no wonder that such rage developed within him, feeling abandoned, neglected, inadequate, and unlovable. It's also not surprising that he kept his feelings bottled up inside him, considering his background. Consider first that he was Canadian. Secondly, he was First Nation. Third, he was a guy. And fourth, he was a friggin' hockey player!

One referee remembers a time during the playoffs when Fleury didn't like a call; he skated up to him and screamed, "You little shitbag asshole. Come outside to the parking lot after the game. I'll kill you."

Looking back at it years later, the referee just shrugged about the incident, saying he'd heard worse. But he mentioned it because it seemed to be a typical story about Fleury during his playing days. It is actually the kind of incident that seems to sum up the nature of the emotional problems that eventually ended his career.

Finding Meaning in Suffering

Fleury had been diagnosed with both anxiety and depressive disorders much earlier in his life but tried his best to hide the difficulties, knowing that he'd suffer ridicule and greater shame. The macho sport of hockey isn't exactly a culture that encourages players to talk about their feelings, especially those that involve anything shameful or forbidden.

About the only emotion they are allowed to express is anger. Well, Fleury had plenty of that in spades.

He also didn't find mental health professionals to be all that helpful, nor did he especially like to talk to them about what happened. It is all the more remarkable that he published an autobiography several years ago documenting in detail the betrayal and abuse he endured at the hands of the coach he trusted. He felt it was important to find his voice, to talk about what happened, so that perhaps he would no longer feel so alone. To his surprise, the public embraced his honesty and offered support in a way that he'd never felt before. He attributes that feedback as more healing than anything he ever received from his doctors.

Fig. 13-1. It was often Theoren Fleury's (the Calgary Flames' player pictured above) rage that fueled his aggression on the ice. He had suffered trauma from sexual abuse, betrayal by his coach, and racism, which led to his uncontrolled violence. Yet over time he came to terms with his emotional problems and became a passionate advocate for survivors of abuse.

At the end of his career, Theo's secrets and depression were so pervasive that he could barely get himself to suit up and get back on the ice. Looking back on his life, he couldn't think of a time when anxiety or depression were not constant companions. He had been self-medicating with any drugs and alcohol he could get his hands on, anything to numb the pain. The one thing he could never seem to do was ask for help. But it turns out the public confession was the turning point of his life. "I can tell you from my own experience," he said, "it wasn't until I asked for help that my life started to change."

Fleury finally came to terms with what happened and was able to let go of his shame. "I'm going to talk about what I want," he announced defiantly, "when I want, with whomever I want." It was in doing so that the healing continued. "And I feel better, and I don't have to hide anything." In a second book, he described in vivid detail the nature of the abuse that had occurred. Eventually, Graham James was prosecuted by the government and sentenced to five years in prison.

Fleury's story is one of incredible courage and resilience, not just about what he did as a hockey player but also what he's managed to do since his career ended. He is one of those rare athletes who managed to reinvent himself as an artist, entrepreneur, and businessman in the mold of Wayne Gretzky, Michael Jordan, and Magic Johnson. In Fleury's case, he launched a reality television show, and when that didn't work out, he started a successful concrete business. Then he ventured into a clothing line before he became a songwriter. Even after a diagnosis of Crohn's disease, he has demonstrated the willingness to bounce back and continue his efforts to fight for important causes related to mental health, sexual abuse, and, more recently, his inflammatory disease.

Fleury separated himself from the game of hockey for many years, still wounded by the way his career ended and the numerous conflicts he faced within the sport. Yet as he looks back on his rather checkered career, he feels grateful for the things he learned along the way, especially the importance of support and caring within a team "and the consequences and that we're all responsible for our actions and our decisions." Even with those gifts, he was also quick to point out "at the end of the day, hockey is just a game. It's not life and death." Saving himself and others is now the primary mission of his life so others might learn and feel encouraged by his experiences.

Theo Fleury feels grateful for what he learned from adversity—what psychologists call posttraumatic growth. It turns out that survivors of abuse, neglect, catastrophes, and other traumas don't necessarily end up crippled by these experiences. Many survivors of abuse, disasters, and catastrophes (according to estimates, as many as 40%) report incredible personal transformations that resulted from their suffering. Like Fleury, they value intimacy in relationships more than ever. They don't take things for granted. And they often discover greater meaning and purpose in life. This is what psychiatrist Viktor Frankl described many years ago when he talked about how even concentration camp survivors could have everything taken from them "but one thing: the last of the human freedoms—to choose one's attitude in any given set of circumstances, to choose one's own way."

In Fleury's case, he came to understand that even though he could do nothing about the deprivations and neglect he had suffered growing up in his family, the racism and oppression he experienced as an aboriginal, or the sexual abuse and betrayal he faced at the hands of his trusted mentor and coach, he could choose to deal with his emotional problems and dismal life circumstances, his shame and guilt, by altering his attitudes about what happened. He could view himself no longer as a victim or even a survivor but rather as the hero of his own life narrative. He also found that his Native roots offered a path to healing with an emphasis on mutual support and spiritual renewal. He asserted that although there were many standard medical and mental health treatments for abuse, addiction, and anger, "for me, the simplest way of dealing with any one of those issues is through community."

More than ever, Fleury tries to leave the past behind and instead focus on the present. "I get less depressed," he says, "when I'm focused on trying to live moment by moment."

Unlike several others mentioned in this book, Fleury doesn't talk about his emotional difficulties as ever being "cured" but rather as part of an ongoing process in which relapses are sometimes inevitable. "I really don't think there's anything wrong with relapse as long as you learn from it." It is all about the coping mechanisms at your disposal to recover from the stressors that trigger self-defeating habits.

It's interesting that Theo Fleury had always capitalized on his reputation as a tough guy, someone who was quick to take offense at the slightest perception of disrespect or to take advantage of anyone's weakness. Now his life is ruled by empathy and compassion for others who have suffered abuse. His greatest growth edge of all is finding forgiveness for those who have most deeply hurt him.

Sources

Calhoun, L. G., & Tedeschi, R. G. (2013). *Posttraumatic growth in clinical practice*. Routledge.

Fleury, T. (2009). *Playing with fire*. Triumph Books.

Fleury, T., & Barthel, K. (2014). *Conversations with a rattlesnake*. Influence Publishing.

Frankl, V. (1959). *Man's search for meaning*. Beacon Press.

Friedman, M. (2015, March 3). Theo Fleury is teaching us how to heal. *Psychology Today*. https://www.psychologytoday.com/us/blog/brick-brick/201503/theo-fleury-is-teaching-us-how-heal

Gore Mutual. (2018, May 3). Theo Fleury: It's what you leave behind. *Gore Magazine*. https://www.goremutual.ca/theo-fleury-it-s-what-you-leave-behind/

Holmes, C. (2018, March 9). Theo Fleury on how depression ended his career. *Grandstand Central*. https://grandstandcentral.com/theo-fleury-on-how-depression-ended-his-career-1c2e482d71a1

Prewitt, A. (2016, July 5). Theo Fleury is giving advice to fellow survivors of abuse. *Sports Illustrated*. https://www.si.com/nhl/2016/07/05/theo-fleury-nhl-player-country-music-singer-addiction-abuse-where-are-they-now

Rendon, J. (2015). *Upside: The new science of post-traumatic growth*. Touchstone.

14

Lionel Aldridge

A Beast Inside Him

He was a giant of a figure, wandering down the middle of the street with an uncertain gait. Six-feet-four, 300 pounds, hunched over, carefully studying the pavement. He was searching for discarded cigarette butts, hoping for a smoke, but he kept getting distracted by the lines wavering in front of him. And the voices.

"You're a fool!" he could hear someone scream at him. "You're a worthless piece of shit!"

He slowly turned around to confront his assailant only to find there was nobody behind him. There were hundreds of people shuffling along, resting on the sidewalks, a few muttering to themselves. But there was nobody behind him. The voice was inside his head.

Skid Row is a square mile in downtown Los Angeles where the homeless can live relatively undisturbed. The sidewalks are littered with tents, sleeping bags, and sometimes just slumbering bodies. It is the only piece of real estate in the world where the Bloods and Crips have a truce in order to coordinate their drug sales. You can see people shooting themselves up with heroin.

Lionel wandered up and down the streets for hours, trying to escape the people he believed were following him. They were clever and secretive. Any time he slipped into a shadow or bolted around a corner with remnants of his famed quickness, he could still hear them mocking him. "You can't escape us," they'd warn him. "No sense in trying. We are everywhere. We are inside you."

Lionel pressed his huge hands against the side of his skull, trying to squeeze the voices outside of his mind. But they were tricky. They were persistent. Nothing would make them go away.

Lionel finally passed out in exhaustion leaning against the wall of a building. When he awoke, he discovered his jeweled Super Bowl ring had been stolen off his finger. Or maybe it had been missing from some other time? He couldn't remember. The ring was a remembrance of his days playing football for the great Vince Lombardi and the Green Bay Packers. He was the only rookie, drafted late in the fourth round, to ever become a permanent starter for the coach, who was notoriously intolerant of newcomers.

Lionel Aldridge, a star defensive end for one of the greatest teams in history—anchoring a defense that won the first two Super Bowls—whose post-football career had led him to be a radio and television broadcaster, was now so broke and disoriented that he called an old friend in Los Angeles to see if he could borrow just three dollars to get through another day. He was not only homeless but also actively hallucinating with acute paranoid schizophrenia.

Early Years

Lionel never really knew either of his parents, abandoned by each of them when he was a young boy. This was the deep South in small-town Louisiana during times of extreme racism. The boy's grandparents were simple sharecroppers, but they tried to instill in him a love of learning and insisted he seek higher education. Yet in his all-black school, he wasn't exactly getting the preparation he'd need to succeed in college. They didn't even have organized athletic programs.

After his grandfather died when Lionel was a teenager, he was forced to live with other relatives in California, and that's when he first realized his physical potential. With his size, strength, and speed, he was a standout in every high school sport. He played basketball and ran track, but football was made for him.

During the '60s, talented African American athletes, especially star high school players, were in great demand in the hinterlands. Schools in the West, in particular, coveted black players who had the size and speed they couldn't find on their own plains or in their small towns and mountains. Thus Lionel Aldridge was offered an athletic scholarship to play for Utah State University, becoming one of a handful of ethnically diverse students on a campus that was almost exclusively white. He would be given support and an education as long as he could perform at the highest level in the stadiums on Saturday afternoons.

While he was attending the university, he met his future wife, Vicky, and they both paid a price for their interracial relationship during a time when this was considered quite controversial in that part of the country. When Vicky's family discovered she was dating a black man, her father intervened, demanding that the school forcibly end the relationship and closely monitor them to make sure they no longer had contact with one another. When they tried to secretly continue the relationship, Vicky was continually attacked as a "nigger lover," and Lionel was threatened with having his scholarship revoked. He would not be allowed to graduate.

Vince Lombardi, coach and general manager of the Green Bay Packers, decided to select Aldridge in the fourth round of the 1963 draft. But he had some concerns because he'd heard his new player was hanging out with a white woman and planning to bring her with him to Milwaukee. The couple had actually been secretly engaged for a year, and when Aldridge told the coach he planned to marry her, Lombardi said he'd support them as long as theirs was a permanent relationship. For the time, this was in itself an unusually brave stand by Lombardi. In what seems incredible only 50 some years later, Pete Rozelle, the NFL commissioner, tried to intervene, warning both coach and player that the marriage was not good for the sport. He tried to forbid the marriage, and it was only Lombardi's power and reputation that permitted him to take a stand in favor of the couple. Since it was illegal for them to marry in the state, they eloped to Las Vegas to begin their life together.

LIONEL ALDRIDGE

PACKERS

DEFENSIVE END • N.F.C.

Fig. 14-1. Lionel Aldridge, seen above, is one of the few rookies Coach Vince Lombardi ever picked as a starter for his championship Green Bay Packers. Aldridge had a rare combination of size, strength, and blazing speed that allowed him to chase down opposing quarterbacks and running backs.

Lionel and Vicky may have had the support of Coach Lombardi, but they didn't have an easy time being accepted by anyone else. Some of the players resented the fact that Lionel had married a white girl. Vicky found it hard to be accepted by any of the other wives, black or white, and she was rarely included in any of their social gatherings. No matter where she sat in the stands, she was often asked to move somewhere else. It was just an added pressure on the couple, who already were dealing with Lionel's ever more volatile mood swings. Over time, he had become even more enraged about things that might trigger him. He was becoming insanely jealous and suspicious of anyone who even looked at his wife. He'd accuse her of having affairs if she came home late from some appointment. He began to become occasionally disoriented. There were even times when he'd come into the huddle during a game and not appear quite sure where he was or why he was there.

Despite all of this, Aldridge was a dominant force on one of the best defensive teams in football history. His huge size, incredible speed, and ability to anticipate plays of the opposing team were significant contributions to Green Bay's championships. In one of his most iconic performances, in the 1965 title game against Cleveland, he was able to help limit future Hall of Famer Jim Brown to just 50 yards rushing. Brown retired after that game in frustration.

Aldridge played at the highest level of his sport for 11 pro seasons, nine of them for Green Bay, where he is still considered a legend today. He played significant roles in the Packers' victories in three consecutive NFL championships and the first two Super Bowls.

Fall From Grace

Like many sports heroes who finish their careers, Aldridge was not quite prepared for what followed afterwards. His behavior had always been a bit strange, if not erratic—a concern of his coaches and teammates that had been mostly overlooked. Yet he was so bright and articulate that many just assumed it was just part of his intense personality. After all, when famous or wealthy people act in peculiar ways, they are most often labeled eccentric rather than crazy. In Aldridge's case, although he was observed to have dramatic mood swings, he was seen as mostly harmless, described as a "big, friendly teddy bear." Nevertheless, some of his teammates had learned to keep their distance at times, not wanting to become the target of his uncontrollable outbursts.

Aldridge was invited to audition as a color commentator, first for radio broadcasts of the Packers games and later for NBC television. It was a new career that provided him with additional opportunities to use his talents and the knowledge of the game that he'd spent a lifetime collecting. He studied hard for his new role, began reading voraciously, and practiced losing his distinctive Southern accent. Everyone believed he was a natural in the media.

Lionel and his wife now had two daughters and appeared to the outside world to be enjoying their new life in Milwaukee. Yet his inner demons came to the fore more and more. He frequently accused Vicky of trying to poison him and control his mind. Sometimes she'd see him talking to himself, carrying on conversations with an imagined other.

During a football broadcast, Aldridge's announcing partner, Jim Irwin, noticed something strange going on. As the game was about to begin, Irwin asked Aldridge standard questions about what to expect from the game that was about to commence. But Aldridge was just sitting unnaturally, still staring out at the field, his eyes never wavering. During the next three hours, Aldridge never moved, never said a word, never responded to anything that Irwin did or said. He just sat there frozen, with an unreadable expression on his face.

What Irwin didn't realize was that the voices inside his friend's head had taken over. They were ridiculing him, telling him he shouldn't bother speaking because he didn't know anything. They were accusing him of laziness, stupidity, worthlessness. "The voices were very scary and confusing," Aldridge later admitted. "I didn't want anyone to find out the terrible things happening inside my head." He felt such shame over what was going on that he did everything in his power to keep the voices a secret.

Over time, the demands inside his brain became more persistent and strident. He believed that people were following him, that the voices had been placed inside his head by enemies who wanted to destroy him. He'd hear accusations that he was a terrible husband and worthless father. To the dismay of his wife and daughters, he'd run around the house searching for an intruder who was obviously hiding from him.

No matter how much he was reassured by family and friends that there was nobody else in the vicinity, Aldridge couldn't get the paranoid delusions out of his head. He would sit in his accustomed chair in the studio during a broadcast, staring into the camera, trying to concentrate on reporting the day's sports events. But the task became increasingly difficult when he started to believe that viewers could see through the camera directly into his brain. He believed this was part of an overall conspiracy to destroy his life, and he felt helpless to do anything to stop the loss of control.

Several more times, Aldridge was discovered frozen in place, unable to go on the air when his broadcasts were scheduled. Others tried to cover for him, but it was increasingly apparent that something was terribly wrong. He was admitted into a psychiatric hospital for treatment but had the further misfortune to be assigned to an incompetent doctor who misdiagnosed his condition and prescribed the wrong medication. Vicky noticed that things only became much worse, and she felt helpless to do anything to reverse the developing trend of increased violence.

Aldridge's behavior became more erratic, then downright dangerous. He started to physically abuse Vicky, who began to fear for her life. One time he held a gun to his wife's head and threatened to kill her if she ever abandoned him. As if to prove his intentions, another time he picked up the family dog and hurled him into the air in anger. His daughter recalled the times the family had to cover for Aldridge when he'd disappear and go missing during one of his "spells." They'd drive around looking for him like a lost dog and bring him home again.

When Vicky had finally had enough, she packed her bags to leave for safety. With little choice, given his dramatic deterioration and stubborn refusal to seek help, she eventually divorced him. He was fired from his job. People were afraid of him. He was a six-foot-four black man with angry voices inside his head who was prone to unpredictable bursts of outrage. Everyone gave him a wide berth and then avoided him altogether.

Aldridge was hospitalized once again in an inpatient unit, this time resulting in an accurate diagnosis and much better treatment with Haldol, an antipsychotic medication. The medicine reduced his hallucinations but came with disturbing side effects, including headaches, dizziness, blurred vision, and restlessness. Tired of feeling like he was living in a fog, he stopped taking the drugs and slipped back into psychotic delusions.

Finally, the voices ordered him to leave his family and his home. He then began a tortured journey for the next few years as he wandered across the country from place to place, sleeping in his car or sometimes outside after he exhausted all his resources. It was during one of these nights that his Super Bowl ring might have been stolen, or maybe just lost. The ring symbolized to him all that he had accomplished in his life. When that disappeared, he felt like he had nothing left.

Aldridge tried to save himself, first through God and religion and then by seeing a succession of doctors who prescribed various medications with limited success. Repeatedly, he couldn't tolerate the side effects that made him feel worse than the disease. It was also difficult for the doctors to get a clear handle on what was wrong and how to best treat the problems. As was the case for so many of the other sports figures profiled in this book, mental illness was poorly understood in this era, and there had yet to be advances in the sort of medications that could better control schizophrenia.

Recovery and New Lease on Life

Eventually Aldridge ping-ponged back to Milwaukee and managed to create some semblance of a stable life. Although Vicky had remarried, she encouraged their daughters to renew a supportive relationship with their father; she still cared about him deeply. Several of his former teammates also came to their sick friend's aid, doing what they could to help him. He had, by this point, agreed to stay on his meds, and he recovered enough that he began speaking as an advocate for the treatment of mental illness. Aldridge claimed he no longer had any bad days and that he was virtually cured: "I deny there is such a thing as paranoia." Like other athletes whose stories have been told in this book, he became a passionate spokesperson for mental health issues and tried to change the stigma associated with the diseases. He wanted people to know that even if his condition could never be exactly cured, it could be tamed. He had learned to do that himself by changing the nature of the voices in his head whenever they did return. He learned to soften their anger and replace the criticism and negativity with something else, something more supportive and benign. The voices were now talking to him in positive ways: "Hey, there's Lionel Aldridge. He used to play for the Packers, and then he got sick. Look how good he's doing now."

Aldridge believed it was partially the medication that helped the voices eventually go away but also that it was God's will. God believed he had suffered enough, so he made the voices stop—at least for a while. He was convinced he'd found his way back home.

His teammates chipped in together to raise money to commission a replica of the Super Bowl ring that he had lost. It was one of the best gifts he'd ever received in his life, in some ways even more meaningful than the original, which only represented winning a

Fig. 14-2. After schizophrenia, medications, and repeated hospitalizations left Aldridge (pictured above) homeless and disoriented, he eventually found some stability and support from former players just prior to his death.

game. *This* ring meant love and faith and friendship. His spirits were also bolstered when he was inducted into the Packers Hall of Fame.

Aldridge tried to work different jobs to support himself, but he never lasted for very long. His disease never really let go of him, and occasional hospitalizations were required, often as a result of his daughters forcing him to get back into treatment. The medications took a toll on his body and his weight ballooned to a point he was unrecognizable from the person he once was during his playing days, a body carved in granite.

Lionel Aldridge died of heart failure at the age of 56, his body worn down. He weighed over 400 pounds.

As sad as his life had become, in some ways Aldridge had felt redeemed by the opportunities he had been given to speak on behalf of those who shared his affliction. Once he had found his powerful voice again, his talks become increasingly in demand, so much so that he began working for the National Alliance for the Mentally Ill. To show their gratitude for his work and honor him after his death, the organization bestows the Lionel Aldridge Champion Award each year to a recipient who has demonstrated courage and commitment to improving the lives of the mentally ill. Past recipients include former Vice President Joe Biden.

Reoccurring Tragedies

We might like to think that the suffering and sacrifices of athletes like Lionel Aldridge or the others mentioned in this book have led to some greater acceptance, if not deeper understanding, of mental illness. Certainly there have been tremendous advances in the development of new, more effective drugs and more successful approaches to psychotherapy. While members of the general public, even those who have attained celebrity status, are permitted to speak more openly about their emotional difficulties, athletes are still considered weak and shameful if they attempt the same sort of openness. They are held to a different standard.

Take Barret Robbins as an example. He was another exceptional NFL player who—with a nine-year career that included an appearance in the Pro Bowl—was one of the best at his position of center. He played in a different decade than Aldridge and mastered a completely different skill set in his sport. The nature of his extreme emotional disorder may have been related to a completely different cause, one that is now gaining increasing interest because of the traumatic injuries that players are known to suffer as a result of banging their heads against one another and scrambling their brains. In Robbins's case, perhaps the sport's pressure and brain bashing didn't help much, but he had a preexisting condition, bipolar disorder, which led to his recurrent difficulties.

Robbins will be known for all time as the player who disappeared before the Super Bowl. In January, 2003, just two days before he was scheduled to be the starting center for the Oakland Raiders in the championship game, he failed to report to the team hotel by the midnight curfew. He had just vanished. This wasn't the first time this had happened. A few times earlier in his career, he had gone missing for a while but had managed to show up in time to suit up. This time, however, he couldn't be located, and the coach had no choice but to cut him.

Robbins had been in the throes of a manic episode, one of many that would follow. He landed in prison and then ended up homeless, panhandling on the street. He was charged with attempted murder, shot three times by the police during an attempted burglary, and convicted repeatedly for drug possession and parole violations. He has since disappeared multiple times, reportedly just wanting to remain invisible.

Like Lionel Aldridge, Robbins has repeatedly attempted to reclaim his life. He has been involved in a multitude of drug rehabilitation and mental health treatment programs, each of which has been time limited. He attributes many of his problems to post-concussion syndrome and drug abuse, both of which were the consequences of playing football. He is still struggling with recovery and hoping for a very different outcome than the tragic stories of many of his colleagues. Although he avoids interviews and attention whenever possible, in one of his last public statements he reported that he was doing well and learning to be more comfortable in his skin. He felt grateful for a fresh start, one that began with accepting the nature of his mental illness and following the treatment protocols recommended by his doctors.

It is the nature of severe mental illness that there is often no permanent cure, especially for those like Lionel Aldridge and Michael Peterson (with paranoid schizophrenia), or like Barret Robbins or Suzy Favor Hamilton (with bipolar disorder and accompanying manic episodes). It is an ongoing process that requires constant vigilance, a stable lifestyle, and supportive care from family and friends. It is just so much more challenging for those who once enjoyed such fame and success as a result of their superhuman athletic accomplishments to accept their limitations and weaknesses. It goes against everything they've ever been taught in their lives.

Sources

Eskenazi, G. (1998, February 14). Lionel Aldridge, 56, stalwart on defense for Packer teams. *New York Times*. https://www.nytimes.com/1998/02/14/sports/lionel-aldridge-56-stalwart-on-defense-for-packer-teams.html

Hendricks, M. (2009, June 23). Bright career clouded by tragic decline. *Milwaukee Journal Sentinel*. http://archive.jsonline.com/sports/packers/48921882.html/

Magner, H. (2014, December 30). The long walk home. *Milwaukee Magazine*. https://www.milwaukeemag.com/the-long-walk-home-lionel-vicky-aldridge/

McDonald, J. (2014, October 14). Former Raider Barret Robbins back in Bay Area, rebuilding his life. *Mercury News*. https://www.mercurynews.com/2014/10/14/former-raider-barret-robbins-back-in-bay-area-rebuilding-his-life/

Oates, B. (1987, October 27). Lionel Aldridge: A long journey and happy days: Former Packer is back on his feet. *Los Angeles Times*. http://articles.latimes.com/1987-10-27/sports/sp-16847_1_lionel-aldridge

Schalin, S. (2012, June 14). Lionel Aldridge: Great man, great career, troubled life. *Packers Hall of Fame*. https://lombardiave.com/2012/06/14/packers-history-learning-something-new-every-day/

Taylor, P. (2015, December 15). The disappearing man: The Raider who went missing before the Super Bowl. *Sports Illustrated*. https://www.si.com/nfl/2015/12/16/untold-super-bowl-barret-robbins-raiders

15

Toward A Deeper Understanding of the Athlete's Life Challenges

T here is by no means agreement among elite athletes, their coaches, the media, the public, and mental health experts regarding what constitutes mental illness. Although within the professional ranks there are standardized criteria for diagnosing such disorders as well as a consensus regarding which behaviors are considered evidence for underlying problems, there is some disagreement within the other groups, mainly influenced by self-serving motives. The media and public, for instance, adore stories of drama, especially when some famous figure goes off on a reckless binge or displays some flamboyant, bizarre behavior. As much as athletes are worshipped as heroes, there is sometimes secret glee that people may feel when one of them self-destructs, which is why such stories so dominate the media.

On the other hand, owners, managers, coaches, and the athletes themselves have a vested interest in minimizing displays of strange, impulsive, aggressive, or eccentric behavior. They are essentially gladiators, or at least entertainers—and the show must go on!

Why Athletes Are at Greater Risk for Mental Illness

It has been assumed for some time that athletes were essentially immune to mental illness because of their extraordinary abilities. Supposedly, their superlative fitness, regular exercise, and support networks help protect them from problems that afflict others. This popular public myth has only been reinforced by the athletes themselves, who present themselves as invulnerable figures too tough to resort to the kinds of remedies available to common folks. The very culture of sport is never to talk about weaknesses and certainly not confess to any sort of emotional vulnerability. For elite athletes, whatever stigma prevents ordinary people from admitting problems and getting help is far more pervasive among those who are paid to play games for a living. They would be seen as cowards.

There are all kinds of reasons to suggest that the makeup of elite athletes would actually prevent them from developing any emotional problems. After all, they are among the most self-disciplined, physically healthy individuals among our species. They are able to run faster, throw farther, leap higher, or carry more weight on their shoulders (literally or metaphorically) than anyone else among us. They perform with grace under extraordinary pressure. They are afforded unimaginable wealth and resources. Just consider that in the United States, where the average 24-year-old earns about $25,000 per year, there are athletes who are paid over $25 *million* annually in salary and endorsements just for kicking a ball, hitting one over a net, or throwing one through a hoop or across a field. Surely with all the advantages of the rich and famous—the best health care, trainers, consultants, managers, agents, and staff—they can better position themselves to function at the highest level.

One problem is that there is a marked difference between what athletes and their coaches see as the difficulties. Coaches tend to minimize psychological issues; they are far more comfortable working with trainers to deal with physical injuries. They don't feel prepared to talk to athletes about more personal problems, so they tend to deny or ignore them when they can. When they see a player working, or even *over*working, as part of training, they view that as a degree of commitment to the job. Yet athletes feel that their coaches don't understand the pressure they are under and measure value by the amount of suffering they are willing to endure.

When Habits Become Addictions

It had been assumed for some time that athletes, because of their idealized status and positions, would have also attained extraordinary mental clarity and immunization against the sorts of things that might plague the rest of us. It is for this reason that so little research has actually been undertaken to determine if this is really the case.

One condition that is clearly more evident in almost all professional athletes—those who must train rigorously in order to maintain optimal fitness and performance—is an addiction to exercise beyond the point where it is healthy. Up to a point, exercise produces all sorts of gains related to fitness, weight control, sleep patterns, reduction of depression or stress, and even increased self-esteem. But there is also a point at which someone loses all semblance of control; there becomes a compulsive need to regulate emotional balance. Other aspects of life related to lifestyle, family, friendships, and work become compromised. Oftentimes, the excessive devotion to the addiction results in physical injuries.

For elite athletes, working out is just a part of their daily lives, often involving as many as eight hours a day of systematic training. This is usually part of a carefully designed program that has been specifically crafted for their sport, fitness level, skill area, and weaknesses. It includes careful attention to their diet, flexibility, strength, and other factors. There are some professional athletes who have been noted for their incredible work ethic. Cyclist Lance Armstrong was famous for being among the first in his sport to weigh his food choices, test his riding position in a wind tunnel, train for hours each day on a simulation trainer, and then actually scout stages days before the scheduled race. Basketball players like LeBron James and Kobe Bryant were notorious not only for their practice regimens prior to a game and during rest days but also for their persistence in practicing shots they missed after the game was over. Football linebacker Ray Lewis has been not only one of the most dominant defensive players in his sport but also the most compulsive trainer; he was known to work out 10 hours a day on weights, running, and exercises specific to his skill position. The same could be said for quarterback Tom Brady, who, although having long passed the age when players usually retire, devoted intense hours every day to perfecting his body and conditioning. And this is a guy who, when he played in college, had been ranked seventh-best quarterback on his team. Even after a stellar career at Michigan, he still wasn't drafted in the NFL until the 199th player was selected. In these cases, it is clearly a matter of commitment and devotion that makes them so exceptional. But sometimes it comes at a cost.

There is a point of diminishing returns at which the demands of the training and sport lead to fatigue, injuries, and overuse syndrome. Sandy Koufax, one of the greatest pitchers of all time, may have been an example of that. He won three Cy Young Awards and five championships trying to strike out every batter he faced, sometimes not trusting his teammates to handle balls hit their way. He played the game in constant agony, yet he pushed himself harder, even when his arm was black and blue. At one point, the inflammation got so bad he was told he was in danger of losing his arm if he didn't slow down or quit. Finally, he had no choice.

Once such athletes retire, they lose a lot of the incentive to continue their regimens, often ballooning in weight. Look at recent photos of stellar basketball players Michael Jordan, Magic Johnson, or Charles Barkley for confirmation of this. Body image fears can also lead some of them to continue pushing themselves to dangerous limits. There is also some evidence that the insane exercise routines become a means of coping with the mood disorders, chronic depression, and anxiety that we have seen manifested in so many of these life stories.

More Prone to Problems?

There is still some debate as to whether professional and Olympian athletes really are more susceptible to emotional disorders than the general population. It would seem from reading the stories in this book that a significant number of them are indeed collateral damage from the wear and tear of their sports, if not from upbringings that predisposed them to make so many personal sacrifices in pursuit of ultimate performance. Almost anyone can rattle off a list of favorite athletes who went off the reservation, so to speak. The ones I've covered represent just a small sample of nominees who displayed florid symptoms of depression, anxiety, bipolar, dissociative, or psychotic disorder, and other mental illnesses.

A comprehensive review of studies that investigated the mental health of elite athletes concluded that, in general, they have at least the same risk of mental disorders when compared to the general population. However, it was also found that there are particular times when they are far more likely to suffer such problems: When their performance falls off, they experience a significant failure, or they approach retirement. As we have also learned, there are certain sports that place athletes at much greater risk, in particular those that have rigid parameters for a lean body shape (figure skating, gymnastics, track).

In one survey of college athletes, half of them said that they experienced major anxiety on a regular basis, and one-third said they struggled with depression at times. It was surmised that the pressures they faced from competition, inevitable injuries, and overtraining contributed to their emotional difficulties. At the professional level, the stress is often many times worse.

Brandon Marshall, a talented NFL wide receiver, had been traded multiple times among more than a handful of teams, mostly because he was such a handful to manage. He was constantly in trouble, not only with teammates and coaches but also with legal authorities. It wasn't until his diagnosis of borderline personality disorder that he began to realize the origin of some of his troubles. He spent three months in a psychiatric hospital trying to come to terms with this label and what it meant for his life. This is the sort of condition that makes it very hard to get along with others. Such individuals are often highly manipulative, controlling, and always out for themselves. They are the kinds of folks who know how to get underneath your skin. But it is precisely because he was a talented, valued, and skilled player that others put up with his antics and he could get away with them for so long.

Marshall found greater meaning during his stay in the hospital. He decided he would devote his life to trying to help people like him rather than tearing them down. He would bring greater attention to problems of mental illness. "This has become my purpose on the planet. Football is my platform."

There's even reason to believe that the incidence of mental and emotional problems is so much higher than can possibly be imagined because such symptoms are often disguised and covered up. We have seen how the very culture of sport is fueled by minimizing pain and discomfort, showing others that no matter what obstacles are in front of you, they are really no big deal, at least with respect to most problems. "Blow out your knee, get into trouble with the law, fail a drug test," baseball player Russ Johnson explained, and the team will help you back. But then, he warns, if you suffer some sort of emotional problem, it's all over: "It's a big mark against you." It's no wonder, then, that such problems are underreported.

In one study of current professional soccer players, one-quarter of them reported significant levels of depression or anxiety. After they retired, emotional disorders became even worse, and 40% of them complained of major symptoms. One example is Aaron Lennon, a British soccer player who had been a superstar as a child and had a distinguished career playing for England in the World Cup until depression and anxiety crippled him. His condition worsened to the point where he was detained by the police for his own protection and placed under psychiatric care.

When the full story came out, Lennon admitted he'd been depressed his whole life but never felt safe talking about it. "I was in a dark, dark place for a long time," he admitted after his release from the hospital, "and now just waking up every day and getting excited to come to training again and enjoying each day again is massive for me. It's hard to put into words. The turnaround from this time last year is massive."

For Lennon, there has been a recovery, but many other soccer players never dig themselves out of that dark place and never find treatment or get the support they so desperately need.

Influences and Risk Factors

There are some essential questions that are interesting to consider. Why do certain people end up as elite athletes? How is it that they chose that path in life, or was it chosen for them? Was it really a function of extraordinary ability that was recognized at an early age, or were they late bloomers who developed their skills through grit and determination?

The same things that are alleged to prevent athletes from becoming as anxious and depressed as the general population are also what sometimes drive them crazy. The status and journey associated with the position become their own risk factors. As we've seen, it takes a certain degree of perfectionism and extreme focus to succeed at the highest level. That leads to an overinvestment in a singular identity, even though it's been found that multiple positive identities help protect people against adversity and developing emotional problems. Athletes, however, are only permitted one way to define themselves, and anything else is seen as a distraction.

In the case of Jim Shea, Olympic gold medalist in the skeleton, it was hardly a coincidence that he chose sport as his obsession. He is a third-generation Olympian—a legacy, so to speak. It was just a family business. His grandfather, Jack Shea, won two gold medals in speed skating during the 1932 Games. His father, Jim Senior, competed in cross-country skiing and Nordic combined events during the 1964 Games.

Fig. 15-1. Jim Shea struggled with severe depression to the point where he experienced anhedonia, a complete absence of pleasure in almost anything. It was only while he was racing down an Olympic skeleton ice track at 80 mph that he ever felt alive, as pictured in his look of jubilation above at the 2002 Salt Lake City Olympics.

Source: Copyright © 2002 Reuters/Juergen Schwarz.

Shea had a lot of problems in school as a result of dyslexia and other learning disorders, limiting him to what he called "the retard classes." He was teased and bullied mercilessly.

His teachers gave up on him. Understandably, he was both depressed and lonely. Out of desperation, he started to lose himself in reckless risk-taking, testing himself in the most dangerous situations. Once he brought that fearless attitude to the organized sports of hockey and lacrosse, he not only felt some semblance of self-worth for the first time; he also felt part of a tribe. He felt like that saved his sanity and certainly the approval of his father and grandfather. In some ways, it was ordained that he would become an Olympian at something.

Given his family history, it was inevitable he would choose a specialty in the Winter Olympics, but he picked the one that was the most dangerous, reckless, and perhaps obscure. The skeleton is that event where an athlete goes flying down an ice track at 80 miles per hour, head first, lying on a sled the size of a cafeteria tray. There are no brakes. No steering mechanism. The only control is exerted by shifting one's weight. There is perhaps no other sport that jacks up adrenaline to such a level.

Here's the most interesting part: Jim Shea suffered chronic depression to the point where he manifested a condition called anhedonia—a complete absence of joy or even minimal enjoyment from almost any experience. His feelings were completely blunted, a state that he just assumed was normal. He just felt empty and numb inside. It was only when he was jumping off a cliff or racing down a mountain that he felt any semblance of arousal. And even that wasn't close to joy, as it was just a physiological rush.

When Shea was selected for the Olympic team as part of his family's destiny, rather than feeling excitement, he only had a sense of foreboding. Sure enough, his worst fears were realized when just a few weeks prior to the Salt Lake City Games, his beloved grandfather was killed by a drunk driver. Jim was so distraught he decided to honor this important figure in his life by putting his grandfather's photo inside his helmet. When he put all his grief and recklessness into his runs down the tube, he won a gold medal. When he realized he had won, anyone watching could see the look of joy and triumph on his face as he took out his grandfather's picture and waved it back and forth (see Figure 15-1). To be clear, it wasn't just this breakthrough moment that released a lifetime of repressed emotions; he had also been prescribed antidepressant medication, which seemed to make a difference. He was fairly certain the drugs gave him a new, or at least different, lease on life because when he stopped taking them, believing he was cured, the depression returned almost immediately.

Accumulative Stress and Living With Fear

So the key point we are considering is that athletes like Shea and so many others may be more at risk for developing emotional problems. Of course it begins with the stress they are under, the constant pressure to perform at the highest level against competitors who are just as talented, obsessed, and driven as they are. Chronic stress produces all kinds of erosion of the nervous system. In addition, the endocrine system floods the body with chemical reactions that, over time, begin to produce distressing symptoms like headaches, sleep disruption, stomachaches, muscle tension, fatigue, irritability, depression, and all kinds of diseases and infections. This often leads to self-defeating coping strategies to manage the distress, such as alcohol and drug abuse, social withdrawal, acting out, displays of rage, and other harmful behaviors.

Imagine what it's like for someone like Shea or the other Olympians we have covered, athletes who spend their whole lives training and preparing for a single minute or two in front of the world. One mistake, and it's all over, especially in sports where the winner is ahead by a hundredth of a second or a fraction of a point.

Imagine, for example, standing on a tower three stories high. If you stare straight ahead, you can see the horizon; look below, and there is a rectangular square of turquoise water. There are thousands of people watching in the stands, with perhaps millions more watching on television. You are about to voluntarily jump off this 33-foot-high platform, spin and flip in mid-air while flying downward at thirty miles per hour, then enter the water like a perfect vertical missile to avoid breaking your spine.

Scott Donie, the most exciting high diver of his generation, was actually upside down, doing a handstand on the 10-meter platform during the 1993 Olympic Festival. The crowd was on the edge of their seats, privileged to watch the Olympic silver medalist perform; he was actually leading the competition once again. There was a hush throughout the venue, with everyone holding their breath. Donie maintained his position as the seconds ticked on. His arms were starting to wobble in a handstand he couldn't maintain. Ten seconds. Fifteen seconds. Twenty seconds. Twenty-five seconds. Thirty seconds. Something was terribly wrong.

Donie remembered thinking to himself that he just couldn't do this anymore, he didn't *want* to do this anymore. He was 27 and had been diving his whole life. But it now seemed pure lunacy to him, launching himself off this tiny platform into water far below. His main worry at this point was how he could get himself off this ridiculous place without killing himself. He wondered if he could just do a "cannonball" or jump feet first. He felt shamed and humiliated, but there was nothing he could say to himself that would make him leave the safety of the platform. He froze completely. All he could think about was how to get off the damn thing. "Forget this. It's over. I'm done."

Anxiety, nerves, and stress were certainly no strangers to Scott Donie. High divers are fearless. "You have to like being nervous," he explained. And over time, he'd learned to welcome and rely on nerves to enhance his performances; he thrived on the pressure.

But all of a sudden, without warning, he got "messed up in his head." He couldn't do it any longer. He couldn't even finish the dive and had to shamefully get himself back down the ladder.

The question that Donie and others asked afterwards was "What the heck happened?" Here was a guy who thrived on stress, who was used to the pressure of deliberately falling at maximum speed off a high tower, doing twists and somersaults on the way down.

In one study of elite divers, it was concluded that to jump off boards for a living, they have to be a little crazy to begin with. The researchers found several more unique risk factors for emotional problems in this particular sport because of the strict emphasis on body shape, risks of injuries, limited self-identity beyond competition, and stressors within the sport itself. Many of these are familiar from the previous discussion of gymnastics.

Donie had been a daredevil most of his life, picking the most dangerous aquatic sport as his specialty. During the height of his fame, he had been recruited to dive off the 50-foot mast of a sailboat—while the boat was rocking and swinging back and forth—for a commercial. He was required to repeat the stunt five times to get the right shot, and he did so without complaint or much concern. Looking back, he could only shake his head.

But that day on the high dive platform, something broke inside of him. All he could remember was feeling helpless. "I had gotten so down, so messed up mentally, that it wasn't fun for me anymore." He couldn't remember what he was even doing up there or what the point was. All he could think about was all the ways he might crash and die.

Yet this is a different sort of story than some of the others in this book. Rather than succumbing to his anxiety, depression, and emotional crisis, Donie found the strength and internal resources to fight back. He had won an Olympic medal in his sport and then simply walked away from it. Done. Over. That's it. But that's not the end of the story by any means.

Fig. 15-2. Scott Donie made the remarkable transition from the high dive to springboard, and later collegiate coach, as a way to cope with his debilitating fears.

Source: New York University, "Silver Medalist and NYU Diving Coach Scott Donie on the Challenges of Sochi," https://www.youtube.com/watch?v=zLMVn6JsAfY. Copyright © 2014 by New York University.

Fearful of high diving, he simply reinvented himself a few years later as a champion springboard diver! He once again made the Olympic team and placed fourth. In some ways, he's even more proud of that accomplishment because of what it took for him to get there.

This is *still* not the end of Donie's story. Like many athletes, after his Olympic career ended, he was hit by serious depression once again. Returning home after winning a medal, he assumed his life would be transformed by endorsement deals, fame, and riches. He had devoted his whole life to diving, and now he expected a payoff.

It was not to be. He was no Bruce Jenner or Michael Jordan, who returned from Barcelona as heroes. He was a participant in an obscure minor sport, and nobody remembered he existed a few days after his event. He gained weight, started smoking, and languished in despair. "I was pretty screwed up," he admitted. "I think I had a number of nervous breakdowns." At one point, he considered suicide and imagined how many flips he could do off a bridge before he ended his life.

So often it has been found that a cure for mental disorders is finding meaning in life, a functional purpose for the suffering, a way to use the pain and life challenges for some greater good. It turns out that Donie found such an attitude in teaching and coaching other divers. He became head diving coach at New York University for 16 years, and more recently, he coached at Columbia University. He has coached nine All-American divers and led several of his teams to qualify for the national championship in both the men's and women's divisions.

What I love most about Scott Donie's story is that he faced and overcame his greatest fear. As a child he was afraid of heights. "I still have a fear of heights!" he admits. Yet he started diving as a sport of choice precisely *because* he was so afraid of them.

He experienced his greatest shame and humiliation at the top of a tower, even after remarkable success in the sport, demonstrating once again that his fear still lived within him. But he refused to surrender. A lesser man would have walked away from diving. He just found other ways to use his fears to teach others to succeed at another level. There are lessons in Donie's experience for all of us.

Lifestyle Issues

The lifestyle of athletes is also an important influence on their emotional state of mind. They travel constantly, living in hotel rooms on the road or in training camps. They have no stable sense of home. They are traded from one city to another according to the whims of their owners. They are constantly separated from loved ones and family. They are a "property," a "commodity," an asset for sale to the highest bidder.

Under such conditions, with little supervision, their inappropriate, self-destructive, even outrageous behavior is not only tolerated by those around them but also enabled in many ways. The most successful athletes have handlers, managers, agents, coaches, public relations experts, friends and admirers, who all profit by keeping the money machine churning out cash. They make excuses for the celebrity who is spinning out of control. They do their best to cover for them as well as for their own benefit.

It's sometimes hard to forget that sport is a game. Professional athletes are being paid to engage in activities that most others spend their own money on, just for the opportunity, joy, and privilege of participating in the sport. Yes, it is also a business—a very lucrative one, at that—for most of the participants. But it is still just a game that many people take *way* too seriously. Brawls break out in the stands between fans of opposing teams. People become seriously depressed if an outcome isn't what they had hoped for and anticipated. All these expectations and illusions of critical importance make the lifestyle of an athlete even more of a pressure cooker.

Early Trauma

Through much of our discussion, I've mentioned how the culture and demands of sport push athletes over the brink because of the pressures they face. Yet the lifestyle doesn't just create emotional problems; it also attracts those who are already quite wounded.

Young people choose to devote their energy and time to a sport not only because of an innate ability or the search for fame and fortune. They also do so for the intrinsic benefits of participation that include social support. They feel a sense of competence at something they excel in, a condition that is considered essential for self-esteem. They also feel a sense of identity as an athlete, one that features heroism and courage, attributes that are especially important to those who have felt like victims during their early lives.

So many professional athletes come from impoverished backgrounds. A disproportionate number of basketball and football players, in particular, suffered abject poverty during their childhoods, especially when you compare them to players in other sports such as tennis or golf. For many of these children who grew up in neighborhoods with violence and deprivation, it seemed as if playing ball was the only way out.

Often such gifted athletes have been singularly unprepared to function well in a far more enriched environment, especially when they are suddenly showered with wealth and fame. Their early experiences growing up with neglect, abuse, violence, and assaults still remain part of who they are and can often be triggered during inevitable times of stress or disappointment.

Physiological Impact

We are just beginning to understand how post-concussion syndrome, which is found to be increasingly common in sports like football and hockey, has delayed effects that manifest themselves as emotional problems in later life. There seems to be fairly conclusive evidence that players who have suffered one or more concussions are three times more likely than their peers to develop major depression.

One well-publicized example of that was hockey great Pat LaFontaine, who suffered severe depression after he retired from the game as a result of catastrophic brain injuries. We still don't know about the accumulative impact of the constant head banging that takes place during routine scrimmages, but an increasing number of forcibly retired players are complaining of constant headaches, seizures, memory loss, and depression.

One other physiological factor that may affect the development of problems is that the peak years for athletic performance coincide with the same ages when early signs of mental disorders first show up. Late adolescence and early adulthood are the most vulnerable life stages in which psychotic disorders, major depression, panic disorder, and personality disorders manifest disruptive symptoms. When these internal changes are exacerbated by increased performance anxiety, public scrutiny, and reduced family support due to constant travel, coping mechanisms are further compromised.

It is also a possibility, if not a likelihood, for many athletes who began their training, and overtraining, at a young age that a number of physical complaints will plague them for the rest of their lives. So many college athletes who played football walk around with nagging injuries and limps as adults. Gymnasts who began their careers during preschool also deal with the lifelong consequences of delayed maturation during their adolescent years. In addition, there are a host of other physical and health maladies that are not uncommon, including limb deformities, osteoarthritis, spinal pathologies, and chronic pain. Then there is the increased likelihood of risk-taking, such as hazardous driving, substance abuse, unprotected sex, and antisocial behavior, in order to duplicate the thrills of the previous elation associated with sport. It is no wonder that problems have become more prevalent.

Transition to Retirement

While we are discussing organic conditions and physiological changes that result from trauma, there is also one other major factor that increases the likelihood that athletes may eventually suffer emotional problems. That process is called aging, and it happens to all of us, regardless of talent and station in life. It is absolutely inevitable that there will come a time when an elite athlete can no longer perform at the highest level. Even though there are a few exceptions when experience and wisdom come more into play, physical decline begins by the age of 25—in some sports, much earlier. This is also the exact average age at which most world records are set. Even though baseball players may not hit their peak until their late 20s, even mental decline begins by age 30.

Of course there are notable exceptions of athletes—quarterbacks Brett Favre and Tom Brady, baseball pitchers Bartolo Colón and Randy Johnson, hockey players Gordie Howe and Jaromír Jágr—who all played at a high level well into their 40s. They learned to compensate for their diminished physical abilities with other skills and accumulated knowledge. But even for them, for all of us, there comes a time when we must accept that optimal, or even adequate, functioning has come to an end. Needless to say, this is a devastating prospect for someone who is used to being among the best in the world at something and now must accept that this is no longer the case. In addition, relatively late in life, without any other marketable talent and often without much of a meaningful education, this person must somehow find meaning and purpose for the next 50 years or so. Who *wouldn't* feel anxious and depressed?

The Olympic organization is trying to prepare their alumni for this stage of life after their careers are over. They mention several areas where problems may arise, beginning with the abrupt loss of structure. Athletes' whole lives are organized around training schedules that begin from the moment they wake up until lights are out. They are told what to eat, where to go, and what activities they may engage in, and they do so with the added structure of their teammates. They are a tribe and feel a sense of belonging. Until it ends. There is a loss not only of dominant culture but also of primary identity.

Both amateur and professional athletes are known for their single-minded focus. They have committed their whole lives and made tremendous sacrifices to do one thing extraordinarily well, whether that is to hit or throw a ball, run at top speed, or do somersaults in mid-air. When the demand for that particular skill ends, there is often uncertainty and confusion about how to fill that hole with something else. Many of the those within this book who have been most successful at adapting to life after sport found ways to use their emotional suffering as a means by which to help others with similar problems. But the vast majority of individuals struggle during the time of transition, and many never find their way again.

Finally, many athletes experience a tremendous sense of grief and loss after retirement. "Nothing could satisfy me outside the ring," confessed boxer Sugar Ray Leonard after retirement. "There is nothing in life that can compare to becoming a world champion, having your hand raised in that moment of glory, with thousands, millions of people cheering you on."

Transcending Body to Spirit

Among athletes who flourish when facing adversity and emotional disruption—or the rest of us, for that matter—there is one overriding factor that assists a high level of recovery and adaptation. It is finding a greater purpose beyond any single limited aspect of ourselves. It means letting go of the ways we define ourselves in order to discover alternative ways of being productive, successful, and purposeful.

Jeanine Shepherd was a renowned cross-country skier, training with the Australian Olympic team for the 1988 Calgary Winter Games. She had been on a training bike ride with her team in the mountains outside Sydney when she was hit by a truck. Her spinal cord was fractured in six different places. She had five broken ribs, a fractured arm and

Fig. 15-3. Jeanine Shepherd is an example of an athlete who completely reinvented herself after her body was crushed in a tragic accident. It is one of the most difficult challenges for athletes in any sport to successfully make the transition from stardom to a satisfying, fulfilling life after their career ended.

collarbone, and various internal injuries. She had lost five liters of blood before they could airlift her to the hospital, where she was not expected to survive more than a few hours.

Her body crushed to an unrecognizable mass, Shepherd still managed to survive. She would be paralyzed from the neck down and restricted to a wheelchair for the rest of her life. When she finally regained consciousness, her first confused thought was to immediately resume her training for the upcoming Olympics. Then she was told that dream was over, as she would never walk again, much less run or ski. The whole meaning and focus of her life was gone; she had nothing else. Depression became a constant companion, and she wondered why she had even bothered to fight so hard for survival when there was nothing left for her.

When her mother asked her one day if life would ever be good again, Jeanine answered, "How could it? Because I've lost everything that I valued, everything that I'd worked towards. Gone."

If an elite athlete has a high dose of one quality, it is determination. In the depths of her despair and depression, Shepherd decided impulsively one day during her recovery at home in a body cast that she would reinvent herself. If her body was no longer responsive to her, no longer a beacon of strength and health, then her spirit would have to serve her instead. If she could no longer ski, no longer function as a world-class athlete, then she would find some other way to soar to new heights. It was actually the prospect of flying that caught her attention.

As soon as that sudden thought occurred to her, she immediately called a local flight school to set up an appointment for an introductory lesson, although she failed to mention that she was in a wheelchair and only had the use of her arms, one of which was still recovering full motion. It took several people to lift and pry her into the cockpit, after which she discovered there were pedals she was supposed to control with her useless feet. Nevertheless, she insisted they continue the lesson, and she contented herself that first day with steering the plane. She was hooked!

During the next year, Shepherd pushed herself in her physical recovery just as hard as she had on that fateful day when she had spent five hours on her bike peddling at maximum effort in the Blue Mountains. With superhuman effort, she was able to take a few steps, then shuffle with two people holding her, then move under her own power. She returned to that flight school again and again and eventually managed to earn her pilot's license. Yet she didn't stop there.

Once she redefined the possibilities of what she might do with a "broken" body, Shepherd went on to earn her instrument's license. Then she attained her instructor's license, teaching others in the same school where she'd first been a student. She was also selected as the first female director of the Civil Aviation Safety Authority. She became the torchbearer of the 2000 Paralympics, held in her native Australia.

"I now know that my real strength never came from my body," she announced. "And although my physical capabilities have changed dramatically, who I am is unchanged. The pilot light inside of me was still alight, just as it is in each and every one of us." That is her inspirational message, not only to athletes who struggle with disappointment, failure, and emotional troubles or mental illness but to all of us who remain stuck in limited beliefs about what is possible.

Sources

Bar, K. J., & Markser, V. Z. (2013). Sport specificity of mental disorders: The issue of sport psychiatry. *European Archives of Psychiatry and Clinical Neuroscience, 263*, 205–210.

Biggin, I. J. R., Burns, J. H., & Uphill, M. (2017). An investigation of athletes' and coaches' perceptions of mental ill-health in elite athletes. *Journal of Clinical Sport Psychology, 11*, 126–147.

Callahan, G. (1996, July 1). Don't look now Scott Donie, driven off the platform by nerves and depression, won the U.S. trials in the springboard. *Sports Illustrated*. https://www.si.com/vault/1996/07/01/208598/dont-look-now-scott-donie-driven-off-the-platform-by-nerves-and-depression-won-the-us-trials-in-the-springboard

Carless, D., & Douglas, K. (2008). Narrative, identity and mental health: How men with serious mental illness re-story their lives through sport and exercise. *Psychology of Sport and Exercise, 9*, 576–594.

Chen, S., Magner, M., Leadingham, M., & Ahmadi, S. (2017). Mental illness and sport. *KAHPERD Journal, 54*(1), 25–34.

Chiu, A. (2010). The Olympic swimmer reveals her secret struggles with cutting and bulimia—and how she beat them. *People, 74*(17), 97–99.

Coyle, M., Gorczynski, P., & Gibson, K. (2017). "You have to be mental to jump off a board any way": Elite divers' conceptualizations and perceptions of mental health. *Psychology of Sport and Exercise, 29*, 10–18.

Gleeson, S., & Brady, E. (2017, August 30). When athletes share their battles with mental illness. *USA Today*. https://www.usatoday.com/story/sports/2017/08/30/michael-phelps-brandon-marshall-mental-health-battles-royce-white-jerry-west/596857001/

International Olympic Committee. (2017, February 28). The six biggest challenges that athletes face when they retire. *Athlete 365*. https://www.olympic.org/athlete365/news/the-six-biggest-challenges-athletes-face-when-they-retire/

Malinowski, E. (2011, July 12). For athletes' peak performance, age is everything. *Wired*. https://www.wired.com/2011/07/athletes-peak-age/

Reardon, C. L., & Factor, R. M. (2010). Sport psychiatry: A systematic review of diagnosis and treatment of mental illness in athletes. *Sports Medicine, 40*, 961–980.

Rice, S. M., Purcell, R., De Silva, S., Mawren, D., McGorry, P. D., & Parker, A. G. (2016). The mental health of elite athletes: A narrative systematic review. *Sports Medicine, 46*(9), 1333–1353.

Shepherd, J. (2012). A broken body isn't a broken person. *TED Talk*. https://www.ted.com/talks/janine_shepherd_a_broken_body_isn_t_a_broken_person?utm_campaign=ios-share&utm_medium=social&source=email&utm_source=email

Stonehouse, G. (2018, May 14). Dark place: Aaron Lennon opens up about mental health issues. *The Sun*. https://www.thesun.co.uk/sport/football/6280709/burnley-everton-aaron-lennon-mental-health-battle/

Team Max (2015, October 14). Know when to jump: Q&A with Olympic silver diving medalist Scott Donie. *MAX*. http://blog.maxmyinterest.com/2015/10/know-when-to-jump-qa-with-olympic-silver-diving-medalist-scott-donie/

Wertheim, L. J. (2003, September 8). Prisoners of depression. *Sports Illustrated*. https://www.si.com/vault/2003/09/08/349196/prisoners-of-depression-mental-illness-still-carries-a-powerful-stigma-in-pro-sports-but-there-are-signs-that-teams-are-finally-facing-the-problem-and-trying-to-help-troubled-athletes

About the Author

Jeffrey A. Kottler is one of the most prominent authors in the fields of health, counseling, psychotherapy, education, and advocacy. He has written over 100 books about a wide range of subjects, including *Divine Madness: Ten Stories of Creative Struggle*; *Change: What Leads to Personal Transformation*; *What You Don't Know About Leadership but Probably Should*; and the best-selling true crime book *The Last Victim: Inside the Minds of Serial Killers*, which was produced as a feature film (*Dear Mr. Gacy*). He has also written dozens of books about mental health and treatment issues, including *On Being a Therapist*; *Creative Breakthroughs in Therapy*; *Stories We've Heard, Stories We've Told: Life-Changing Narratives in Therapy and Everyday Life*; *Relationships in Counseling and the Counselor's Life*; *On Being a Master Therapist*; *Secrets of Exceptional Counselors*; and, most recently, *Living and Being a Therapist: Selected Writings of Jeffrey Kottler*.

Jeffrey has been a counselor, therapist, supervisor, and educator for 45 years, having worked at a preschool, middle school, mental health center, crisis center, hospital, medical school, refugee resettlement agency, nongovernmental organization (NGO), university, and community college as well as in private practice and disaster relief settings. He is also the founder of Empower Nepali Girls, a foundation that supports and mentors at-risk children. He has served as a Fulbright scholar and senior lecturer in Peru and Iceland and worked as a visiting professor in New Zealand, Australia, Hong Kong, Singapore, and Nepal. Jeffrey is Clinical Professor in the Menninger Department of Psychiatry and Behavioral Science at the Baylor College of Medicine in Houston, Texas.

Index

LSD, 13
Lyme disease, 6

M

Maddux, Greg, 6
Marantz, Andrew, 73
marijuana, 7, 26
Marshall, Brandon, 164
Mauch, Gene, 109
Mays, Willie, 21
McEnroe, John, 1, 4
McKinley, Kenny, 2
Menninger Institute, 96
mental illness. *See* emotional disorders/mental
    illness
Merckx, Eddie, 55–57
Metta World Peace. *See* Artest, Ron
Michael Peterson Classic surf tournament, 35
Michaels, Al, 109
Mingus, Charles, 30
Mont Ventoux, France, 132
mood swings, 68
"Moon Rocket", 24
Moore, Donnie, 109–116
Morgan, Joe, 14
Morning of the Earth, 26
mountaineering, 103–104. *See also* climbing/climber
mouth-to-mouth resuscitation, 24

N

Nastase, Ilie, 4, 68
NBC television, 156
New York Mets, 6
New York Time, 77
Neyer, Megan, 97
NFL championships, 155
Niccol, Andrew, 73
Nike, 42

O

Obree, Graeme, 51–65, 131
    brief triumph, 57–59
    comeback, 62–64
    darkest hour, 55–57
    early life, 53–54
    escape from suffering, 52–53
    fame and misfortune, 59–61
    self-acceptance, 61–62
    ups and downs, 54–55
Ormsby, Kathy, 39–40

P

Pantani, Marco, 131–145
    blame game, 142–144

as climbing specialist, 135–136
    deep depression, 139–141
    self-doubt, 134–135
Payne, Angie, 97
Perez, Tony, 14
perfectionistic paradox, 8
performance-enhancing drugs (PED), 26, 41, 86, 131,
    136, 139, 143–144
Peterson, Michael, 23–35, 160
    board-shaping business, 25–27
    chase, 33–34
    club championship, 26
    cult status, 28
    death, 41
    emotional instability, 25
    illicit drugs use, 26, 29–30
    international recognition, 27
    Morning of the Earth, 26
    self-administered drugs, 30
    single mother, 24
    stories and legends, 30–32
Peterson, Tommy, 24–26
physiological impact, 170
Piersall, Jimmy, 117–130
Piniella, Lou, 4
pitchers/pitching
    Ellis, Dock, 9–21
    Moore, Donnie, 109–116
Pittsburgh Pirates, 9
Plath, Sylvia, 30
potassium cyanide, 108

R

Rabe, Bahne, 97
recovery and adaptation, 172–174
retirement, 171
Richards, Mark, 29
Rigby, Cathy, 97
risk factors, 164–166. *See also* influences
road cycling. *See* cycling/cyclists
Robbins, Barret, 2, 159–160
Roberts, David, 107
Robinson, Jackie, 15
Rodman, Dennis, 1, 4
Roe, Nicholas, 54
Rose, Pete, 14, 21
Rousey, Ronda, 4
Runner's World, 41
running/runner, 38–48. *See also* Hamilton,
    Suzy Favor
Ruth, Babe, 7
Rypien, Rick, 2

S

schizophrenia, 29, 145
sex worker, 37–38
shaping boards, 27